IMAGES
of America
KEIZER

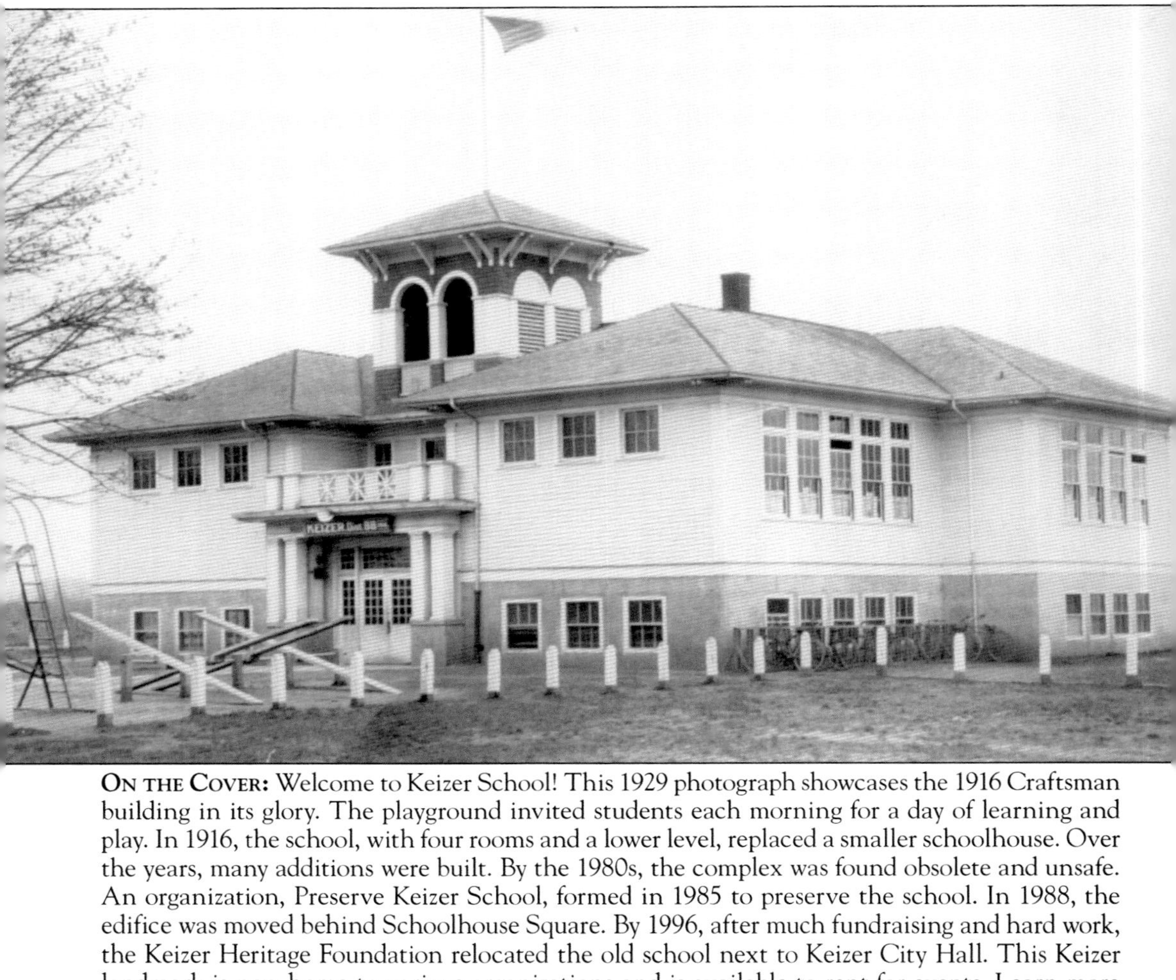

On the Cover: Welcome to Keizer School! This 1929 photograph showcases the 1916 Craftsman building in its glory. The playground invited students each morning for a day of learning and play. In 1916, the school, with four rooms and a lower level, replaced a smaller schoolhouse. Over the years, many additions were built. By the 1980s, the complex was found obsolete and unsafe. An organization, Preserve Keizer School, formed in 1985 to preserve the school. In 1988, the edifice was moved behind Schoolhouse Square. By 1996, after much fundraising and hard work, the Keizer Heritage Foundation relocated the old school next to Keizer City Hall. This Keizer landmark is now home to various organizations and is available to rent for events. Learn more at keizerheritage.org. Keizer Heritage Museum, PO Box 20845 (980 Chemawa Road), Keizer, OR 97307. (Blake family photograph.)

IMAGES
of America

KEIZER

Tammy Wild and Keizer Heritage Museum

ARCADIA
PUBLISHING

ISBN 978-1-4671-3261-9

Published by Arcadia Publishing
Charleston, South Carolina

Printed in the United States of America

Library of Congress Control Number: 2014942098

For all general information, please contact Arcadia Publishing:
Telephone 843-853-2070
Fax 843-853-0044
E-mail sales@arcadiapublishing.com
For customer service and orders:
Toll-Free 1-888-313-2665

Visit us on the Internet at www.arcadiapublishing.com

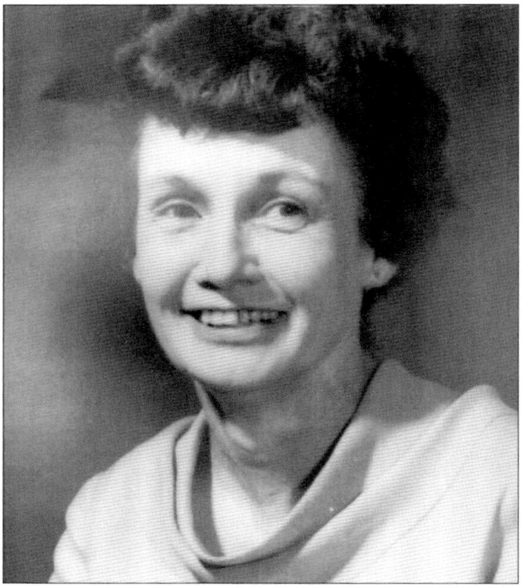

We are indebted to the visionary work of Ann Lossner and her decades of interviews, articles, and books, which have preserved Keizer history.

Contents

Acknowledgments

We are indebted to those who had the foresight to preserve our history and the volunteers who created the Keizer Heritage Foundation, which restored the historic 1916 school building. A hearty thank-you is given for the help and support from the Keizer Heritage Museum (KHM) committee members: Al Rasmus (the scanning king), Daisy Santana Hickman, Evelyn Melson Franz (her firsthand experiences are highly valued), Gary Young, JoAnne Beilke, Lyndon Zaitz, Ray Hansen, and Terri Hoag, who made this book possible. Many thanks go to Bob Wild, who partnered with Tammy in this project with care and patience along with her supportive family.

This work was made possible by community contributions of family stories, treasured photographs, and mementos. We appreciate our local businesses, schools, Keizer City Hall, Keizer Fire District, and Keizer Chamber of Commerce for sharing their scrapbooks. Thank you to all who assisted this endeavor; Keizertimes, Dick Hohnbaum, and Loreen Ostrander Wells for preserving Clear Lake history; and the Arcadia Publishing staff.

We are inspired by those who have documented Keizer history: Ann Lossner for her devotion in recording Keizer's past, Roger Hawley, Lucile Cummings Bagley, Steve Neal, photographer Gerry Lewin, Jerry McGee, and all the families who wrote down their memories and occurrences.

Thanks to all those who have preserved Salem heritage photographs and documents to tell the story of Oregon's history: Bush House Museum, Oregon State Library, Oregon State Archives, Salem Public Library, Willamette Heritage Center, oregonpioneers.com, and the *Statesman Journal*.

The photographs in this book are courtesy of the KHM or the following contributors' collections, unless otherwise noted. Abbreviations used in this book are as follows:

Blake	William and Ida Blake (John Blake, Pat Blake LaRock)
Claggett	Ben and Mabel Claggett (Keith Claggett)
Gallagher	Jim and Barbara Gallagher
Herber	Rosalie Herber (Tyrene Herber Denlinger)
Jones	Alice Rose Jones (Corie Jones)
Keefer	Daniel and Myra Keefer (Fred Schaeffer)
Keizur	Keizur family (Ginger Riley Powers, Gary Keizur)
McCarty	McCarty Family Collection
Melson	Evelyn Melson Franz
Pearmine	Lester Pearmine Jr. (Ron Pearmine)
Sangster	Katherine Barry Sangster
Saucy	Paul and Tracey Saucy Collection
SJ	*Statesman Journal*
SPL	Salem Public Library Historic Photograph Collections

INTRODUCTION

Many local stories about the past two centuries can be found at the Keizer Heritage Museum. After looking around Keizer, a person could be forgiven for thinking it is a relatively new settlement. Unlike other Oregon cities, it does not have a downtown filled with 19th-century buildings. Keizer does have two structures in the downtown core that date to the early 1900s: the Frank Evans house, near the corner of River Road and Dearborn Avenue (currently the café Mommy and Maddi's), and the old Keizer School, which found new life as the Keizer Heritage Center at the civic center campus on Chemawa Road.

The mild climate of the Willamette Valley made it a favorite winter camp for the Native American Kalapuya people. The animal life, trees, river, and smaller waterways, along with the rich soil abundant with the native camas and other vegetation, provided a land on which they could live and thrive for thousands of years. Reports of plentiful wildlife brought fur trappers from the Astor Fur Company to this area in 1812. Their fur-trading post was on a bluff overlooking the Willamette River in what is now southeast Keizer. William Wallace was one of the leaders of the group. The lodging they built was known as the Wallace house or fort. This area became known as Wallace Prairie.

In 1834, at the request of Native Americans of the Flathead tribe who desired to know about "the book of heaven," the Board of Missions of the Methodist Episcopal Church selected Rev. Jason Lee to lead a group of 70 people on a journey to this new land. Their mission on the Willamette River was just a few miles north of what would later become Keizer. Flooding in Mission Bottom forced the missionaries to move south. Reverend Lee was a founding father of Salem, Oregon, and of the educational institution of the region.

After the Wallace fort and trading post was abandoned, there was little activity in the region until 1843, when Thomas Dove "T.D." Keizur and his party rode into the Willamette Valley and claimed the fertile land that would develop into the core of the city (present-day Shari's Restaurant). The city's name comes from these earliest settlers.

John Force, of the 1842 immigration, worked with the Jason Lee mission in constructing the first mill in Salem. His land claim and large "mission" home on Wallace Prairie was said to have been a stop for travelers, just as the John and Reeda (Keizur) Ford house was also used for lodgers. A large, heartily built barn on the Force claim was known as the Jason Lee Barn.

Early pioneer families risked their lives to trek out West, bringing with them seeds, plant cuttings, and livestock to aid settlement in the new frontier. The bountiful land had varying ecosystems of river bottom, grasslands, and stands of tall, old-growth evergreen fir and other native trees.

Pioneers played instrumental roles in the founding of this new territory. T.D. Keizur was a representative of the Champoeg district in the 1844 provisional government. The Keizurs (the surname has been variously spelled), Pughs, and Horace Holden played vital roles in organizing the new territory, including involvement in the Cayuse Indian War and with the Oregon Rangers, a precursor to the Oregon National Guard.

The Keizurs brought with them breeding horses, including their prized Morgans, along with oxen and cattle. The Claggetts imported the first Angora goats to Marion County and were known for their registered Clydesdale horses, which won accolades at county and state fairs. They also raised fine sheep and racehorses. Later, families brought mink to raise commercially. The Savage and Saucy families operated local dairies that supplied fresh milk.

T.D. Keizur and Horace Holden are recorded to have planted the first apple trees. Imagine walking through the quiet farm country when the creeks were filled with fish and crawdads, and orchards lined the single-lane dirt road that led north to Champoeg. Springtime was filled with the smell and lovely sight of blossoms on apple, cherry, peach, pear, and prune trees. Groves of filberts (hazelnuts) and walnuts were plentiful. Huge trees grew from the plantings of early pioneers. Area nurseries sold quality stock across the country. Farm fields produced bountiful crops of asparagus, blackberries (Loganberries), celery, corn, dandelion, green beans, hay, hops, onions, peppermint, strawberries, and wheat, among others. Hop and prune dryers dotted the landscape to preserve and ready the harvest for market.

The serene, wide-open spaces could be explored on horseback. Common sounds of the day included the whistle of the sternwheelers maneuvering on the river, the singing of the electric wires strung between the telephones, and train whistles on the nearby tracks as the railroads took passengers and cargo to their destinations.

In the 1940s, subdivisions of new homes began to change the farmland. Soon, businesses other than agricultural industries were established, and the town started to take shape. The roads were given names, not just rural route numbers, and were widened and paved. New schools were built to accommodate growth. With resilience, the people endured the ebb and flow of floodwaters from the Willamette River. Installation of dams and dikes mitigated the risks from this natural disaster, and development increased.

Readers can learn and reminisce within these pages, covering pioneer days through the 1960s. More information and photographs can be found at the Keizer Heritage Museum. By purchasing this book, you are helping efforts to display the early years of this neighboring community of Salem.

Officially a young city, Keizer was incorporated in 1982. Join us in a travel back in time, revisiting how it was before the modern day and paying respect to those who have gone before.

One

First Settlers

The town's founding families left everything behind and ventured west to a land with new promises. These were strong, resourceful people. The names of the original settlers were Keizur (three families), Pugh (four families), Claggett, Fisher, Ford, Force, Penter, Purdy, Smart, Smith, Spong, Stephens, and Zieber. In the Clear Lake area, holders of the donation land claims were George Lesley and Jeremiah Stevenson. Claims of Zieber and Smith included land in both communities.

A map from 1851 labels the area south of Mission Bottom (the site of Rev. Jason Lee's first Methodist mission complex) as "Wallace Prairie," a reference to the early fur trappers who resided there. In 1852, a descriptive plat map of Marion County townships notes the area as having "gently undulating bottoms" and "soil first rate clay and sandy loam." "Doke's Ferry" and the road leading from it are the same as today's Spong's Landing Park and Chemawa Road. The higher land to the east of the river was rich with timber fir.

In the early 1850s, only 18 families laid claim to the Keizer area, their lands totaling approximately 7,655 acres. However, some of these donation land claims included parts of other communities, such as Hayesville, Clear Lake, Chemawa, and North Salem. The City of Salem now extends its boundaries to such an extent that the claim of one of the Keizurs for whom the community is named is almost wholly within Salem.

These pioneers took an active part in government. They served on school boards, commissions, and in minor political offices. They signed petitions for and against roads, for prohibition of liquor, against the incorporation of Salem and then for it; for a district court, for a charter for the Oregon Institute, and for a toll bridge across Lake Labish. As the population increased, travel along the Willamette River grew. Riverboats stopped regularly at Spong's and Beardsley Landings, bringing farm workers, freight, and passengers.

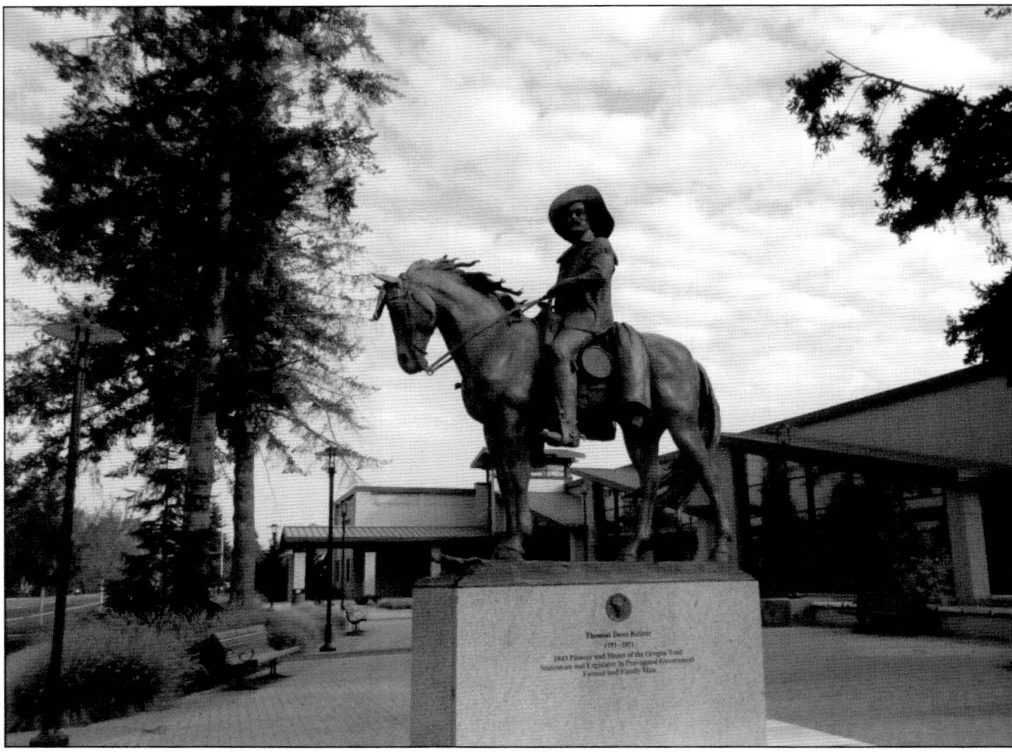

The unveiling of the Thomas Dove Keizur statue took place at Keizer Civic Center on January 30, 2010. More than 140 descendants witnessed the likeness of their patriarch mounted on his beloved Morgan horse. Keizur was an 1843 Oregon pioneer and founder of the Oregon militia. The Keizur clan may spell their name in various ways, but they all know where their roots were established. (Tammy Wild.)

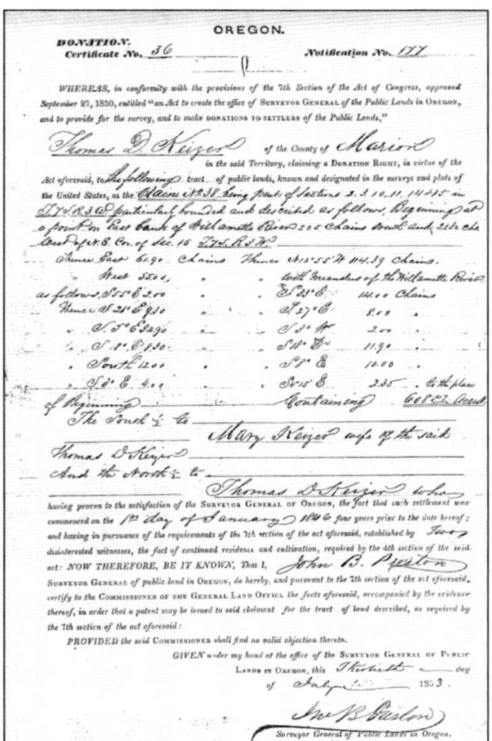

OREGON.

DONATION.
Certificate No. 36 Notification No. 177

WHEREAS, in conformity with the provisions of the 7th Section of the Act of Congress, approved September 27, 1850, entitled "an Act to create the office of SURVEYOR GENERAL of the Public Lands in OREGON, and to provide for the survey, and to make DONATIONS TO SETTLERS of the Public Lands,"

Thomas D. Keizer of the County of Marion in the said Territory, claiming a DONATION RIGHT, in virtue of the Act aforesaid, to the following tract of public lands, known and designated in the surveys and plats of the United States, as the Claim No. 38 being part of Sections 2, 3, 10, 11, 14 & 15 in T. 7 S. R. 3 W. particularly bounded and described as follows, Beginning at a point on East bank of Willamette River 2.25 chains South and 21.12 chs West of N.E. Cor. of Sec. 15 T. 7 S. R. 3 W.

Thence East 61.90 chains Thence N. 12° 55' W. 114.39 chains.
" West 55.00 " " with meanders of the Willamette River
as follows, S. 55° E. 2.00 " " S. 35° E. 14.00 chains
Thence S. 21° E. 9.30 " " S. 27° E. 8.00 "
" S. 5° E. 32.90 " " S. 3° W. 2.00 "
" S. 1° E. 8.30 " " S. 18° W. 11.90 "
" South 12.00 " " S. 8° E. 10.00 "
" S. 6° E. 4.00 " " S. 4° 15' E. 2.35 " to the place of Beginning Containing 608.22 Acres

The South ½ to Mary Keizer wife of the said Thomas D. Keizer And the North ½ to Thomas D. Keizer who having proven to the satisfaction of the SURVEYOR GENERAL OF OREGON, the fact that such settlement was commenced on the 1st day of January 1846 four years prior to the date hereof; and having in pursuance of the requirements of the 7th section of the act aforesaid, established by Two disinterested witnesses, the fact of continued residence and cultivation, required by the 4th section of the said act: NOW THEREFORE, BE IT KNOWN, That I, John B. Preston SURVEYOR GENERAL of public land in OREGON, do hereby, and pursuant to the 7th section of the act aforesaid, certify to the COMMISSIONER OF THE GENERAL LAND OFFICE the facts aforesaid, accompanied by the evidence thereof, in order that a patent may be issued to said claimant for the tract of land described, as required by the 7th section of the act aforesaid:

PROVIDED the said COMMISSIONER shall find no valid objection thereto.

GIVEN under my hand at the office of the SURVEYOR GENERAL OF PUBLIC LANDS IN OREGON, this Thirtieth day of July 1853.

Jno B. Preston
Surveyor General of Public Lands in Oregon.

In 1843, the Keizurs and their horses and cattle settled north of Salem on the west side of the Willamette River. By the spring of 1844, they had re-crossed the river and settled near the head of what was called Keizer's rapids. Thomas and Mary's name was spelled "Keizer" on their Donation Certificate No. 36 (pictured). Each had equal shares of the 640 acres. (Ginger Riley Powers.)

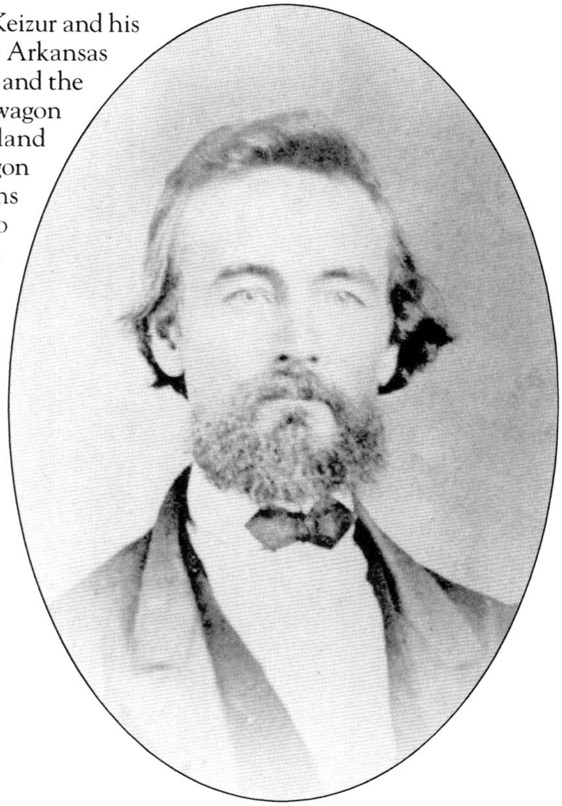

Natives of North Carolina, Thomas Dove Keizur and his family traveled west to Tennessee, then to Arkansas and Missouri, joining the "great migration" and the Oregon Emigration Company. The 1843 wagon train was the first to complete the overland trek to the Willamette Valley in the Oregon Territory. The family consisted of five sons and five daughters, eight grandchildren, two sons-in-law, and a brother of a son-in-law. (Ginger Riley Powers.)

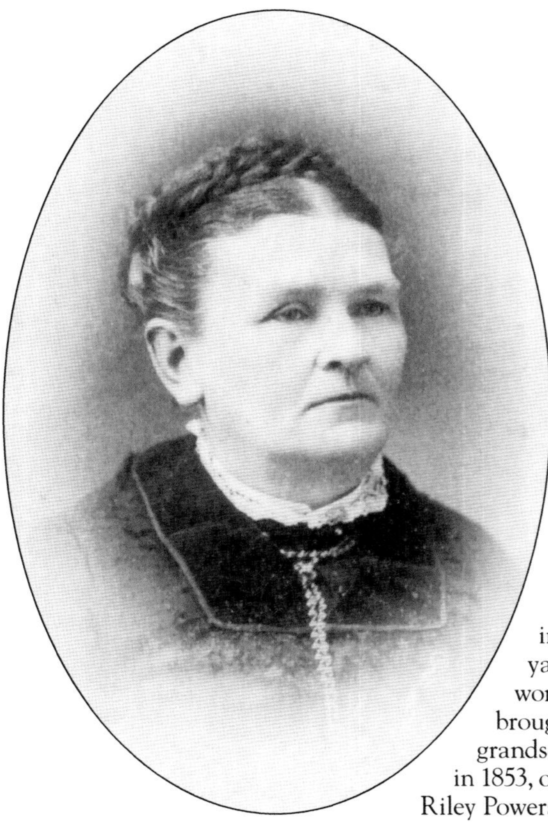

Mary Gurley and T.D. Keizer were born on the same day in 1793 in North Carolina. An industrious woman, Gurley raised cotton, spun yarn, and knitted socks that Thomas Keizer wore on his wedding day in 1828. The socks were brought across the plains and worn by sons and grandsons at their marriages. Gurley died at age 60 in 1853, only 10 years after arriving in Oregon. (Ginger Riley Powers.)

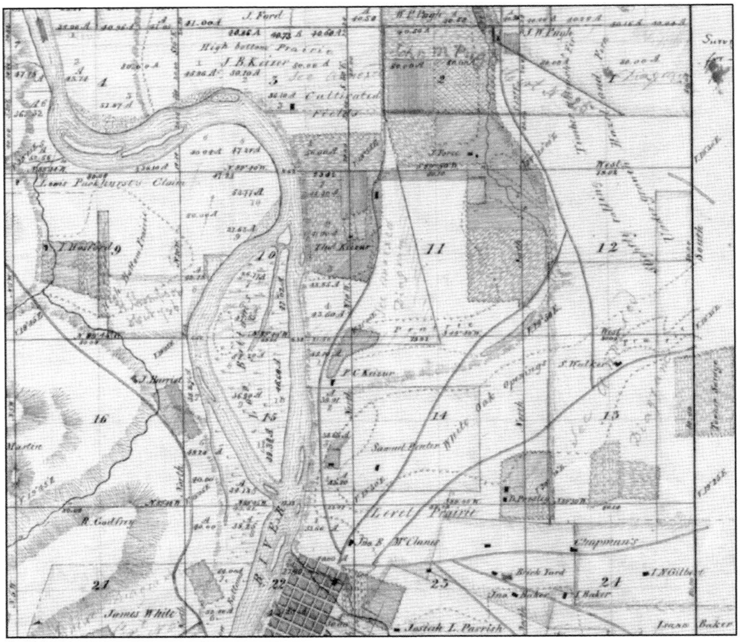

This neatly drawn 1852 original land survey shows the Keizer family land claims along the Willamette River. Note the cultivated fields and land descriptions, with "bottom" and "prairie" lands described. The city blocks of Salem are visible to the south. Today's roads are clearly defined. (Bureau of Land Management.)

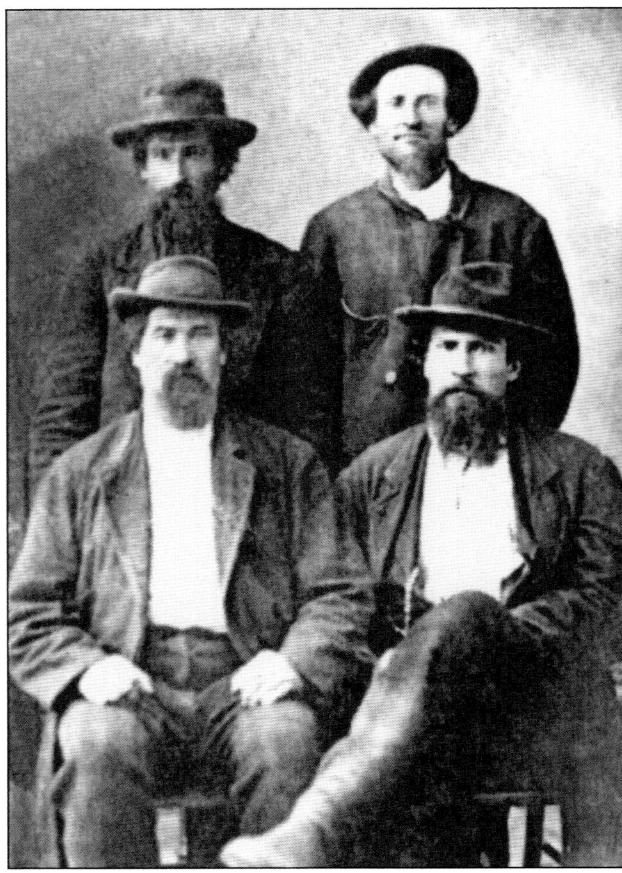

Very few photographs exist today of the Keizer ancestors. Thomas and Mary Keizur had ten children: five sons and five daughters. The brothers shown in this undated photograph are, from left to right, (seated) Pleasant Cicero and Francis Marion; (standing) William Henry Harrison and Thomas Cullwell. The oldest brother, John Brooks, died in 1870. Before 1900, William H.H. and Francis Marion moved to Idaho. (Ginger Riley Powers.)

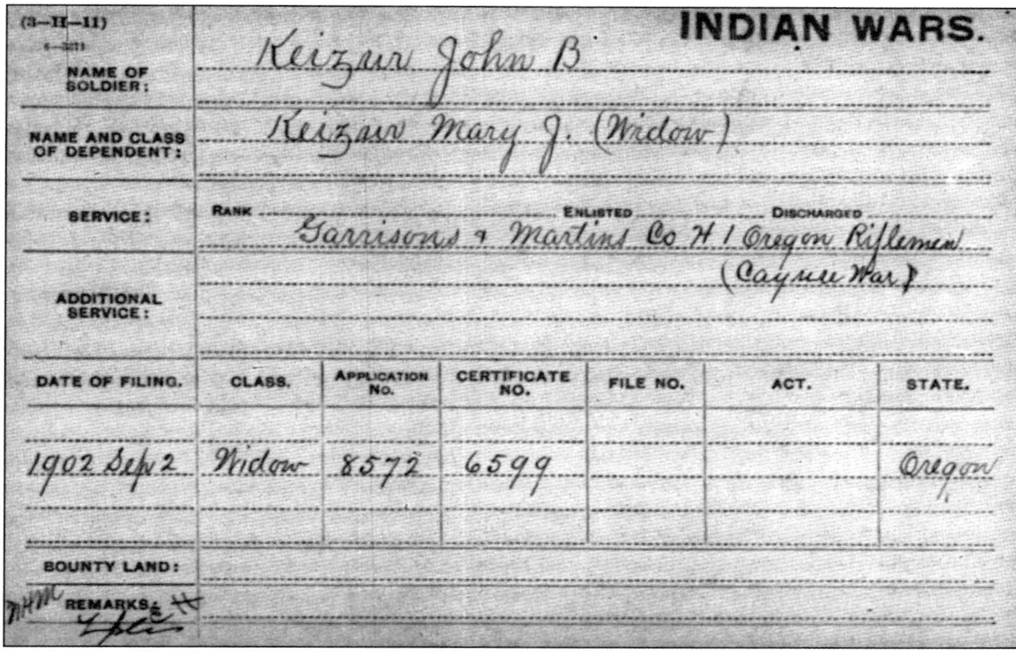
(3—II—11)

INDIAN WARS.

NAME OF SOLDIER: Keizur John B.

NAME AND CLASS OF DEPENDENT: Keizur Mary J. (Widow)

SERVICE: RANK ...... ENLISTED ...... DISCHARGED ......
Garrisons & Martins Co H 1 Oregon Riflemen (Cayuse War)

ADDITIONAL SERVICE:

DATE OF FILING.	CLASS.	APPLICATION NO.	CERTIFICATE NO.	FILE NO.	ACT.	STATE.
1902 Sep 2	Widow	8572	6599			Oregon

BOUNTY LAND:

REMARKS:

Area men enlisted with the Oregon Riflemen during the Cayuse War, including Capt. Thomas Dove Keizur and his sons Pleasant C. and John B. Keizur. Note the variation of the last name on this document. Silas and Will Pugh served with the company of volunteers in the war, William as captain and Silas as second lieutenant. Another area farmer, Horace Holden, was documented to have enlisted. (US Pension Files.)

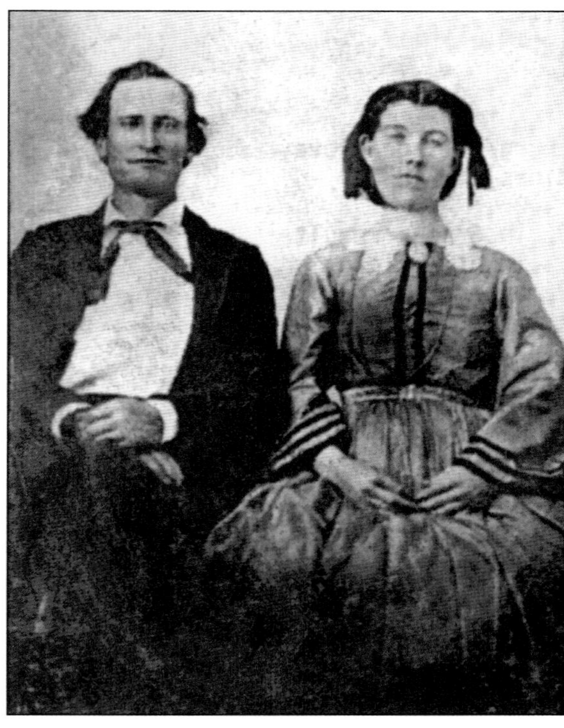

Thomas Cullwell Keizur and Sarah Isabella Ramsey were married in Salem on November 22, 1855, by Daniel Bagley, minister of the gospel, at the Ramsey dwelling. They settled in the Roseburg/Cottage Grove area and had 12 children. "Cull" died from an accidental shooting in 1906 in Dorena. (Ginger Riley Powers.)

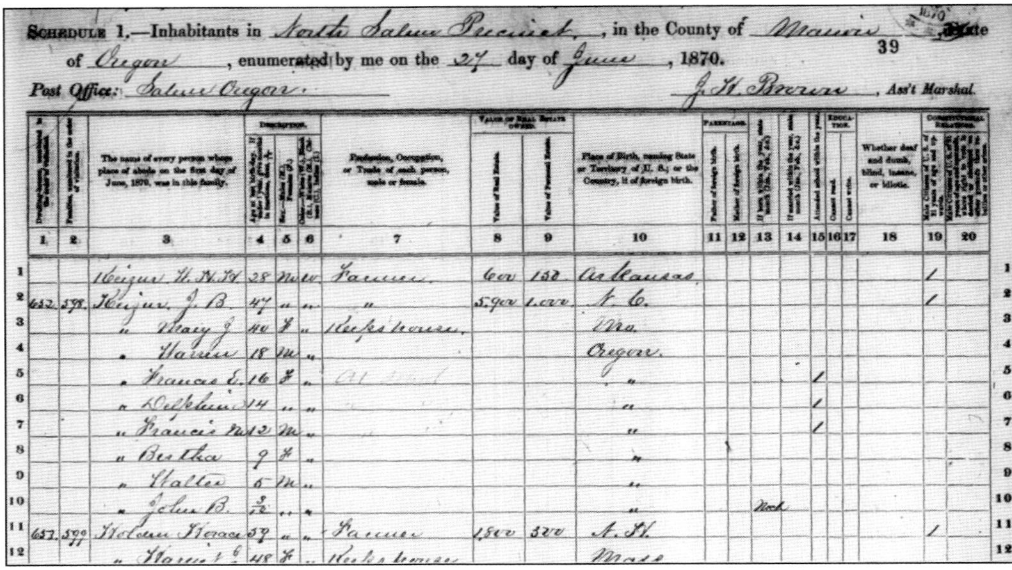

SCHEDULE 1.—Inhabitants in North Salem Precinct, in the County of Marion, State of Oregon, enumerated by me on the 27 day of June, 1870. 39

Post Office: Salem Oregon. J.W. Brown, Ass't Marshal.

	1	2	3	4	5	6	7	8	9	10	13	15	19
1			Keizur W.H.H.	28	M	W	Farmer	600	150	Arkansas			/
2	652	598	Keizur J.B.	47	"	"	"	5,900	1,000	N.C.			/
3			" Mary J	40	F	"	Keeps house			Mo.			
4			" Warren	18	M	"				Oregon			
5			" Frances E.	16	F	"				"		/	
6			" Delphine	14	"	"				"		/	
7			" Francis M.	12	M	"				"		/	
8			" Bertha	9	F	"				"			
9			" Walter	5	M	"				"			
10			" John B.	3/12	"	"				"	Mch		
11	653	599	Holden Horace	57	"	"	Farmer	1,800	300	N.H.			/
12			" Harriet	48	F	"	Keeps house			Mass			

Enumerated in the June 1870 census for Marion County, North Salem Precinct, are William Henry Harrison Keizur and his brother John Brooks and his wife, Mary Keizur. The couple had seven children living at home. Also listed are neighbor Horace Holden and his wife, Harriet. The Holdens purchased a portion of the John Force land claim that was on the west side of the road from the Keizurs. (US Census.)

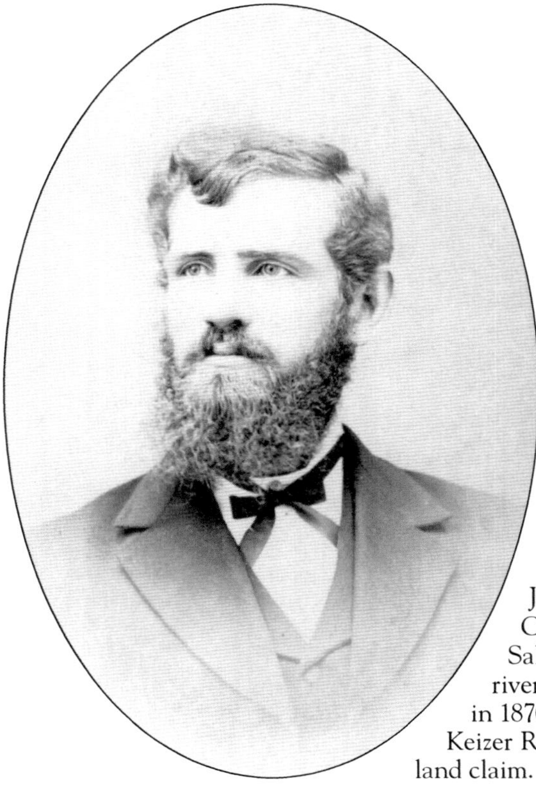

John Brooks Keizur was born in 1824 in North Carolina. He married Mary Jane Herron in Salem in 1851. They raised eight children on the riverfront farmland next to his parents. John died in 1870 at his residence. Cummings Elementary and Keizer Rapids Park are located on the old J.B. Keizur land claim. (Ginger Riley Powers.)

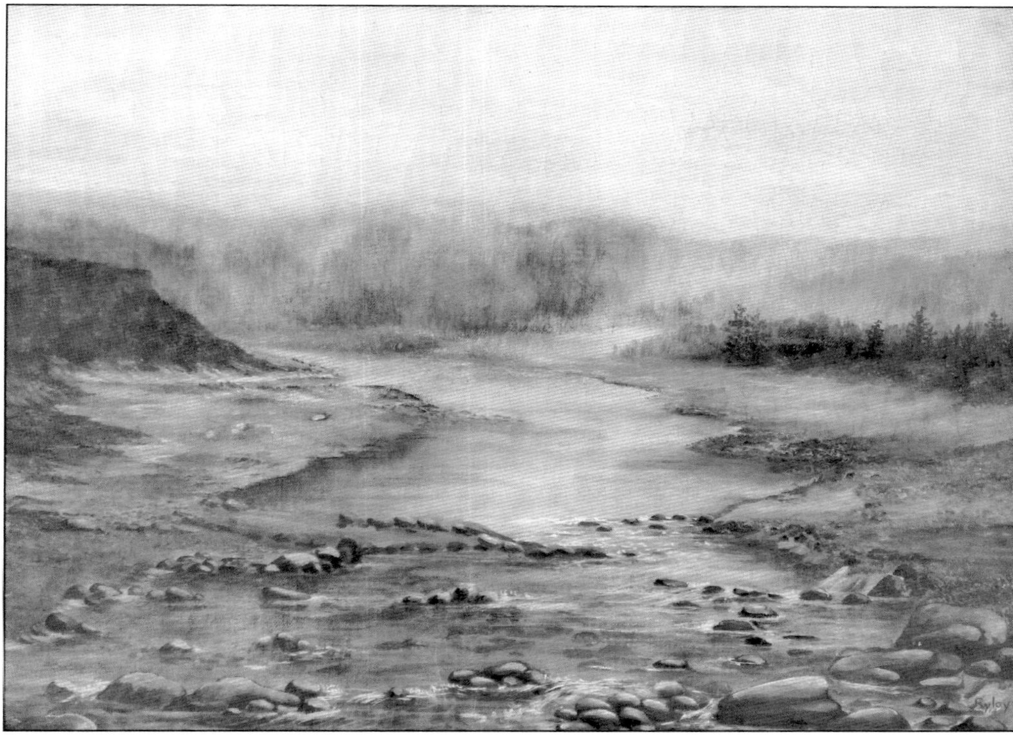

Evelyn Bertha Keizur Ryley, daughter of John Brooks and Mary Jane Keizur, painted from her memory this scene of the property of her grandfather, Thomas Dove Keizur. T.D. is said to have been buried on the knoll of his property, overlooking the river. The exact location of the grave and T.D. Keizur's bodily remains are still a mystery. (Ginger Riley Powers.)

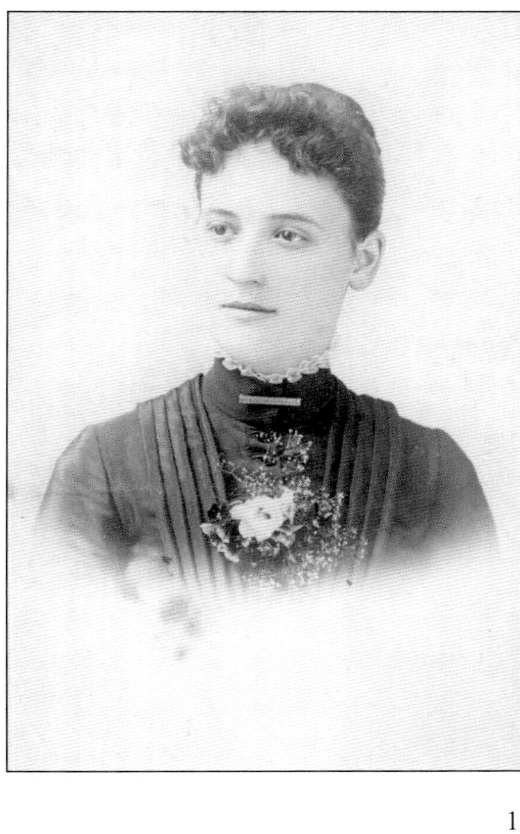

Evelyn Bertha Keizur Ryley was the daughter of John Brooks and Mary Jane Keizur. Bertha, as her name is sometimes listed, married Richard Hibbert Ryley in 1899 and had three children. The family later moved to Texas when son Adaulphs K. Ryley returned from service during World War I. (Ginger Riley Powers.)

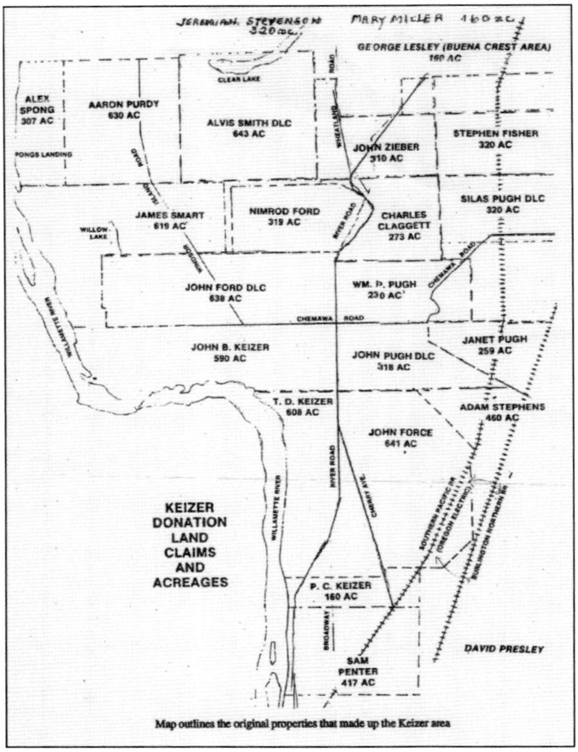

Note the Keizur families' land claims along the Willamette River. Sam Penter and John Ford are sons-in-law of T.D. and Mary Keizur. This map of Keizer donation land claims and acreages was compiled from early maps by Ann Lossner in her research of the Keizer area and pioneers. Her books and research materials are available at the Keizer Heritage Museum. (KHM.)

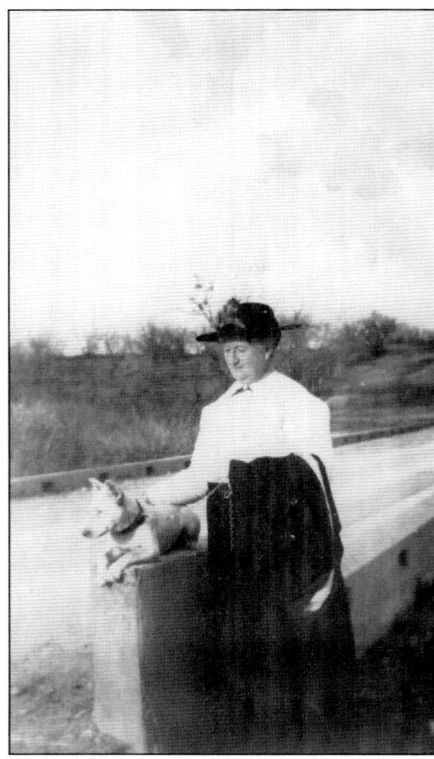

Mabel Zieber Keizer poses with her dog in 1916. Her husband was Sylvanus Franklin Keizer, grandson of T.D. Keizur. "Frank" died in 1900 in Alaska. Mabel later married his brother, John Brooks Jr. Mabel's family, also early settlers, came across the Oregon Trail in 1851. (Courtesy of the Oregon State Library.)

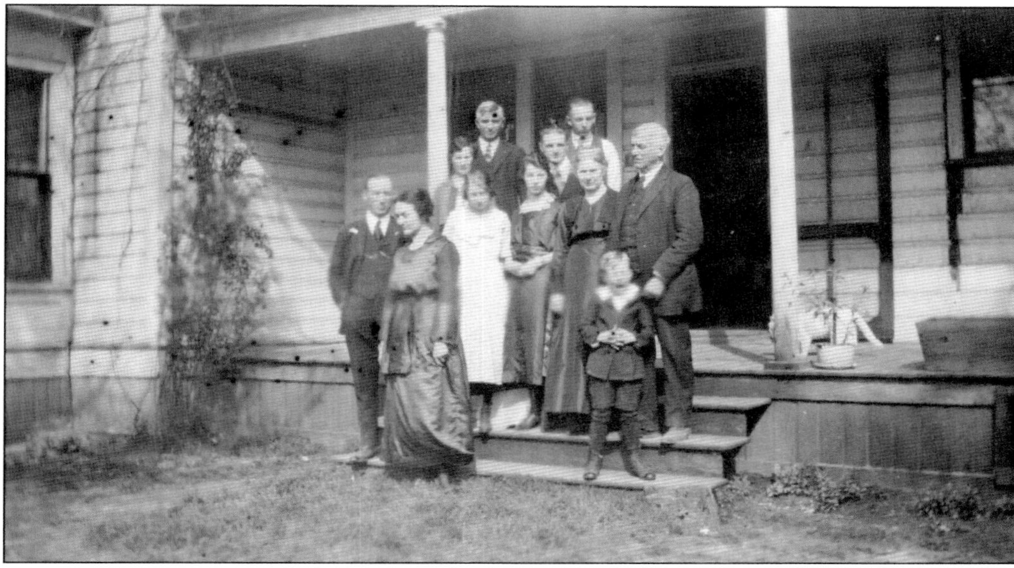

Emil Keizur and Cora Speelman (left) were married on September 1, 1912, in Baker, Oregon. The two older folks on the right are Estelle Pugh Keizur (wife of Lafe and daughter of W.P. Pugh), and Marcus Lafayette "Lafe" Keizur (son of John Brooks Keizur). The others are unidentified. The location of this scene is not known. (Gary Keizur.)

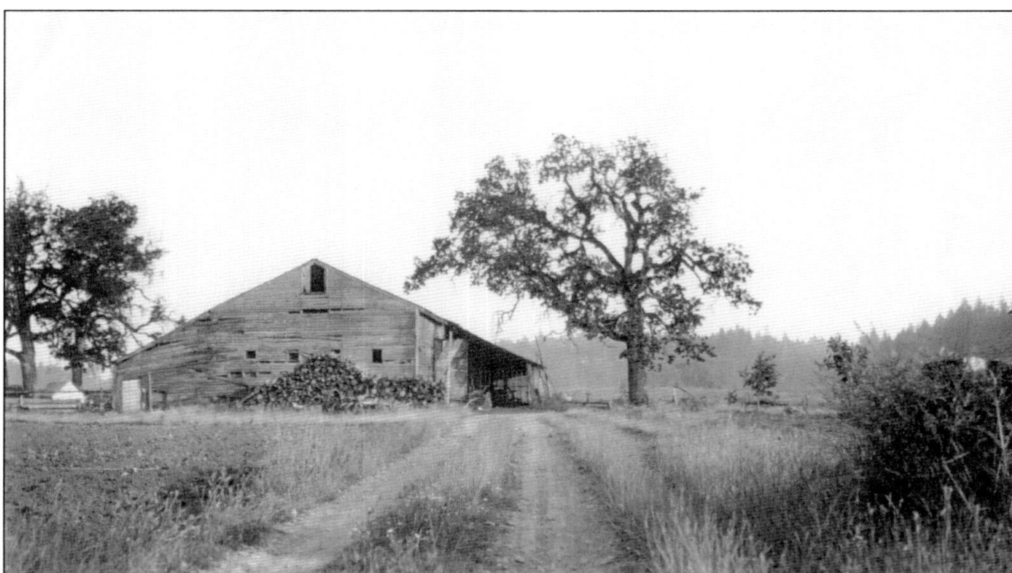

The "Jason Lee barn" is seen here at Wallace Prairie, over 500 acres of land owned by Asahel Bush and managed from 1922 to 1941 by David Saucy Sr. According to Gladys Webb Fitts, the large inside support timbers, measuring 10 inches by 12 inches, were hewn by ax. No nails were used; the beams were notched and dovetailed, with wooden pegs. The barn was located behind the farmhouse at what is now Arnold Street. (Paul and Tracey Saucy Collection.)

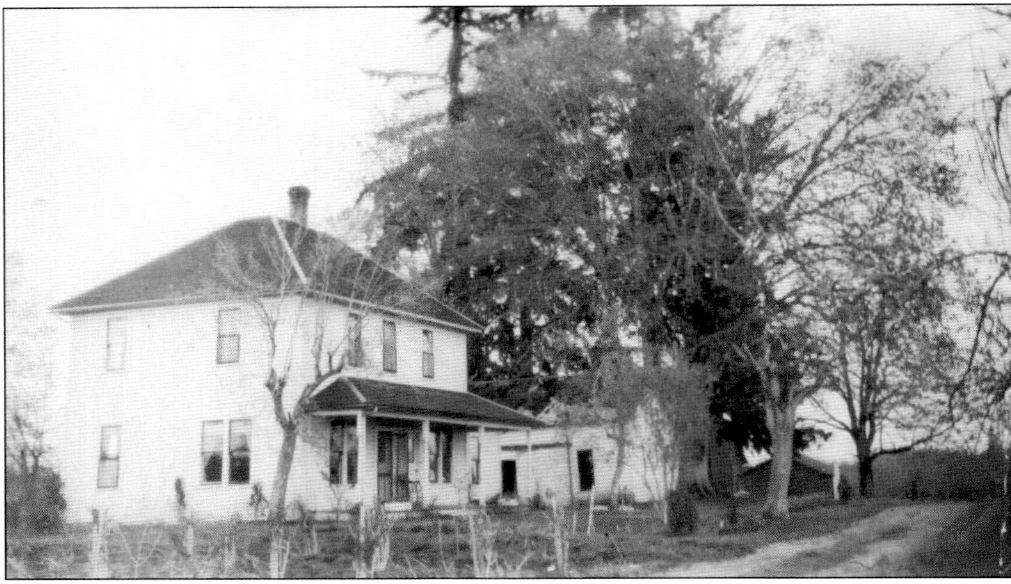

In 1927, Roy and Etta Melson purchased 34 acres of the John Force donation land claim. The farm extended from River Road on the west to Claggett Creek on the east. It consisted of walnut, filbert, and cherry orchards, a swale, a pasture, and an oak grove. Before 1940, the creek was known for crawdad and trout. (Melson.)

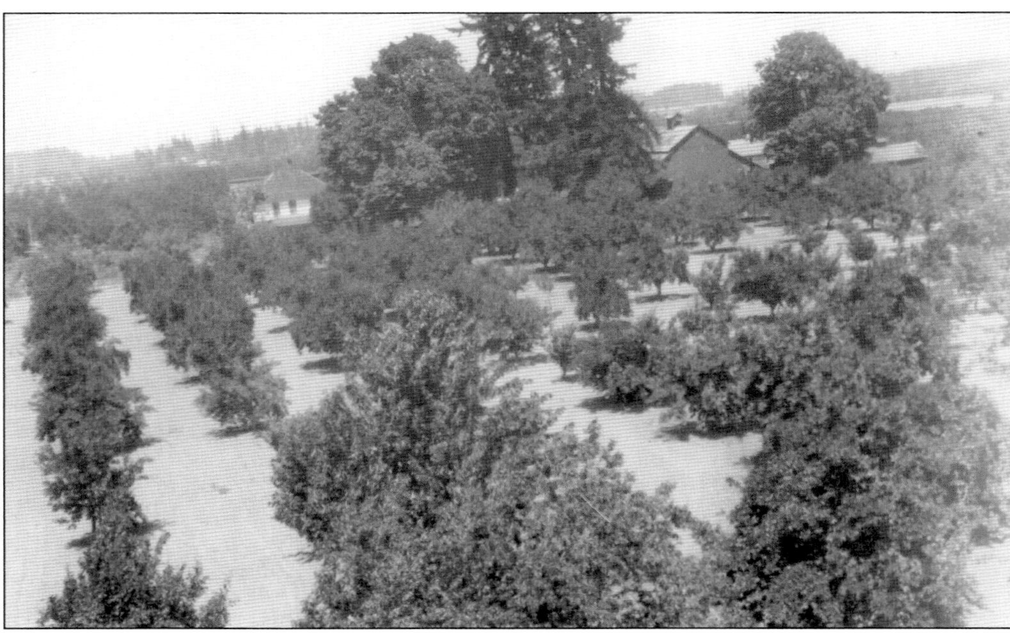

Along with the large two-story farm home that from early days housed travelers, the property consisted of a prune dryer, a barn, a smaller house, and a rabbitry. Evelyn Melson Franz recalls the most delicious apples from heirloom varieties that were well-established trees when she was a child. "Pound" pears were not good for eating and made a loud thump when they fell. (Melson.)

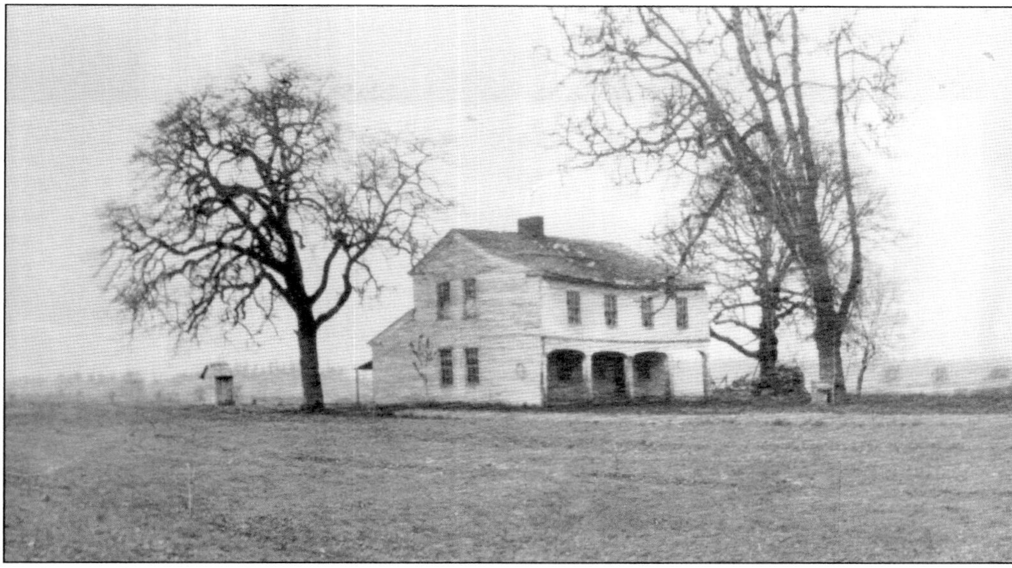

Beda "Reeda" Keizur, daughter of T.D. Keizur, and John Ford were newlyweds in 1842 when the young couple joined the Applegate wagon train. Ford was born in 1818, Reeda in 1822, both in North Carolina. They settled their 638-acre claim in 1844 and began selling their land in 1862. Their claim, north of the other Keizur claims, included the Keizer School grounds. Ford died in 1875. (KHM.)

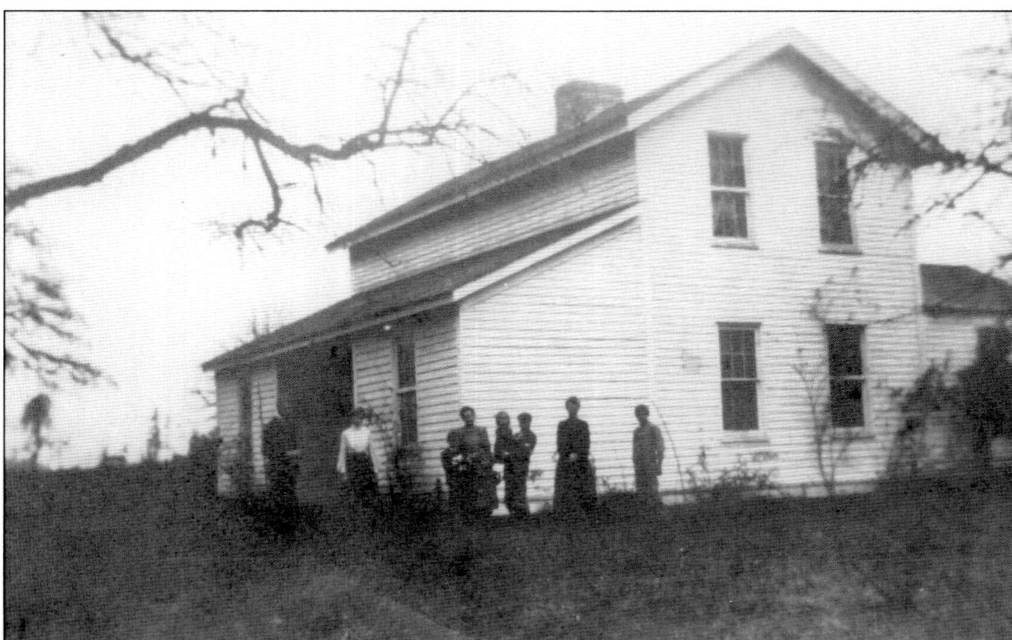

The Daniel and Myra Keefer family pose in front of their home in 1910. This home was the former dwelling of William Claggett, who purchased the original John and Reeda Ford house. The Fords kept a room available to welcome weary travelers in the early days. The foundation timbers rotted, and the home was replaced in 1917 by Daniel Keefer and his son, Hal, with a Craftsman house on Trail Avenue. (Keefer.)

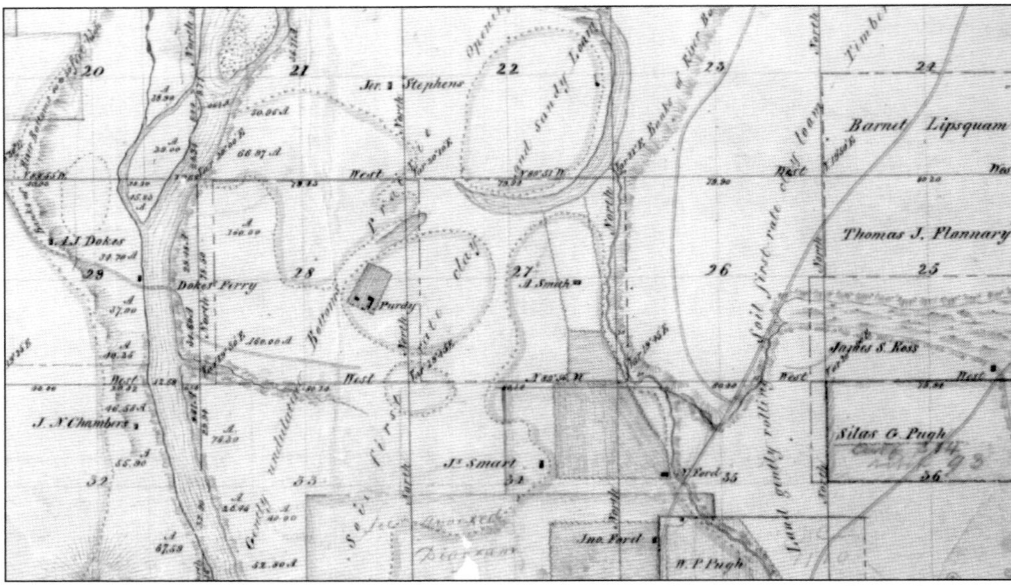

This 1852 survey shows the northern land claims along the Willamette River. Farmlands are noted with descriptive words. "Doke's" (Doaks) Ferry and road look the same as today (now Windsor Island Road and Spong's Landing Park). Other descriptive terms include "Prairie" and "North Banks of River Bottom" (Verda Lane area). (Bureau of Land Management.)

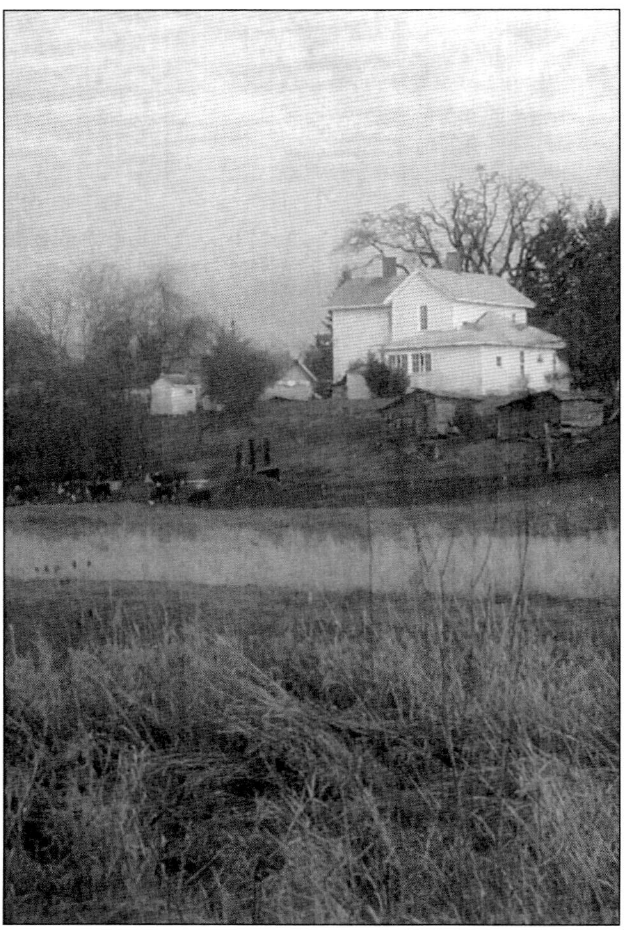

The John and Sally (Claggett) Pugh house at 4845 Verda Lane stands on the ridge above Claggett Creek. The home, built around 1875, is Keizer's oldest. Huge rocks for the foundation were hauled from the Santiam River. Plumbing and a bathroom were installed in 1930 by the Savage family. The Savages built the small one-bedroom house on the south side. Keizer View Dairy was on this property. (Tyrene Herber Denlinger.)

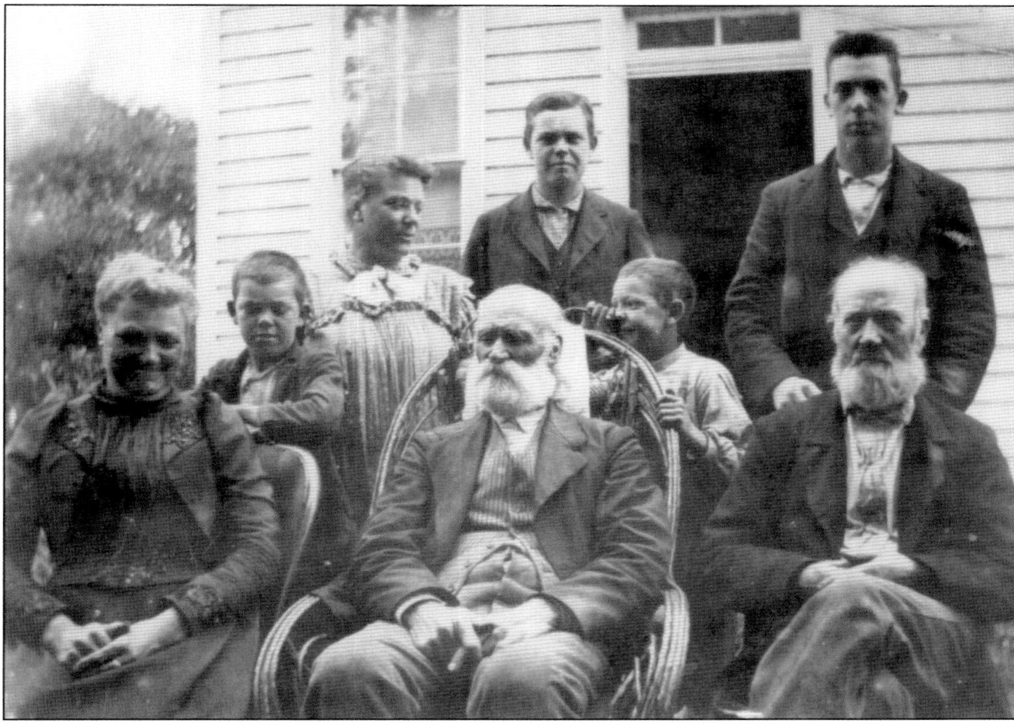

Members of the Silas and Sarah Rose Pugh family have gathered for a photograph. They are, from left to right, (seated) Sarah Jane Rose Pugh, Commodore S.D. Rose (Sarah's father), and Silas George Pugh (Sarah's husband); (standing) George Beaty (son of Josephine Pugh and Frank Beaty), Josephine Pugh Beaty (daughter of Silas and Sarah Pugh), Carl Beaty (son of Josephine), Otto Beaty, and George Pugh. S.D. Rose died in 1899. (KHM: Carrie Alexander.)

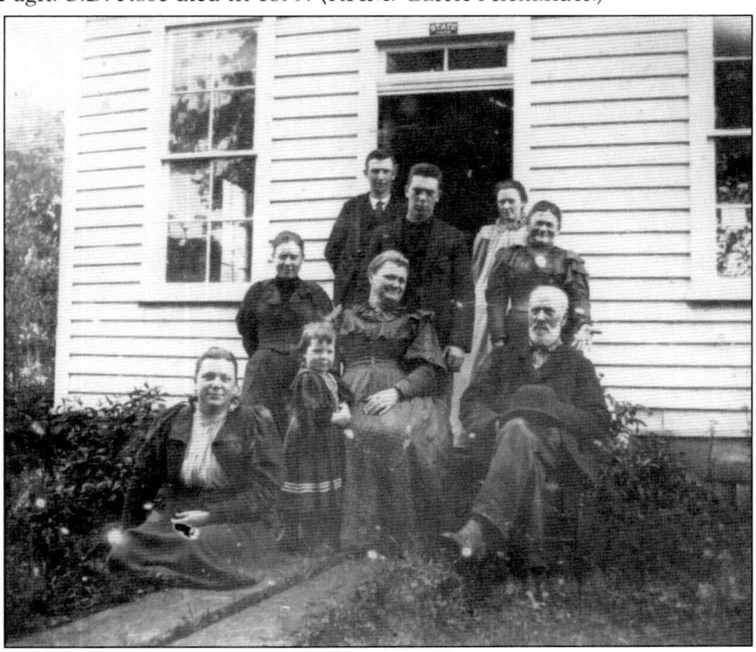

Silas and Sarah Rose Pugh's home and land claim included part of Lake Labish as well as the clay banks above the lake. Silas started a brickyard and made the bricks for the buildings at the Indian School. Most of those structures were demolished in 1977, more than 100 years later. (KHM: Carrie Alexander.)

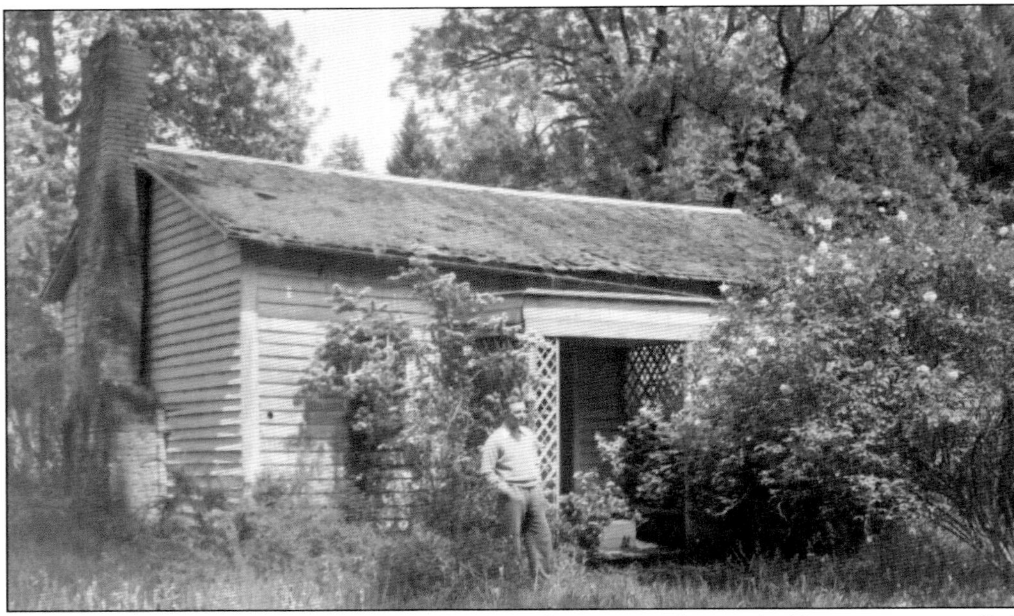

The Zieber house, Fernhazel, was originally a log cabin. Later, siding and additions were installed. John Zieber was the father of Eugenia, wife of Asahel Bush. She died at the age of 30, after the birth of her fourth child. John Zieber's grandson A.N. Bush, as a young boy, used to stay in an attic room of the cabin. Stuart Bush had the house demolished. This photograph is from 1947. (SPL: Ben Maxwell.)

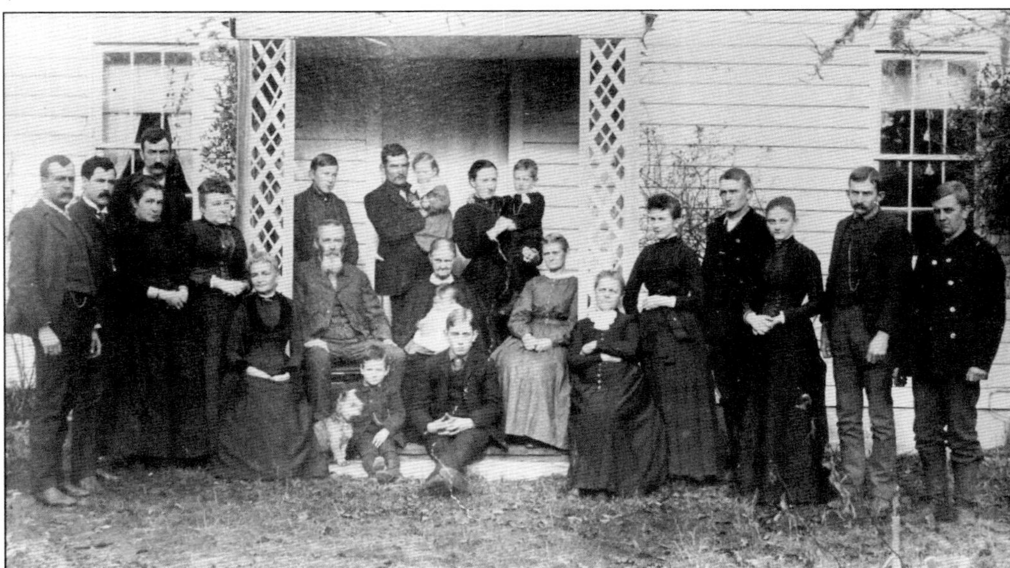

Posing here around 1888 are members of the Zieber, Painter, and Keizer families. They are, from left to right, (on ground) Russell Keizer and William Mumper; (seated) Charlotte Zieber (wife of Albert), Albert Zieber, Eliza Sloan Zieber (holding Cornelia Keizer), Octavia Zieber, and Ella Painter Mumper; (standing) Fred Zieber, Bert Zieber, Eugenia Zieber Campbell, Lucian Campbell (rear), Eliza Zeiber, Tom Zieber, Frank Keizer (holding Margaret), Mabel Z. Keizer (holding Phil), Octavia Painter Nolan, Phil Painter, Zulette Painter, Jack Painter, and Charlie Mumper. (KHM.)

Irma Keefer poses "in a 150 year old wedding trousseau." This is one of many photographs with friend Frances Welch at the old Zieber homestead about 1917. The hickory tree at the house was grown from nuts sent from Pottstown, Pennsylvania, at the request of John Zieber. Irma Keefer lived on Trail Avenue and was a neighbor of the Ziebers and Claggetts. She became a music teacher. (Claggett.)

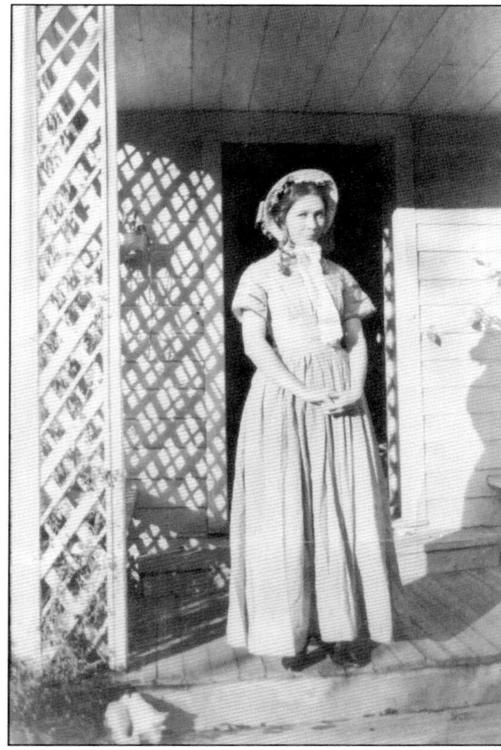

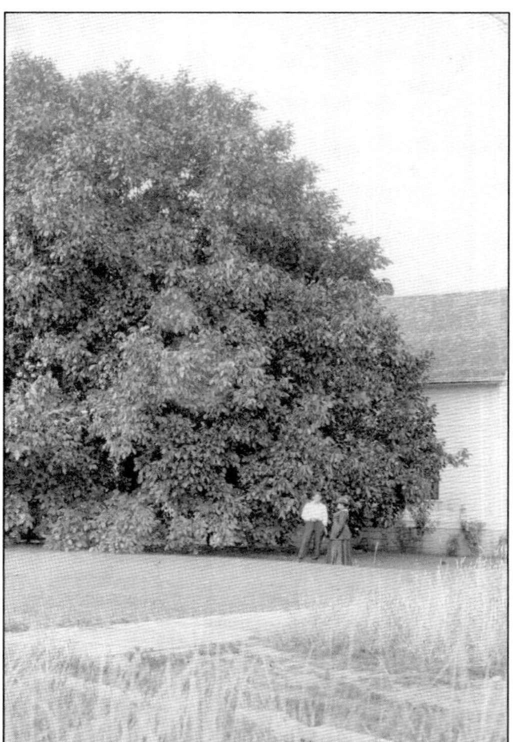

The inscription on the back of this postcard photograph reads: "Walnut tree at home, 1541 N. Front Street. It was the largest tree in the Willamette Valley at one time at the home where Ron and Maxine Clark were born in 1924 and 1912." Ann Lossner notes in her book, *Looking Back*, that Cicero "P.C." Keizur planted walnut trees that grew quite large. His claim was in the same area. (KHM: Maxine Clark Dugger.)

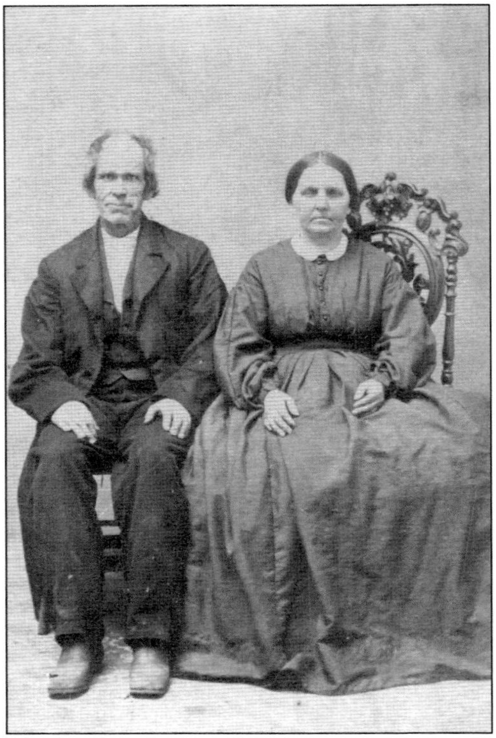

Charles and Mary Irvine Claggett were natives of Kentucky who migrated to Missouri, where their son William was born in 1840. The family left for Oregon in 1852, with 12-year-old William driving one of the two teams of four-yoke oxen. They arrived in October and took up a 320-acre, heavily timbered claim on present-day Trail Avenue, north of Will Pugh's property. (Claggett.)

Shown here is the 1872 warranty deed from E.M. Bamford to William D. Claggett for a portion of the donation land claim of John Ford and his wife, Beda Ann "Reeda" Keizur. The deed reads in part, "Thence west to the north east line of road leading from Salem to Spong's Ferry." John Ford's brother Nimrod had a neighboring claim. Reeda served as a medical practitioner. John Ford died in 1875. (Claggett.)

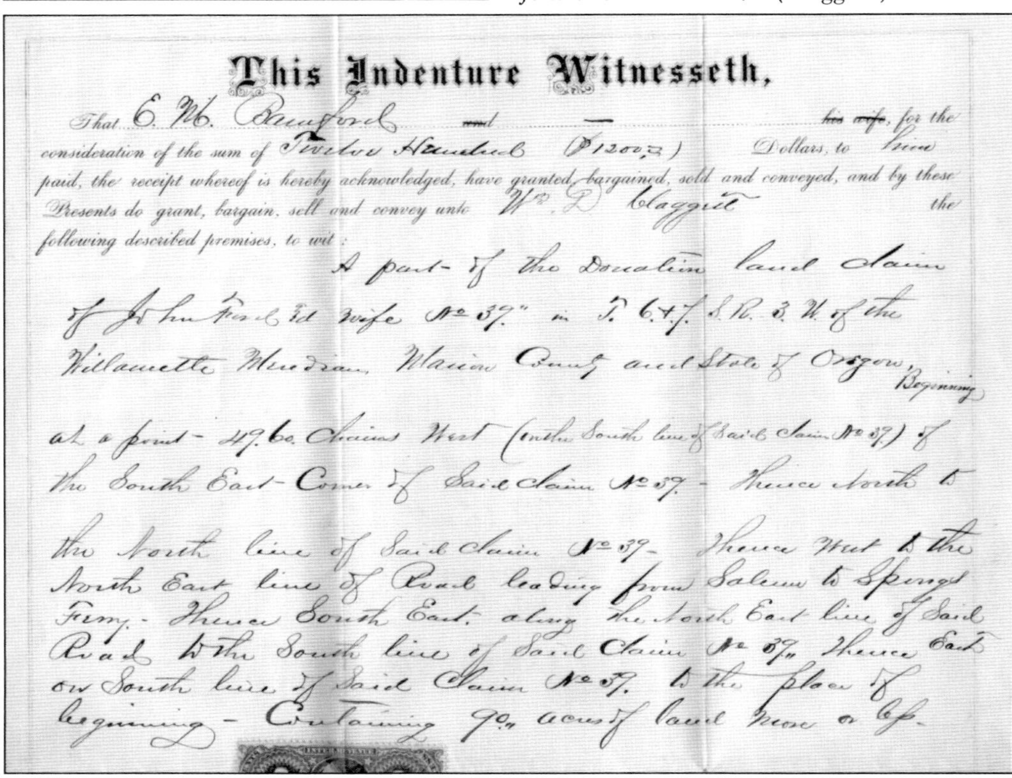

This Indenture Witnesseth,

That E. M. Bamford ~~and~~ — ~~his wife~~, for the consideration of the sum of Twelve Hundred ($1200.00) Dollars, to him paid, the receipt whereof is hereby acknowledged, have granted, bargained, sold and conveyed, and by these Presents do grant, bargain, sell and convey unto Wm. D. Claggett the following described premises, to wit:

A part of the Donation land claim of John Ford & wife No 37 in T. 6 & 7 S. R. 3 W. of the Willamette Meridian Marion County and State of Oregon, Beginning at a point 49.60 chains West (on the South line of Said Claim No 37) of the South East Corner of Said Claim No 37 – Thence North to the North line of Said Claim No 37 – Thence West to the North East line of Road leading from Salem to Spongs Ferry – Thence South East along the North East line of Said Road to the South line of Said Claim No 37 – Thence East on South line of Said Claim No 37 to the place of beginning – Containing 90 acres of land more or less.

Hugh Linza McNary's family emigrated from Kentucky in 1845. Hugh married Margaret Claggett in 1860 and later moved to the Claggett claim, where the younger five children were born and lived on the knoll above what is now McNary Golf Club. The McNarys' 10 children served the community in various ways. Margaret died in 1878 at age 43. Both are buried at Claggett Creek Cemetery. (SPL: Al Jones).

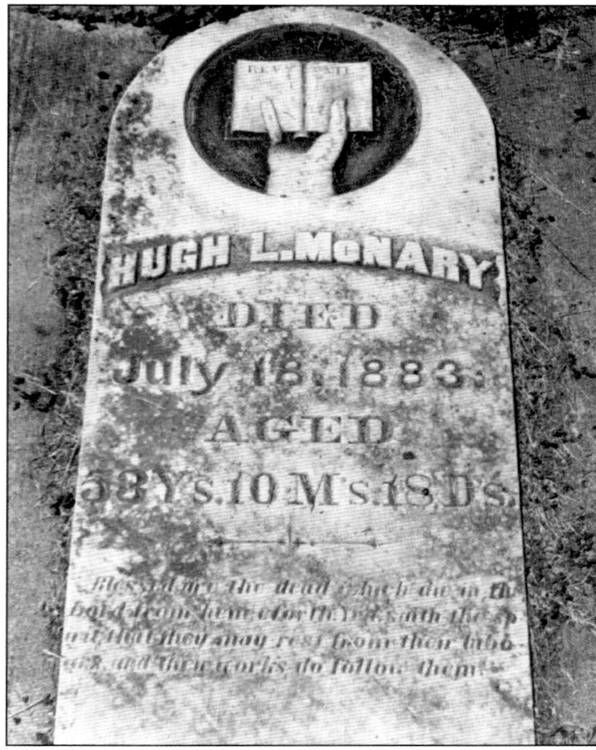

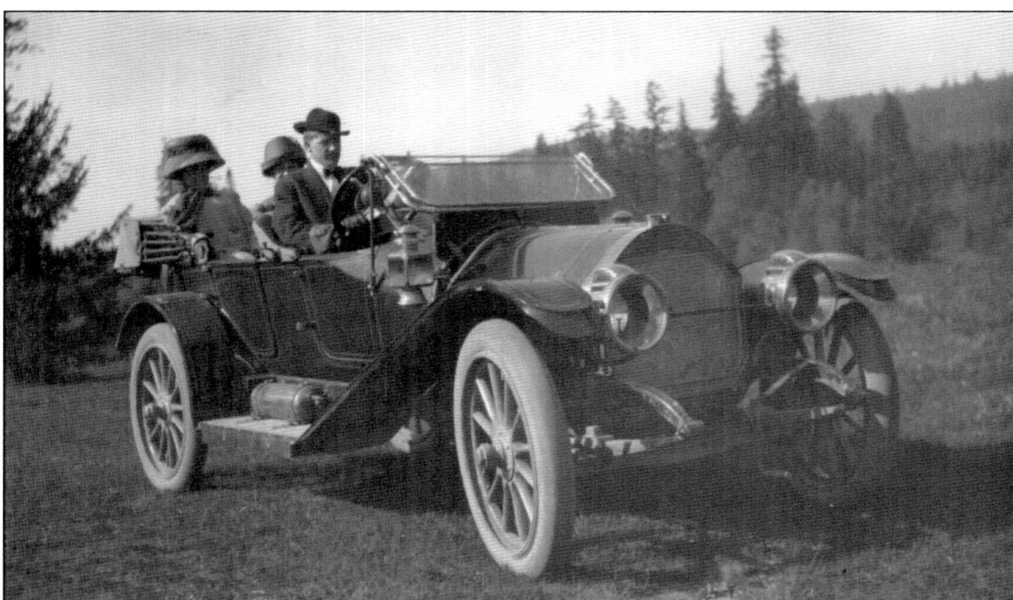

Sen. Charles McNary and unidentified women are out for a drive in one of the first Buicks in Salem. McNary married Jessie Breyman in 1901 at her parents' Salem mansion. Tragedy befell the popular couple in 1918. Just south of Newberg, she died in an automobile accident while visiting in Oregon from Washington, DC, for her mother's funeral. (Courtesy of the Oregon State Library.)

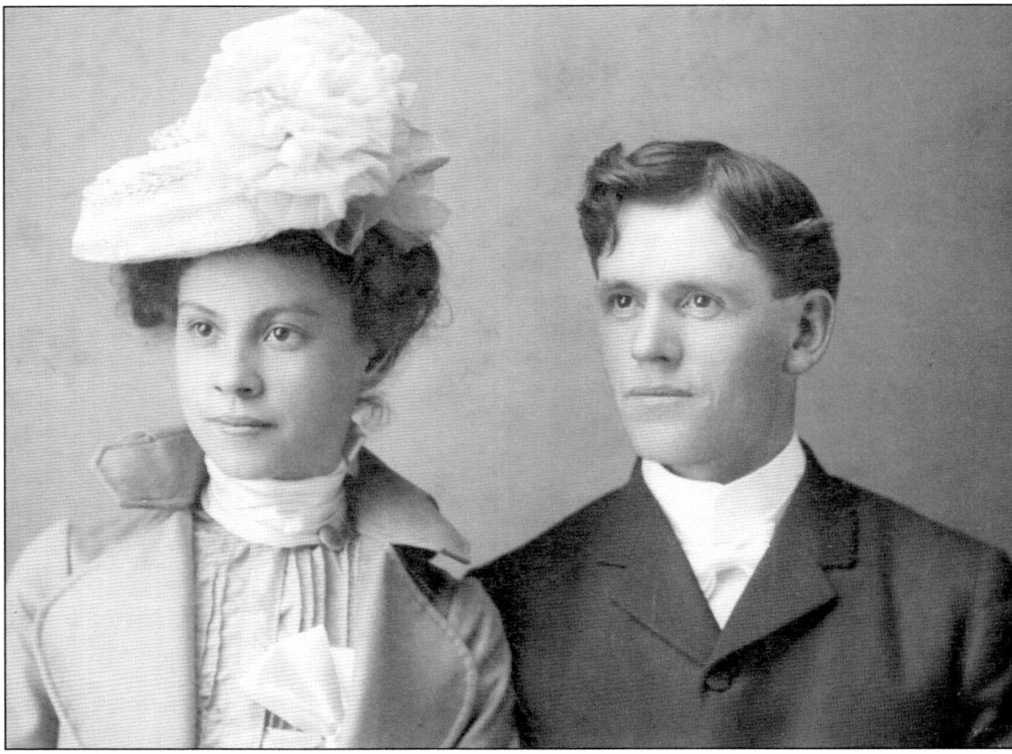

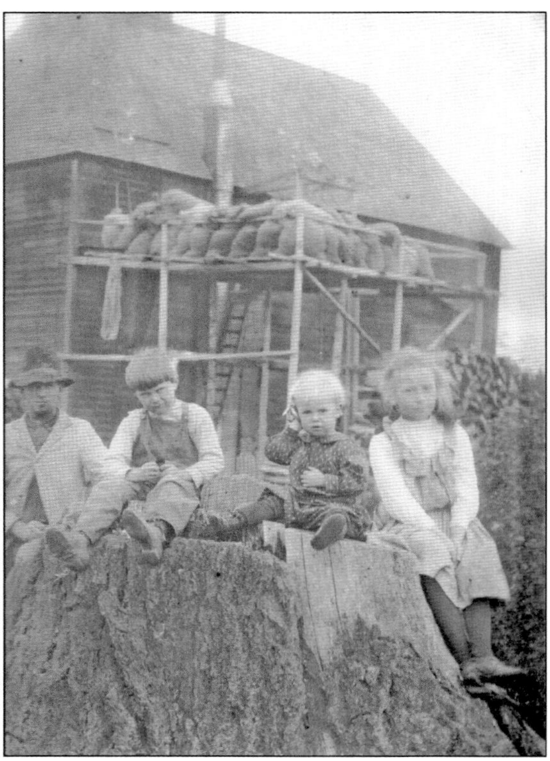

Charles William "Charley" Claggett and his wife, Della (Goodrich), were married on March 26, 1902, at her parents' home near Chemawa. They had three children before Charley's untimely death in September 1912 after an accident while baling hops near Chemawa. Charles was the son of William D. and Eliza Jane (Parrish) Claggett. Della was the daughter of William Goodrich and later married Calvin Patton. (Claggett.)

Charley Claggett poses here with his children, from left to right, Charles, Lloyd, and Reta, in front of a hop dryer. Sadly, Charley was involved in a tragic accident while engaging in baling hops near Chemawa, breaking his leg and injuring his head. He was hospitalized for several days and was mostly unconscious for that time. This photograph was probably taken shortly before the children's father died in September 1912. (Claggett.)

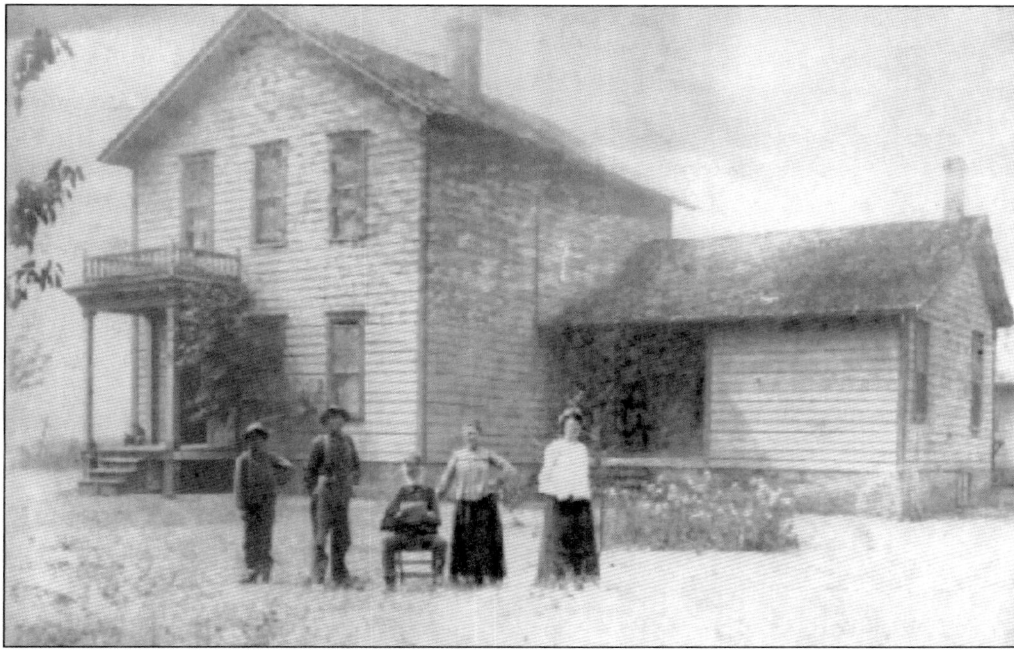

In 1902, Minnie Frogley's parents, Obed and Lucricia Gaines, purchased 238.9 acres from F. and Pauline Levy as part of the original James Smart donation land claim. The date of the house's construction is unknown, but, as it was indicated on a map in the Marion and Linn County Atlas in 1878, it is assumed to have been built prior to that time. Pictured are, from left to right, Obed Frogley, Alfred Frogley, Obed Gaines, Minnie Frogley, and Bessie Frogley. (KHM: Frogley.)

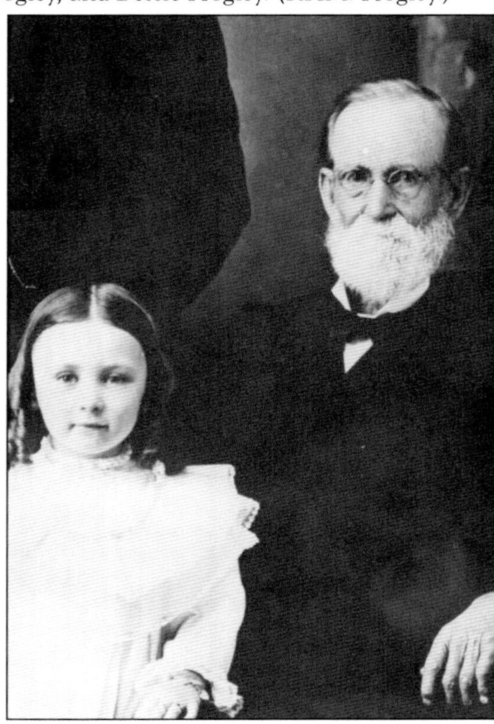

Horace F. Holden was born in Boston in 1810 and went with his parents to the Hawaiian Islands. In 1844, he came to Oregon and purchased a portion of the John Force donation land claim. Holden led an adventurous life, including being shipwrecked and kidnapped. He later authored the book *Narrative of the Shipwreck*. He participated in the Indian wars of 1855 and 1856 and died at age 72. (SPL: Ben Maxwell.)

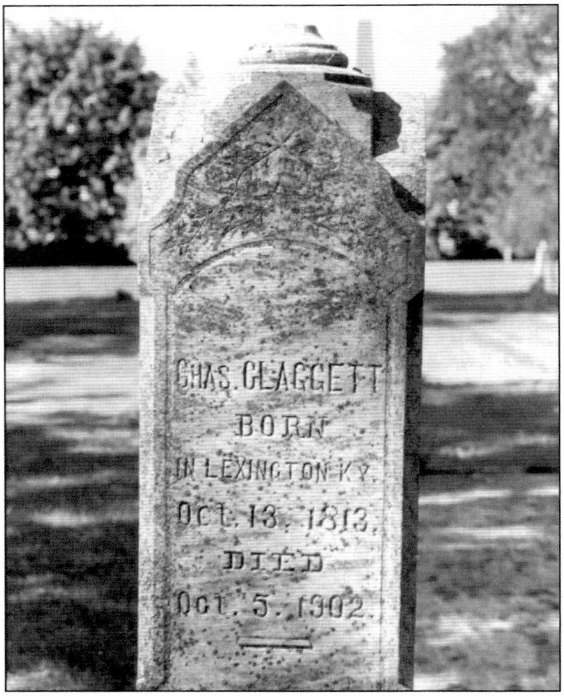

On the bluff above McNary Golf Club is a small cemetery off Wheatland Road. Remembering the past and honoring loved ones is part of community life. Alvis and Sally Smith settled their homestead in 1848 and established this graveyard at the death of their infant daughter. The Claggetts purchased the land, later owned by grandson Charles McNary. (SPL: Al Jones.)

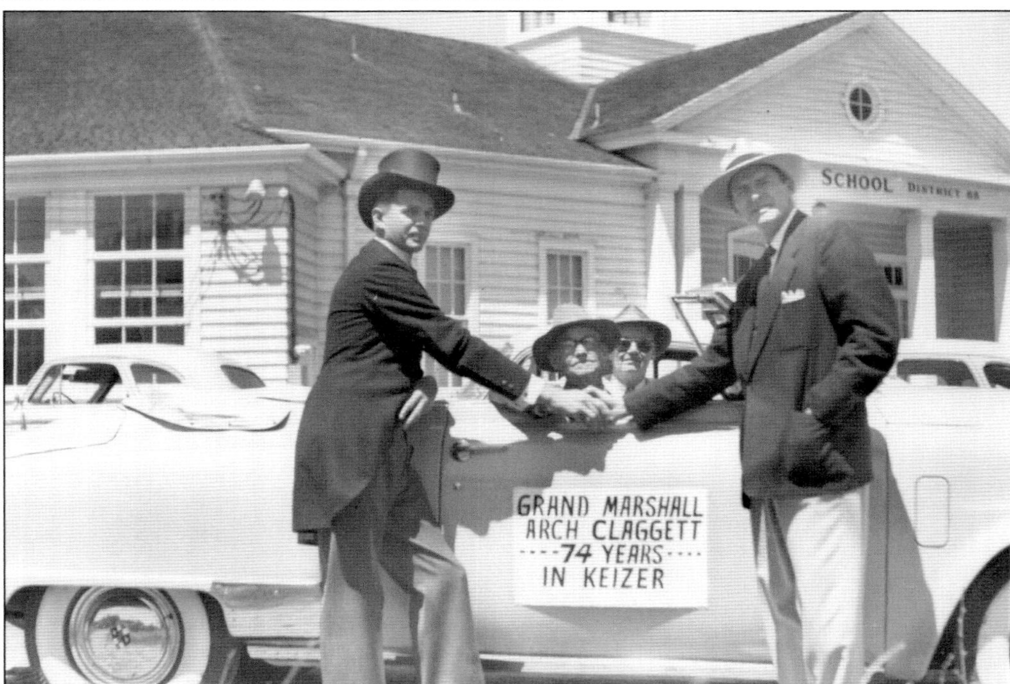

Archie Claggett (center, in car) was the grand marshal of the Keizer Days Parade. Archibald, the son of William D. and Eliza (Parrish) Claggett, was a lifelong Keizer resident. Like his brothers, he farmed their father's property, which they inherited. He successfully raised seed from onions, turnips, and beets. His most profitable venture was with dandelion seed. (KHM.)

Two

Early Families

By the end of the 19th century, the early pioneer families had grown, many marrying their childhood friends who lived nearby. Some moved to other parts of the West. Farms became well established. T.D. Keizur and Horace Holden are noted for planting some of the first apple trees. Charles Claggett's daughters married men from prominent families: McNary, Pugh, and Savage. The names Keizer, Claggett, and McNary would remain part of the area's history far into the future. The McNary grandsons, John and Charles, became notable attorneys in Marion County. Their positions propelled them into state and federal government, yet "Charley" retained his Keizer hometown roots and family property until his death. The city of Salem proudly displayed buildings designed by Pugh sons, and the old Pugh land claim continues to have cattle grazing.

A local school, churches, Sunday schools, and a cemetery were established to meet the needs of the growing outskirts. New families settled on farmlands, and the Frogley, Blake, Hoffman, Bowden, and Weeks families still work their established nurseries and farms along the river. Hop farms have supplied a traditional crop. A Chinese settler, Hop Lee, ran several of the well-established farms. Along the dirt Champoeg/Saint Paul road, which would later become River Road, were other farms including those of the Clark, Pearmine, Melson, Wells, Evans, Cummings, and Keefer families. A variety of fruits, nuts, and other crops were harvested. Filbert nuts (hazelnuts) are prized throughout the world. Prunes were dried in big dryers that dotted the region and shipped to far-off lands. On the south end, where Keizur-Penter land claims were located, was the site of the Marion County Poor Farm.

In 1910, William D. Claggett filed a plat with the county for the first subdivision, known as Claggett Fruit and Garden Tracts, dedicating roads for public use. The Oregon Electric Railway was convenient for travel and commerce. More subdivisions were developed in the 1940s. By the 1950s, businesses were established in the growing community.

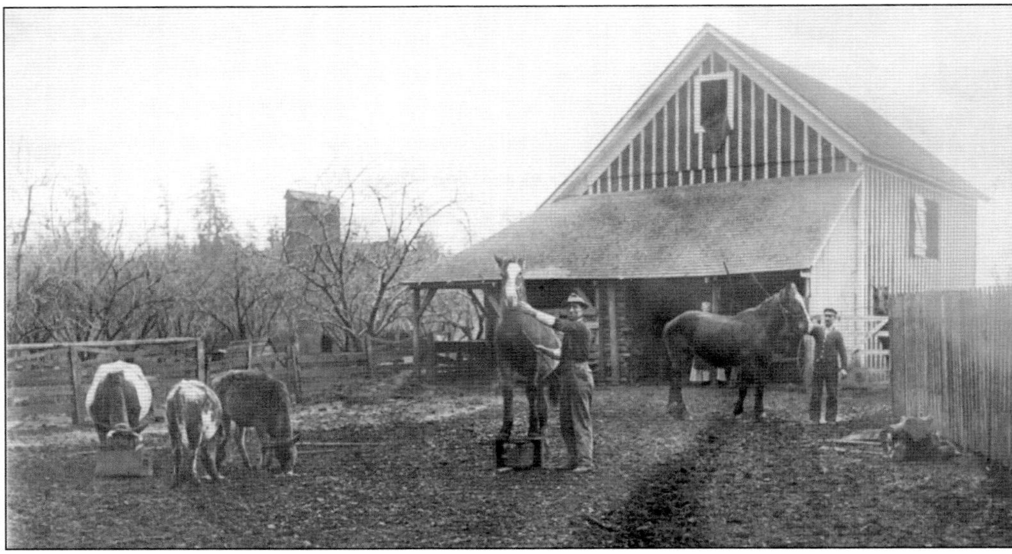

This photograph of the Pearmine farm offers a glimpse into rural life and the caring of livestock. Note the orchard at left and the horse standing on a crate (center). George W. and Frances Pearmine arrived in Salem in 1891; in 1893, they purchased property in Keizer north of Weeks Drive Northeast from River Road to Cherry Avenue. The farming tradition continues today on the Pearmine farm in Gervais. (Pearmine.)

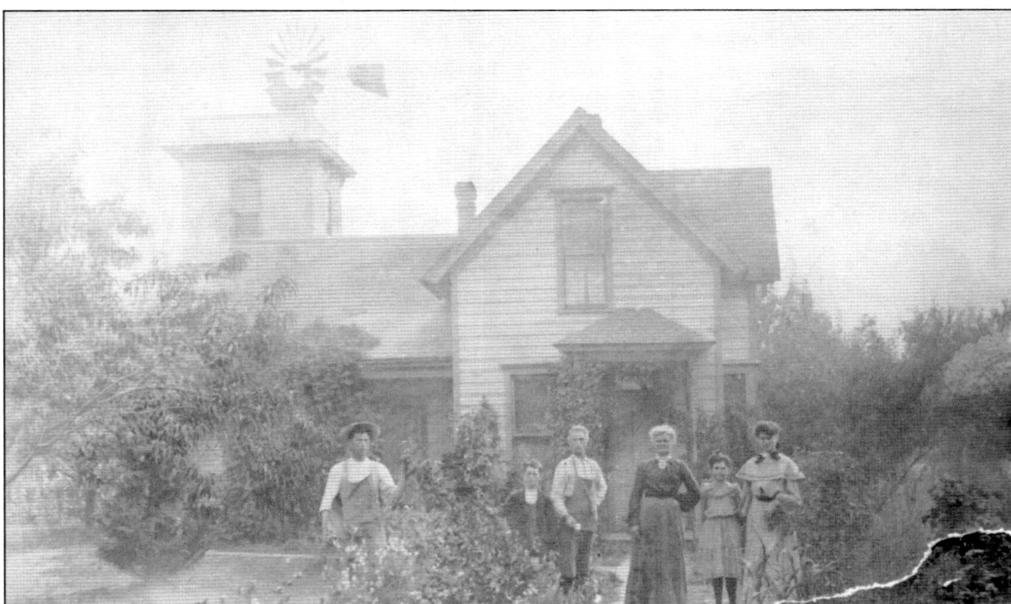

Shown here is the Pearmine family home along River Road. Those thought to be pictured here are, from left to right, Walt, Lester, George Walter and Frances (parents), Clarissa, and Elsie Pearmine. Prunes were their livelihood; the Pearmines had their own dryer and joined marketing groups to sell their produce. Later, Walter and Lester operated their own orchards and farms. Lester Jr. and his wife, Milo, purchased the Springer farm and sold it in 1958 for the Palma Ciea subdivision. (Pearmine.)

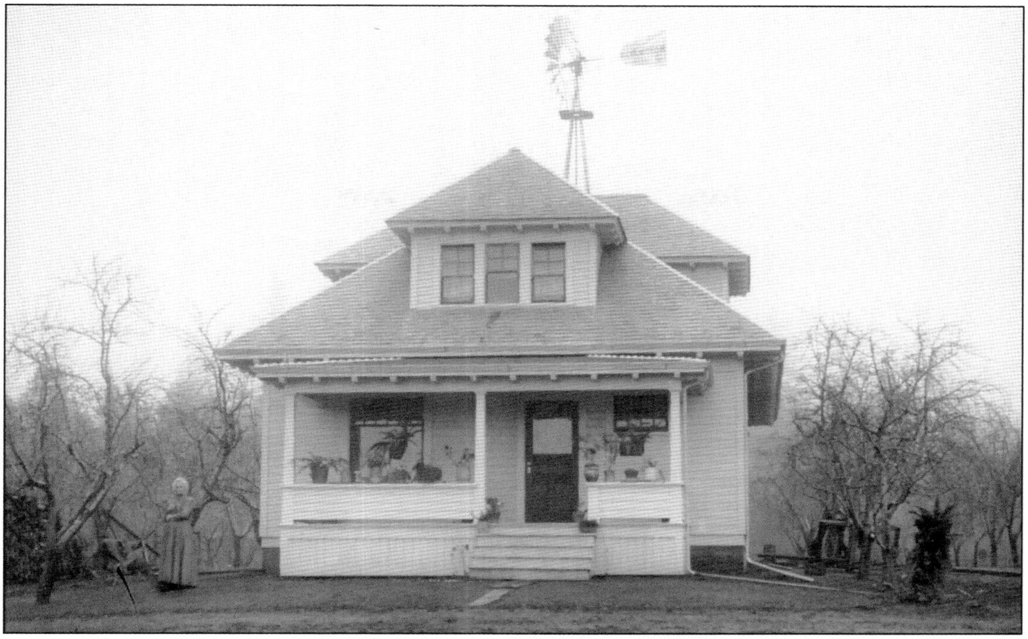

This photograph, labeled "The home place," shows the farm on North River Road at what is now Cherry Avenue, just north of Weeks Drive. Frances Sauff Pearmine (Mrs. George Walter) is standing on the left. Note the plants displayed on the front porch. Milo (also known as Viola) Coonradt Pearmine, wife of Lester Jr., created a beautiful family keepsake album. (Pearmine.)

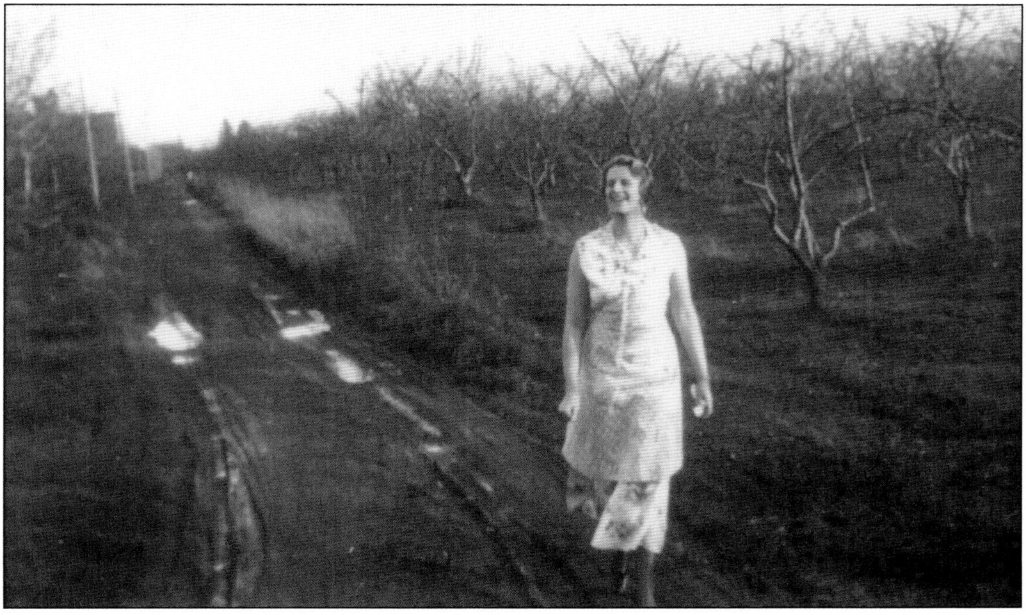

Lucile Cummings (Bagley) walks through the orchard along Cummings Lane. She was the daughter of Dora and Carroll Cummings. Years after the death of Carroll, Dora married his brother, Arthur. An accomplished vocalist, Lucile was a featured soloist on *The Bell Telephone Hour* and at New York's Radio City Music Hall. The farm was on the original John Keizur land claim, where Cummings Elementary is today. (KHM: Cummings.)

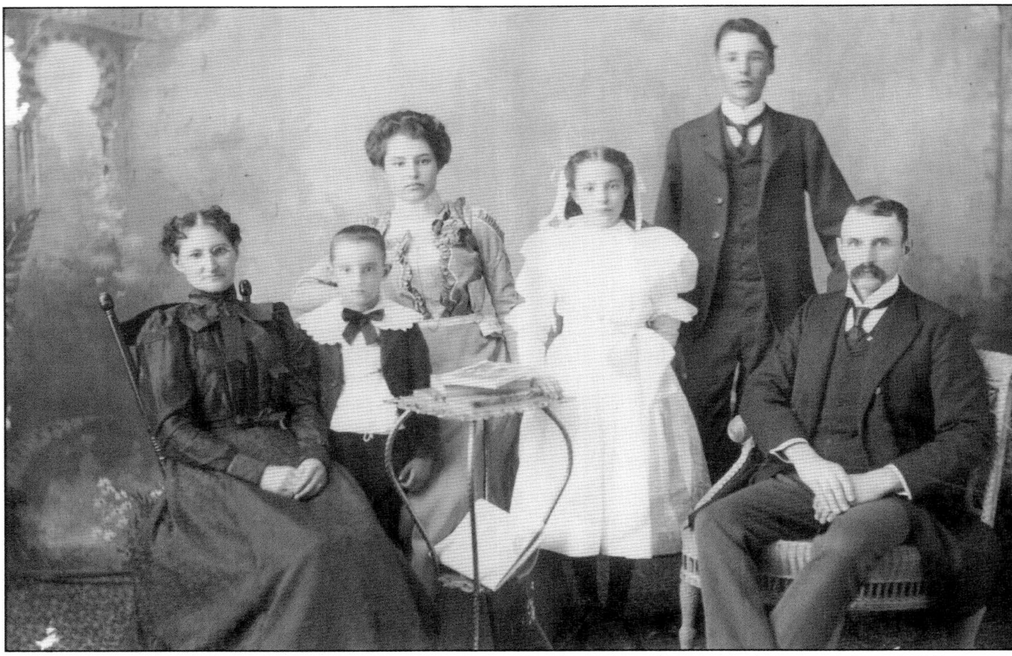

George and Matilda "Til" Weeks are shown with their family around 1900. The children are, from left to right, Lloyd, "Dimma," Lena, and Wilbur. The farm started in 1888 as a peach farm on the banks of the Willamette River. By 1908, a nursery business had been started. The Weeks Berry Nursery has continued on various properties in the Keizer area for over 100 years, with five generations farming in Oregon's Willamette Valley. (KHM: Weeks.)

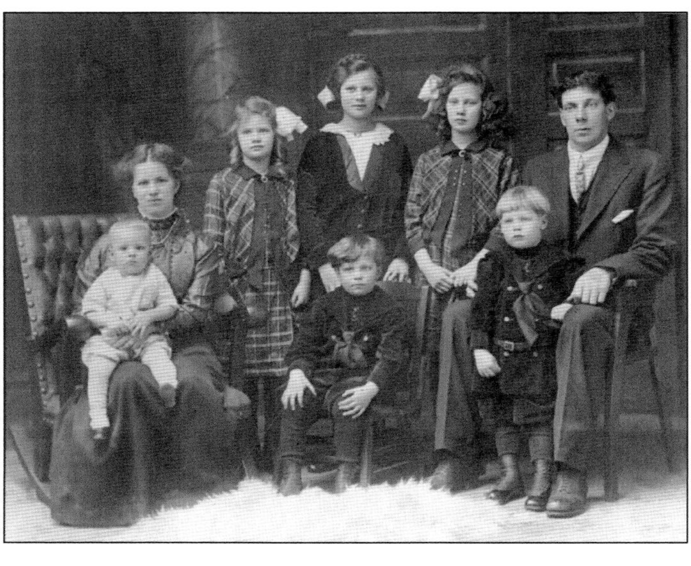

The Bowden family poses for a photograph around 1915. From left to right are baby Tom, Ada, Violet, Doris, Jack (seated), Ivy, Gordon, and father Harry. The Bowdens arrived about 1906. While building their home, the family lived in the hop dryer on Louis Lachmund's ranch on Windsor Island Road. The Bowdens planted orchards of prunes, apples, walnuts, and filberts. Their prune dryer was the last in Marion County. (KHM: Bowden.)

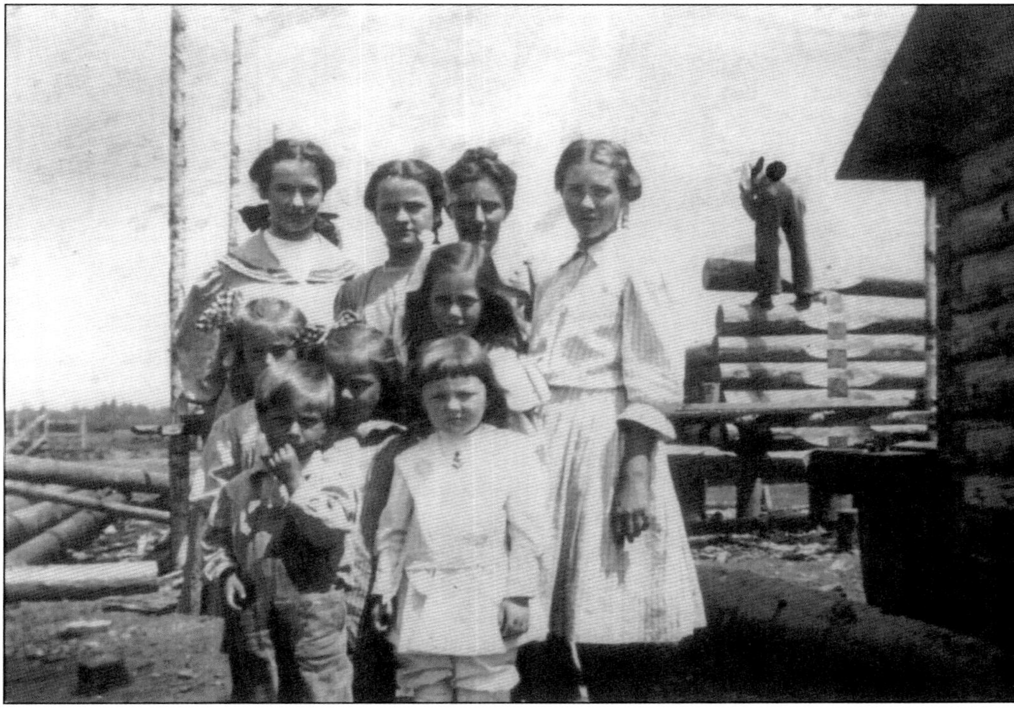

The Blake log house is seen here in 1907 in the only known photograph taken during its construction. Mother Ida Blake (back row, second from right) poses with her children. The Blakes traveled from California to attend the 1905 Lewis and Clark Exposition in Portland and were inspired to move to Oregon. Will Blake found two Norwegians at the coast with the skills to build the log house. (Blake.)

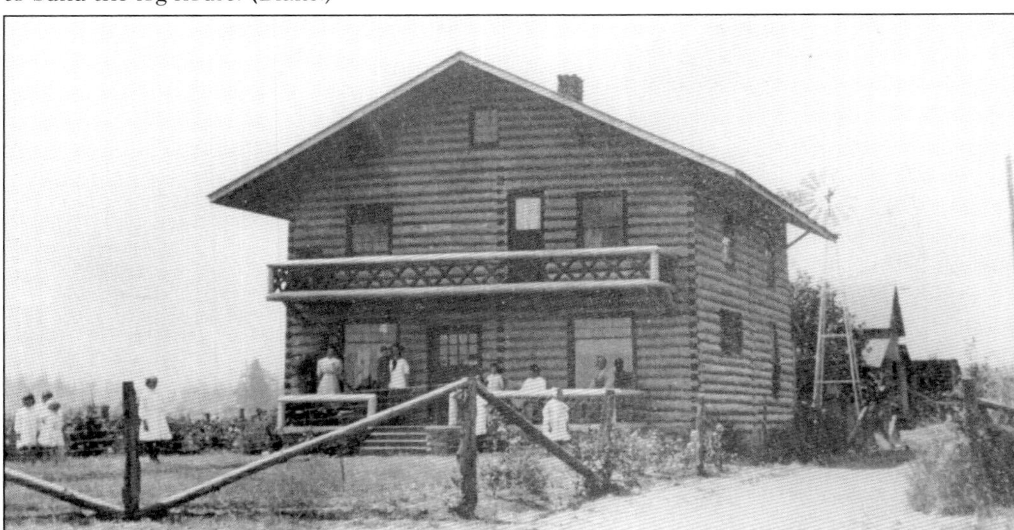

The Forestry Building exhibit at the 1905 Lewis and Clark Exposition in Portland is thought to have been the inspiration for the Blakes' log house. They first lived in their barn. Note that in the early days, the home had decorative porch railings, which were later removed. William and Ida cleared the land and planted orchards and berries on their lake farm. (Blake.)

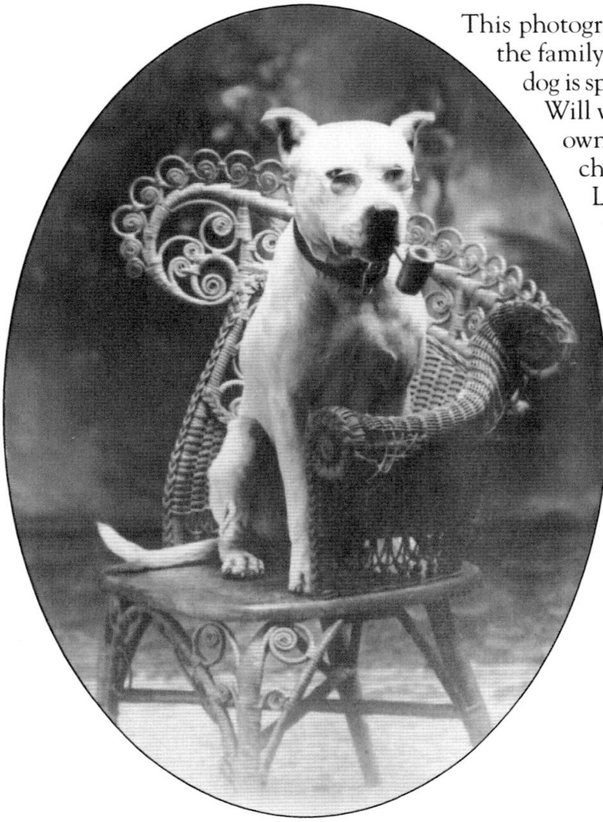

This photograph of the Blakes' dog was included in the family album. In emulation of Will Blake, the dog is sporting a pipe. Many photographs capture Will with a pipe in his mouth. The farm, now owned by the third generation of Blakes, has changed over the years. Formerly Willow Lake Nursery, it is now a premier site for weddings and events and is known as Log House Garden. It remains a working farm as well. (Blake.)

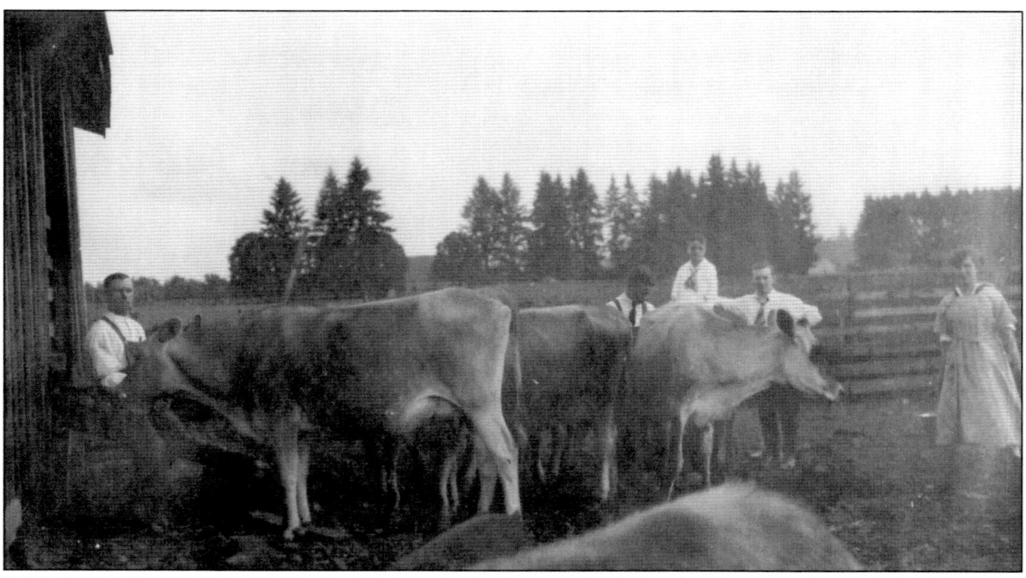

Will (far left) is seen here with children and cows on the lake farm. Alice (far right), the oldest Blake daughter at home, was a very capable helper with all the farm chores. A huge apple tree grew along a property line that no one could identify. When Philip Blake was a small boy in the 1920s, he used to jump over the planted firs and cedars designed to shade the house. (Blake.)

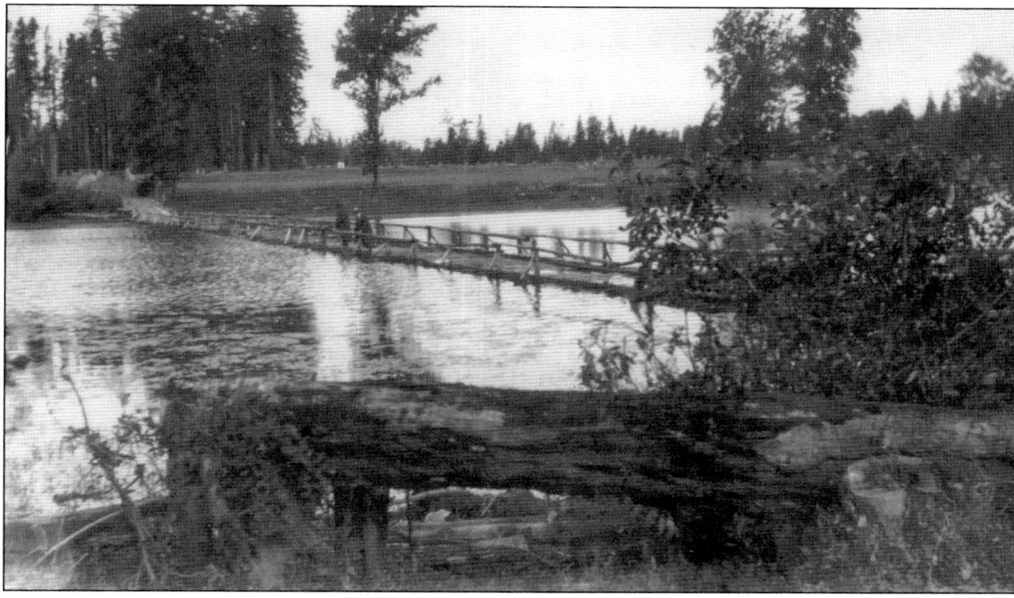

This is a view of Willow Lake (previously known as Bybee Lake) with the floating bridge that the cows used to cross. The bridge is toward the south property line. The bridge was replaced in the 1940s with fill, and a road was put on top for access to the west side of the lake. (Blake.)

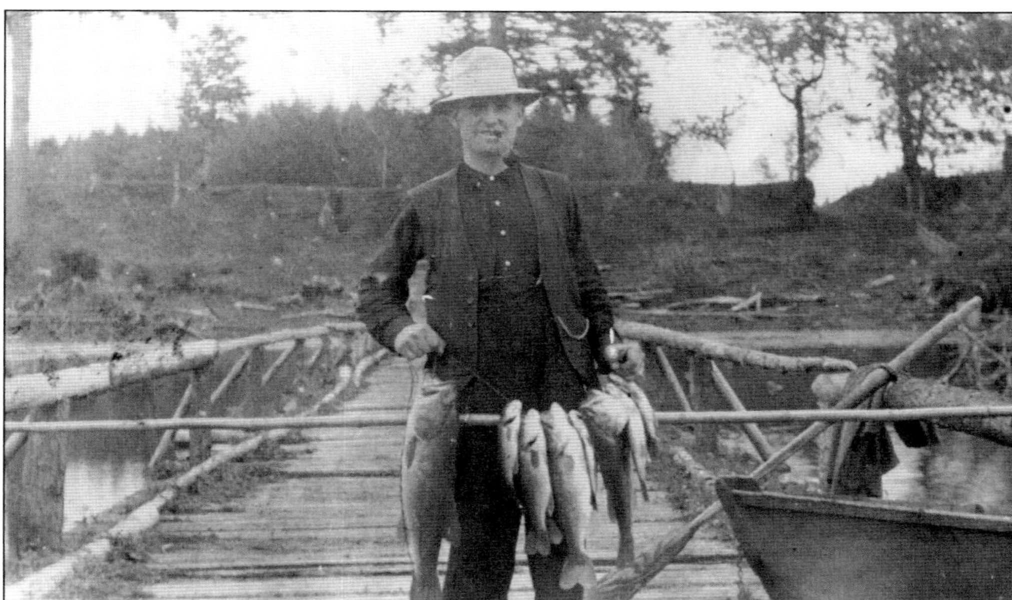

Will Blake poses with his catch of the day. Family and friends enjoyed boating and picnicking at Willow Lake. The logs for the Blake home came from the lake area. Willow Lake is two miles long, north to south. The beautiful blue lake, fed by springs and the river, was teeming with fish. The floating bridge gave way in the 1940s. (Blake.)

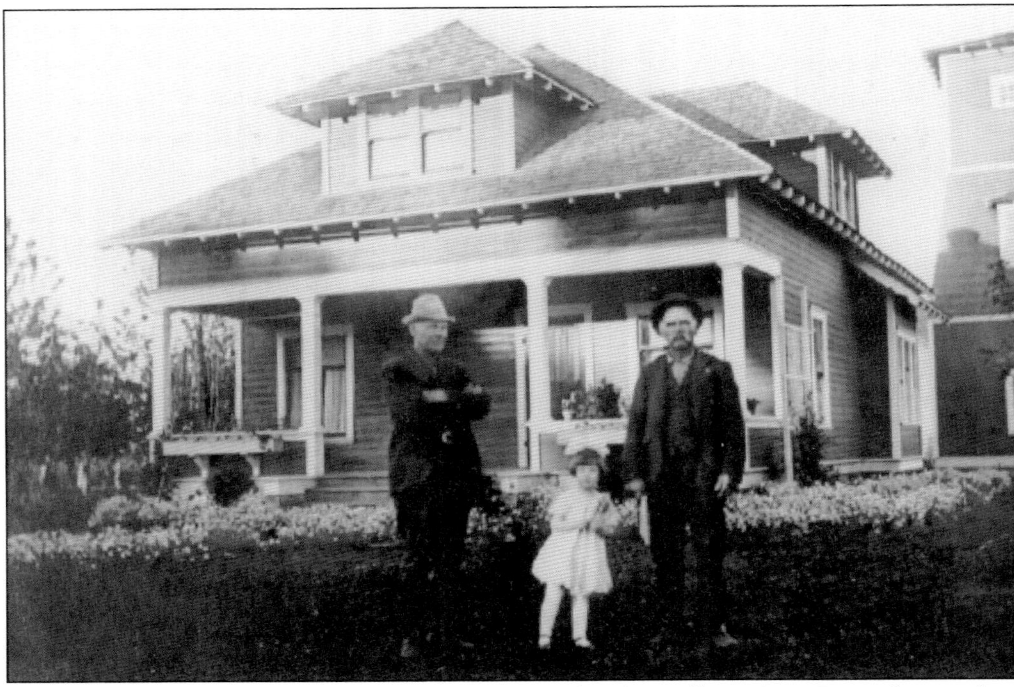

Across from the Blakes' home on Windsor Island Road is the Hoffman farm. Posing here in front of the house are John (right), son Roy Hoffman (left), and granddaughter Zelda Unruh. The house, water tower, machine shed, woodshed, and garage (formerly carriage house) were built in 1914 by John and Roy. (KHM: Hoffman/Olson.)

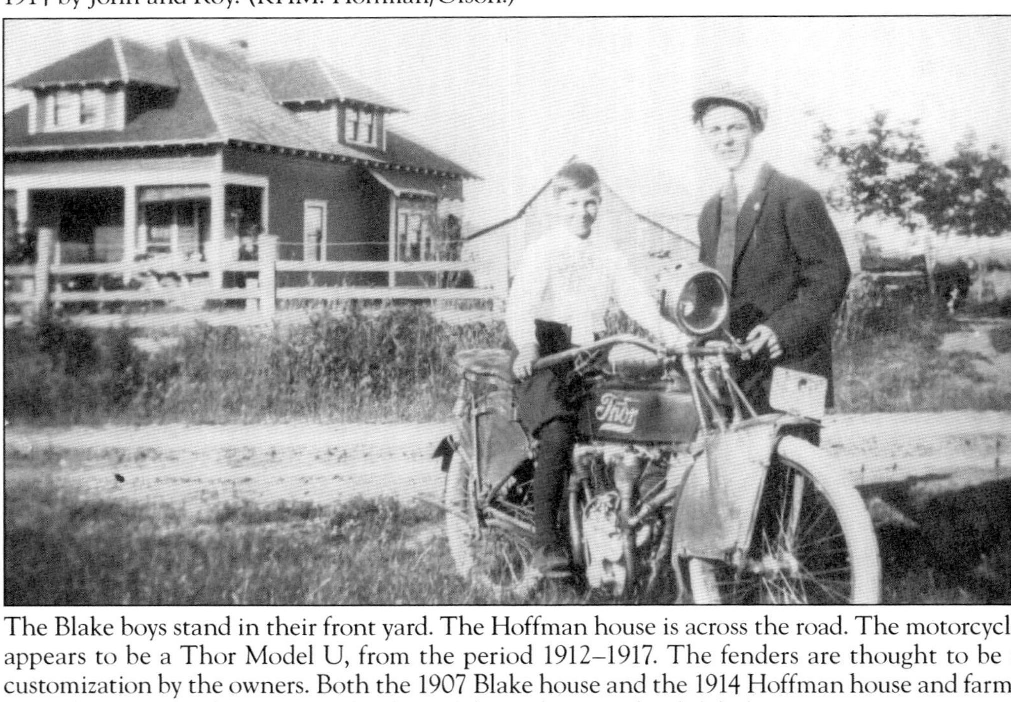

The Blake boys stand in their front yard. The Hoffman house is across the road. The motorcycle appears to be a Thor Model U, from the period 1912–1917. The fenders are thought to be a customization by the owners. Both the 1907 Blake house and the 1914 Hoffman house and farms are today much as they were in the days of these photographs. (Blake.)

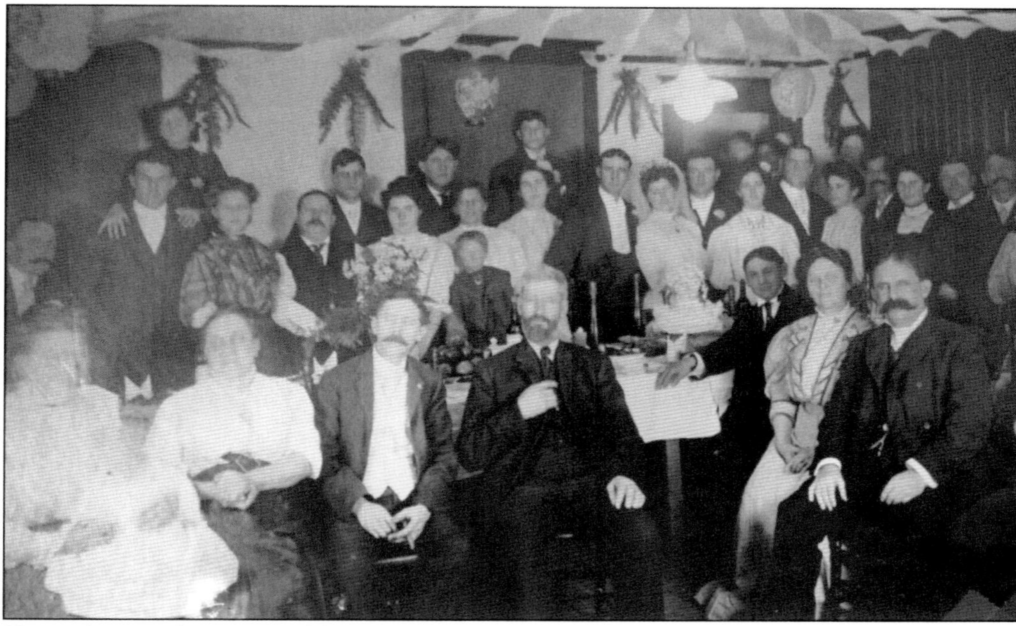

Shown here is the 1907 wedding of Caroline M. Mankertz and Fred A. Kurtz. The bride and groom are standing behind the wedding cake. The father of the groom, G. Fred Kurtz, is at front center with his hand on his chest. The father of the bride, August Mankertz, is fifth from the left in the rear wearing a vest. Fred and Caroline's daughter Barbara Kurtz Smith was the co-owner of Tele-Treat Drive-In. (KHM.)

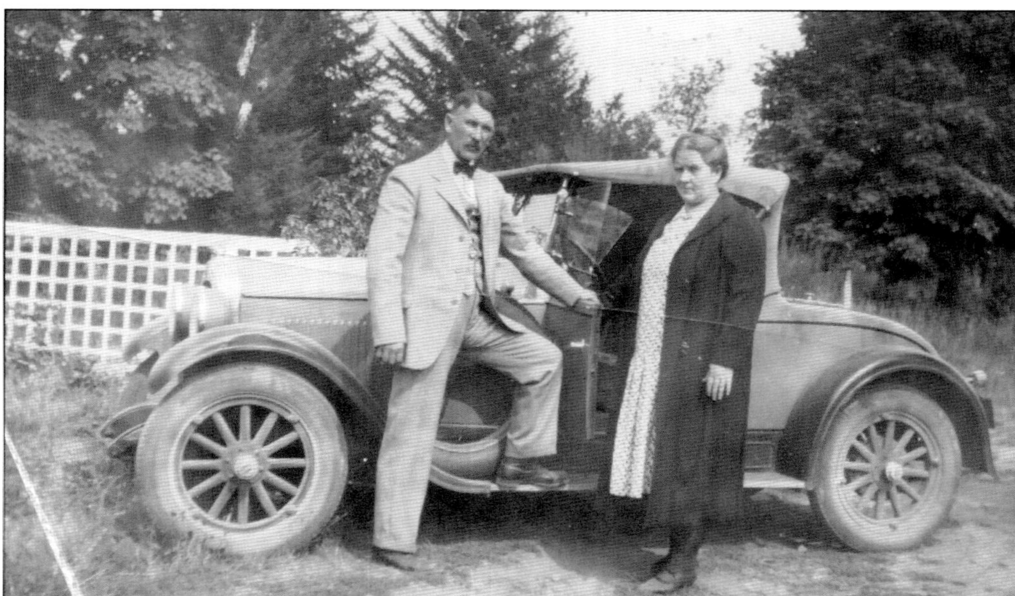

John Charles and Katherine "Kate" Barry pose with their car at their home on Ridge Drive about 1927. Their home was near the site of the future Little League fields. They could see the Chemawa Indian School from their property. (Hersch Sangster.)

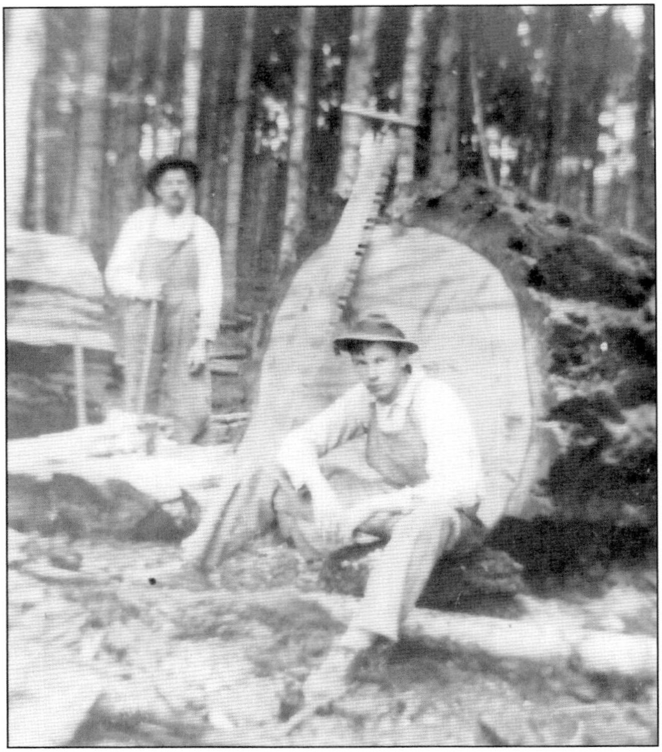

Daniel Keefer (left) and his son, Hal, cut timber to expand their farm on Trail Avenue. The farm had two woods, known as the "little woods" and the "big woods." The Keefers built their new home, near the old house, in 1917 before Hal entered the Army. The house is there today and is part of the property in the former Wilark Park, now the Bob Newton Family Park. (Keefer.)

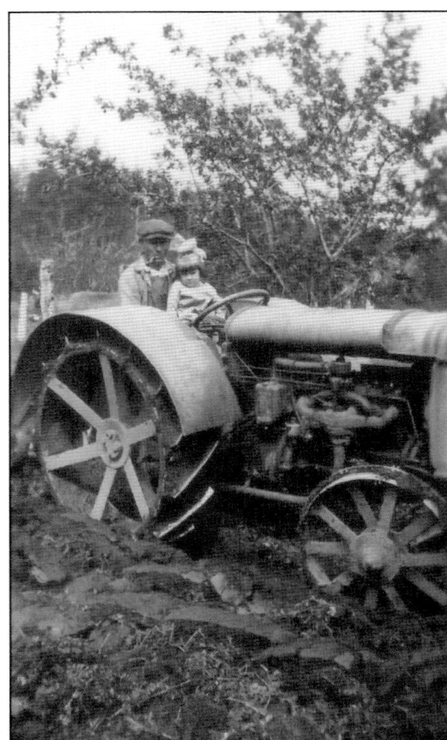

Harry Keefer is on his tractor with a child, presumed to be Margret Keefer (Canary). The farm was sold off to build the Wilark Park subdivision, but the Keefers' Craftsman house still stands on Trail Avenue. Daniel and Myra Keefer and their eight children were active in the community with school, music, and the grange. (Keefer.)

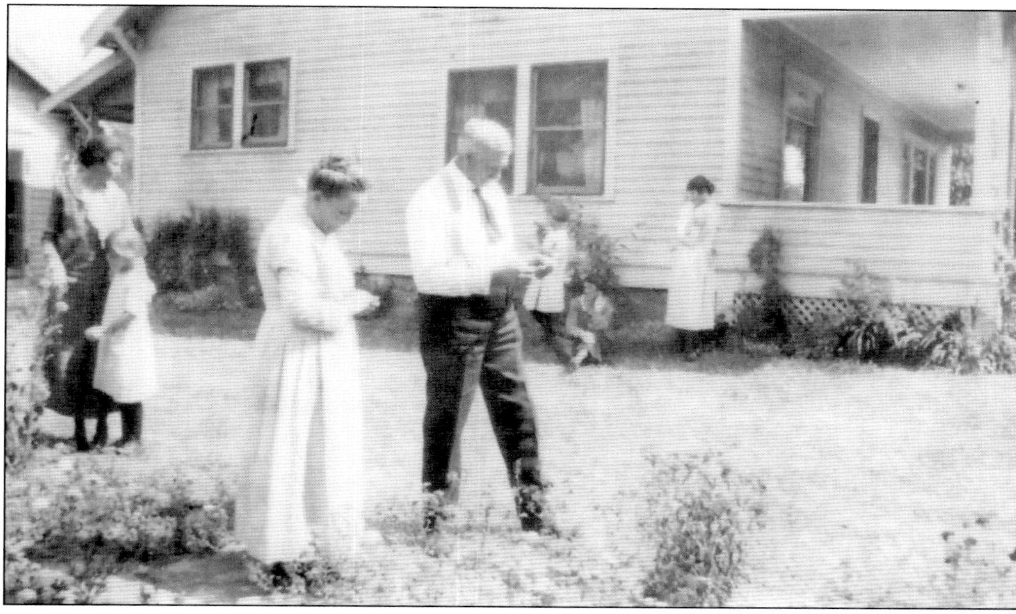

The Keefer family walk in their yard, admiring the flowers on the north side of their house. A fence was installed in front to prevent passing cows from devouring the planted flowers. To the south is a creek that is now part of Wilark Park. The 1917 home remained unchanged until the 1960s, when the 40-acre Wilark Park subdivision was developed. (Keefer.)

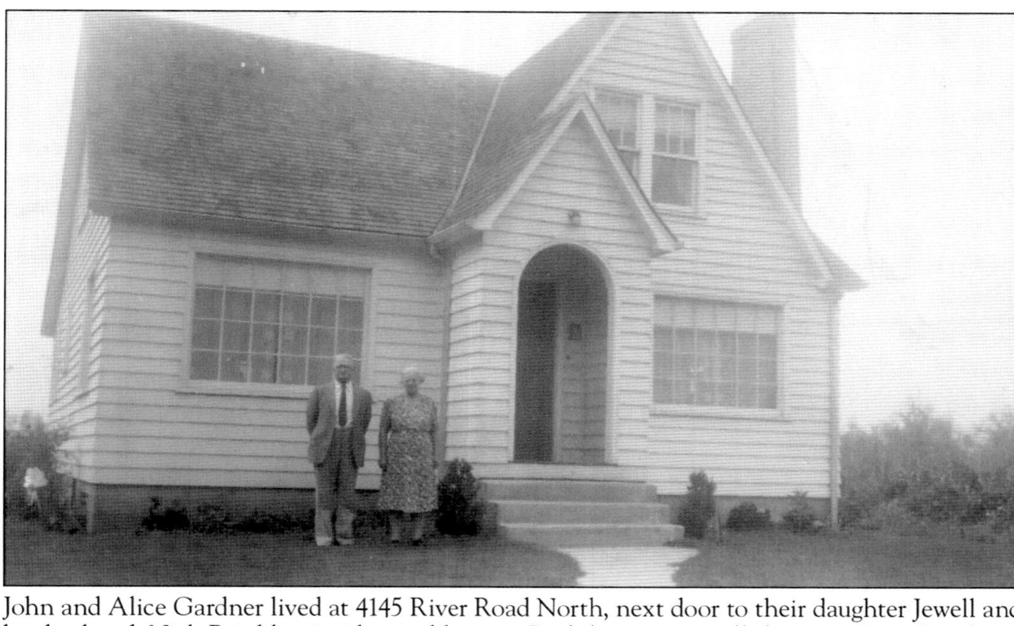

John and Alice Gardner lived at 4145 River Road North, next door to their daughter Jewell and her husband, Nick Brinkley, in identical houses. Both houses are still there on River Road and are used as businesses. The Brinkleys were co-developers of the Man-Brin Gardens neighborhood. (KHM: LaVaun Gardner White Buck.)

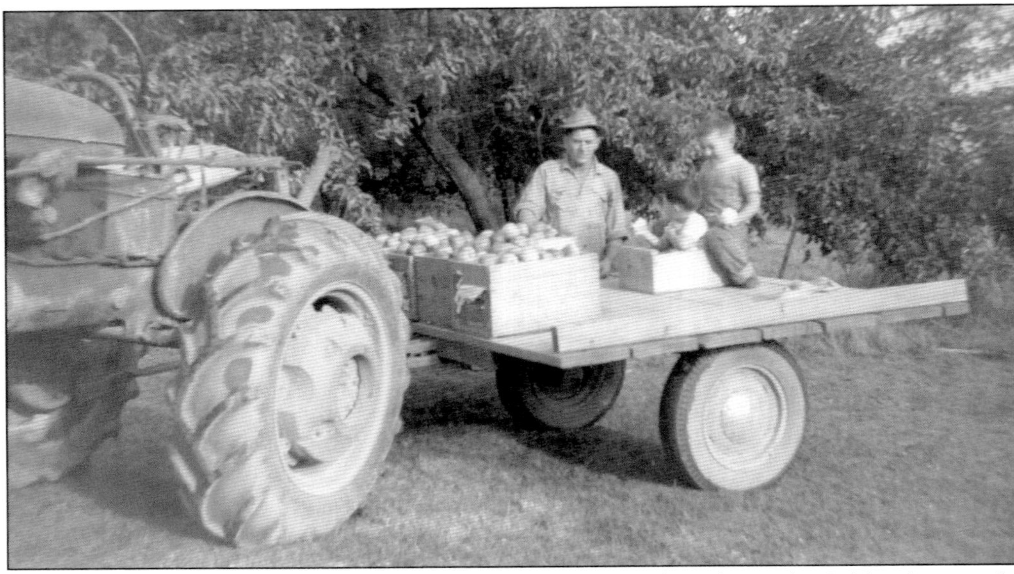

Dave Schlag and his grandsons Steven and James Schlag pick apples at the Schlag farm in the Clear Lake area in October 1957. Mina Schlag's parents, Amos and Adaline Smith, lived north on Wheatland Road. David's parents, Frederich and Carolina Schlag, also lived in Clear Lake, arriving in 1919 and purchasing 80 acres on the east side of Wheatland Road. It later became the Schmalz farm. (KHM: Ann Lossner collection.)

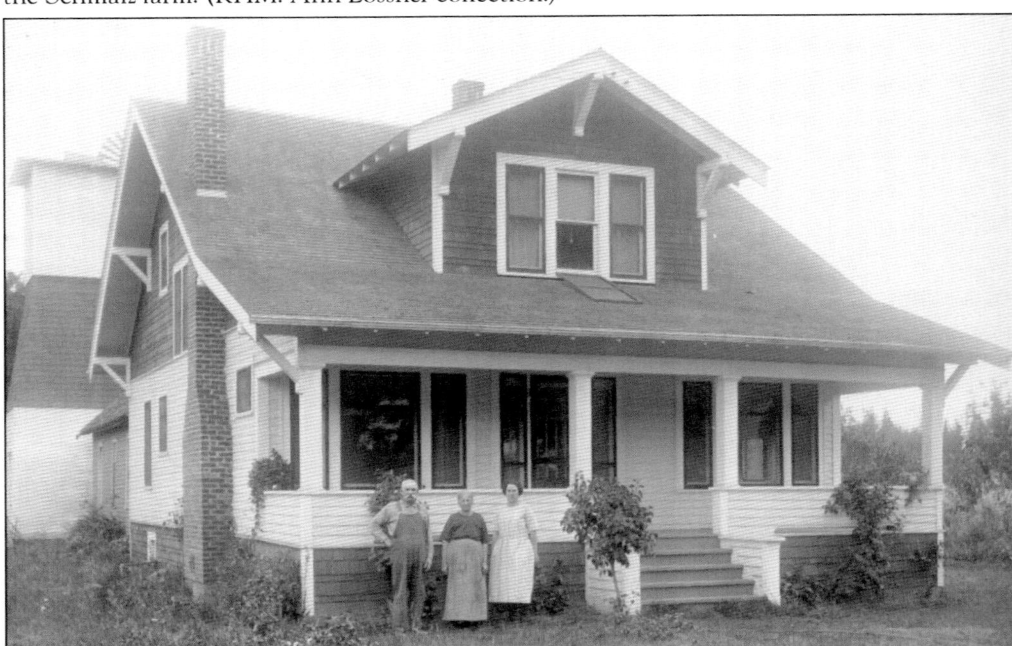

This is Amos and Adaline Smith's house, built in 1922 on Wheatland Road (previously called River Road), north of the current Jays Drive. The Smiths owned 24 acres in "downtown" Clear Lake. Their daughter, Mina (seen at right here, with her parents), and her husband, David Schlag, lived nearby. The Smiths gave the newlyweds 10 acres and a small house under construction; Mina and David purchased additional land and cleared it for farming. (Terri Thompson-Hoag.)

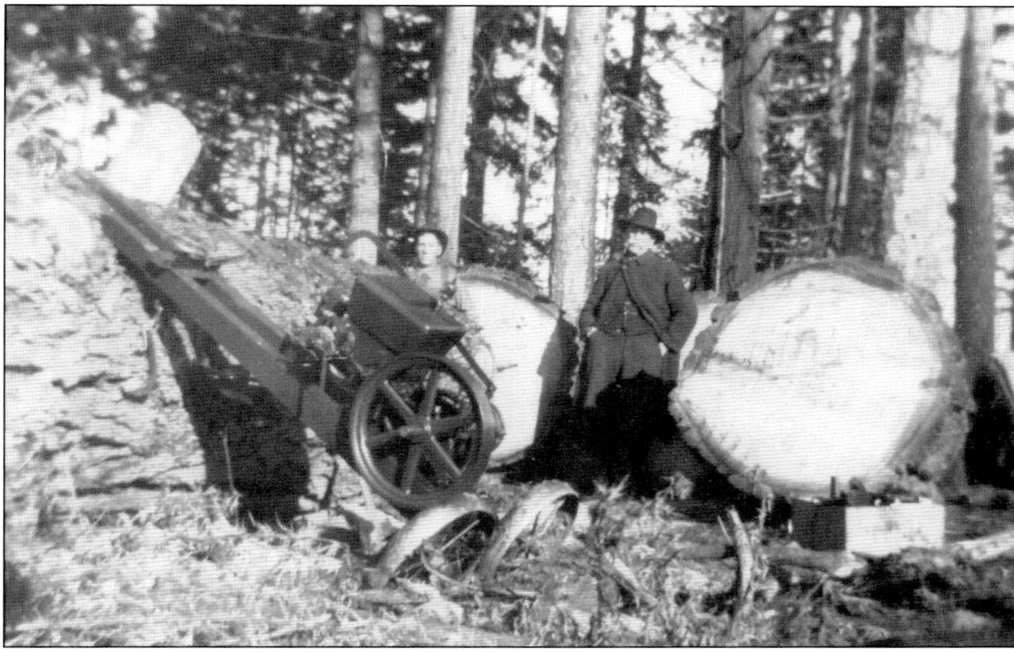

Guy Smith (left) logs with his father, Amos, at his farm on McLeod Lane. The property was thick with old-growth fir timber. Guy's parents, Amos and Adaline Smith, lived farther north in Clear Lake on Wheatland Road. Their family came from Kansas in 1920. Guy and Golda Smith had two daughters, Betty Jean and Orall. (Terri Thompson-Hoag.)

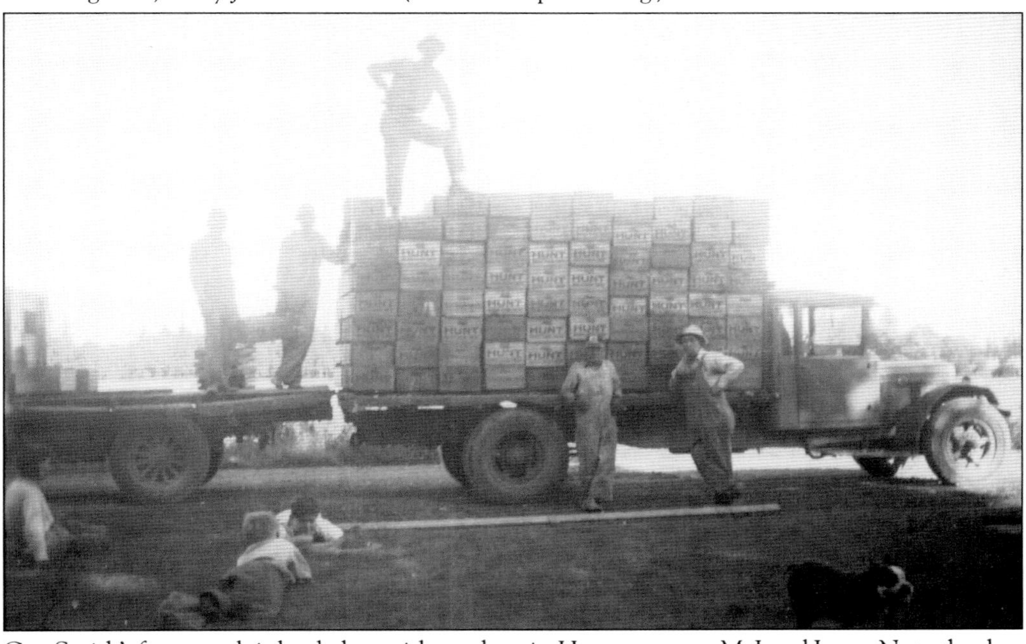

Guy Smith's farm truck is loaded up with produce in Hunt crates on McLeod Lane. Note the dog, as well as the boys relaxing on the ground. Many growers worked with co-ops to help process and sell their produce. Working the fields was hot, tiring work, yet a proud satisfaction rewarded the farmers when the harvest was gathered. (Terri Thompson-Hoag.)

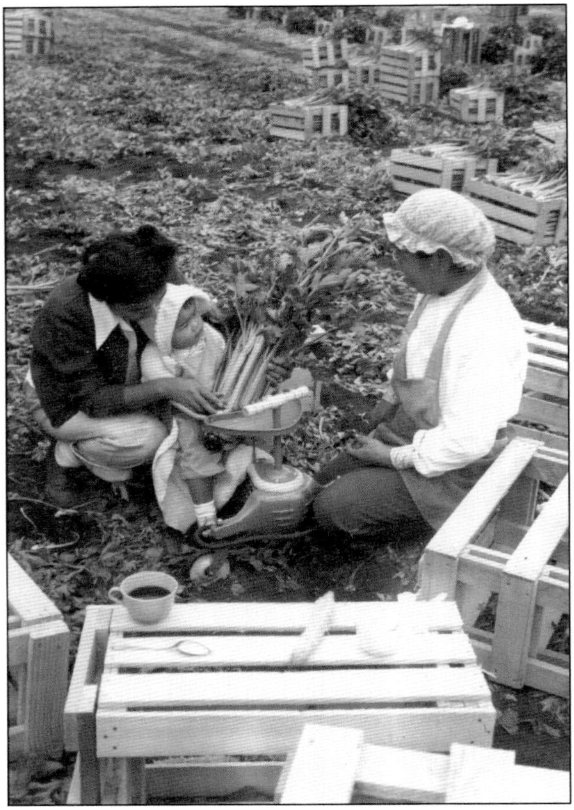

A news article described Roy K. Fukuda as a pioneer celery grower on a commercial scale in the "Labish Meadows" area. Many Japanese, Chinese, Korean, and American Indian children were involved at school, sports, and other activities. Sad times came in 1942 during World War II, when Japanese neighbors were evacuated to Tule Lake or other sites. Some served in the military, but only a few returned. (Saucy.)

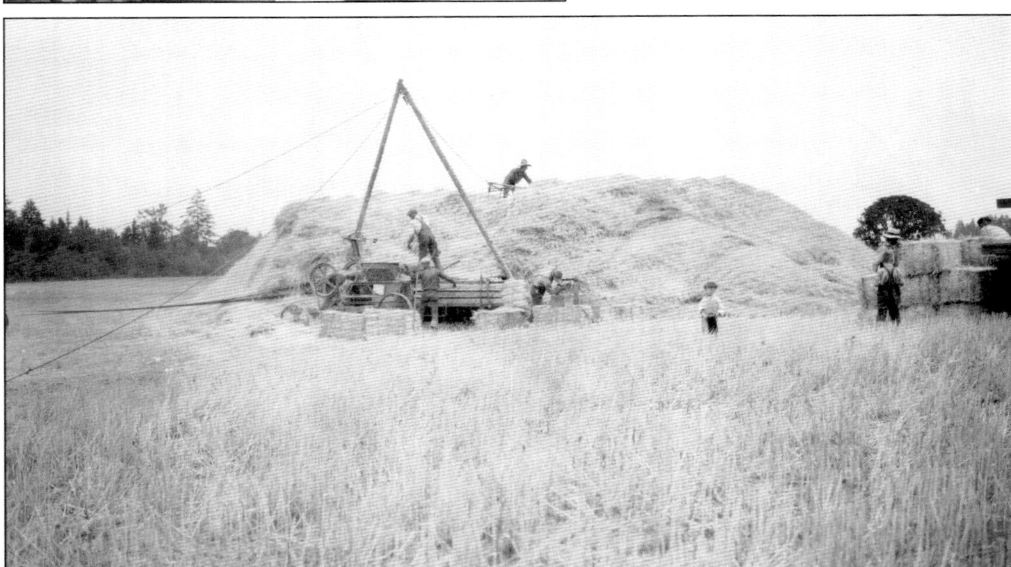

The David Saucy Sr. family and farm workers bale hay on the Wallace Prairie farm owned by Asahel N. Bush. The property bordered Cherry Avenue and extended past Claggett Creek. The Oregon Electric rail line ran through the farm property, which also included the Painter's Woods. (Paul and Tracey Saucy Collection.)

Roy and Etta Melson stand in front of their old farmhouse. The River Road farm was part of the John Force land claim. Force was one of the immigrants who arrived in the Oregon Territory in 1842 to support the Jason Lee Mission. Etta Melson loved her flowers and created an elaborate rock garden. These beautiful irises would be the future symbol of the incorporated city of Keizer. (Melson.)

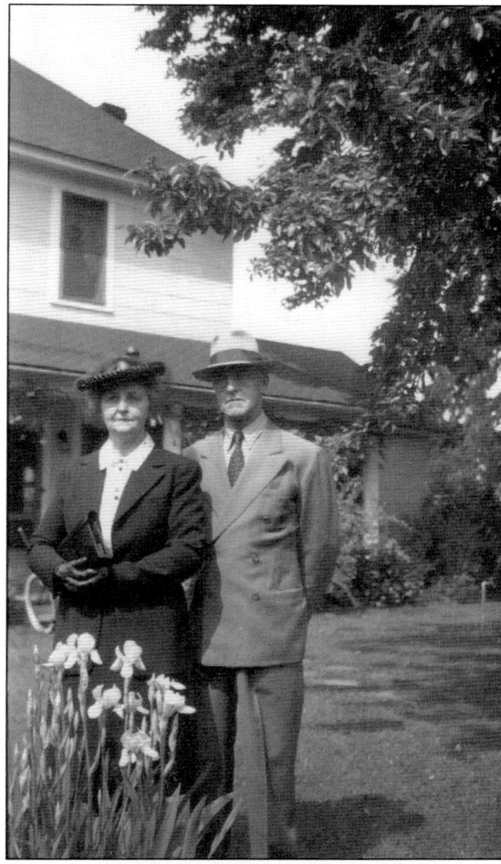

The Melson kids pose in 1931 on their farm with Lewis's Model T. Lewis was a senior at Salem High School. Evelyn Melson Franz recalled: "Mother wanted a picture with the ceramic frog (on radiator) and the sun was just right for a short time. None of us were very happy—as is obvious—to pose for the photo. Keizer was a quiet, nonpopulated area in those years." (Melson.)

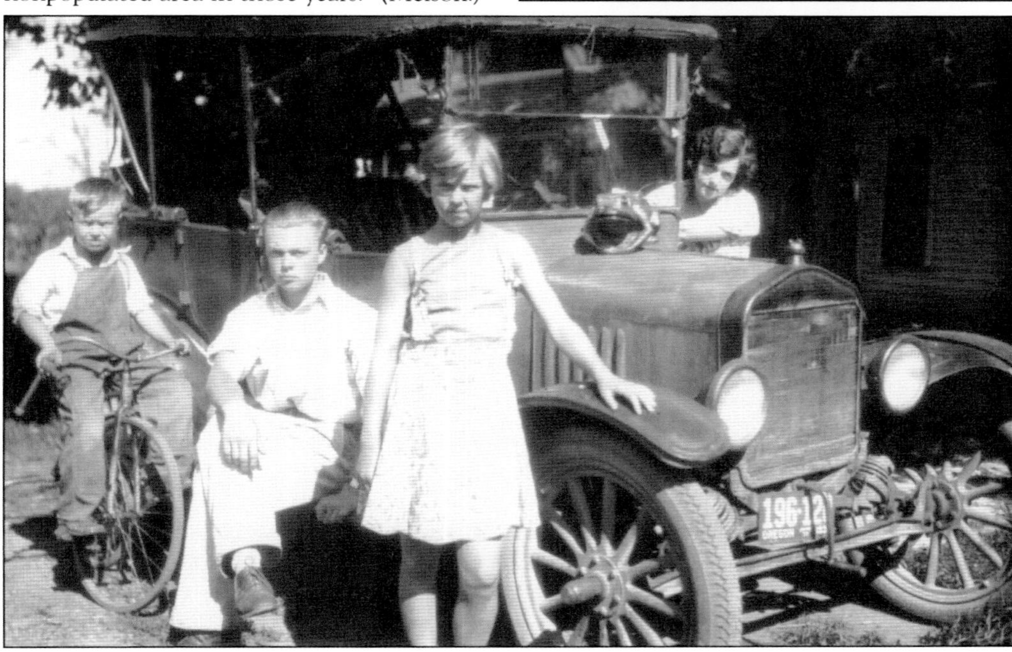

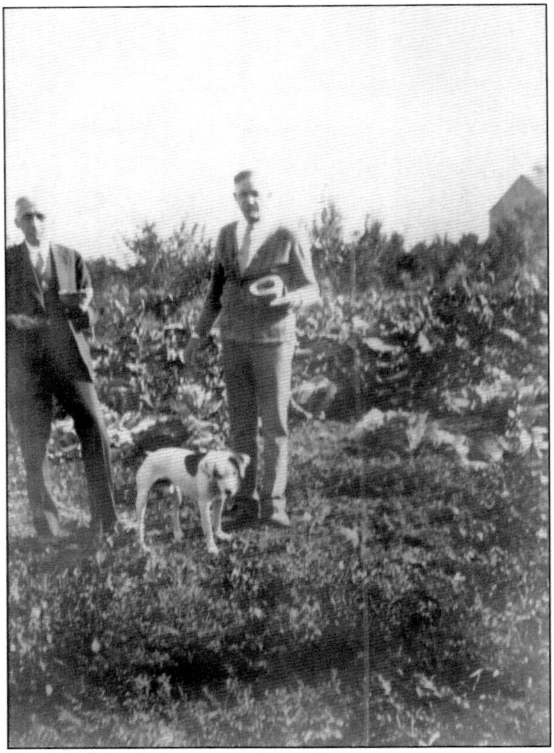

Keizer-born US senator Charles McNary (right) eats melons from the field with his brother-in-law Walter Stolz in the 1930s. McNary served in Washington, DC, for 27 years, yet maintained his love of the land and returned often to his home on his grandfather Claggett's claim property. With Oregon pioneer roots, McNary hosted family reunions. (Claggett.)

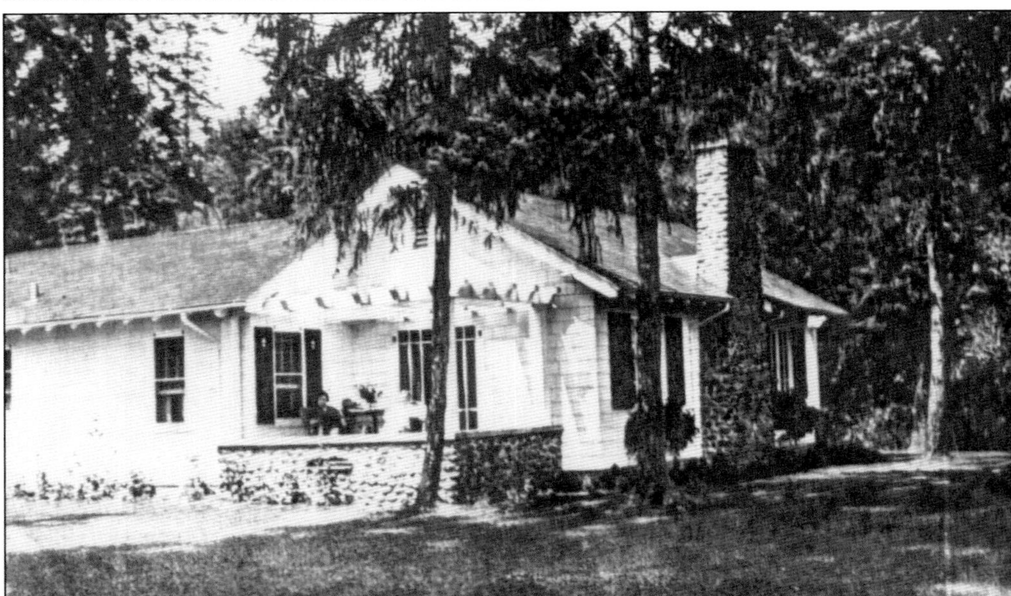

In 1923, Sen. Charles McNary designed plans for a relaxing Cape Cod–style farmhouse, named Fir Cone, on his grandfather Claggett's homestead. The simple home had a large stone porch where he would often conduct business with his personal secretary. Inside was a huge stone fireplace where a big iron kettle hung from an heirloom Claggett "crane." Fir tree designs were carved into the green window shutters. (KHM.)

Acquaintances since childhood in Salem, Senator McNary (pictured) and Herbert Hoover worked together in the nation's capital. As assistant majority leader, McNary became known as the man who ran the Senate during Hoover's presidency. He was among the first Senate leaders to make frequent use of the telephone to win votes. (KHM.)

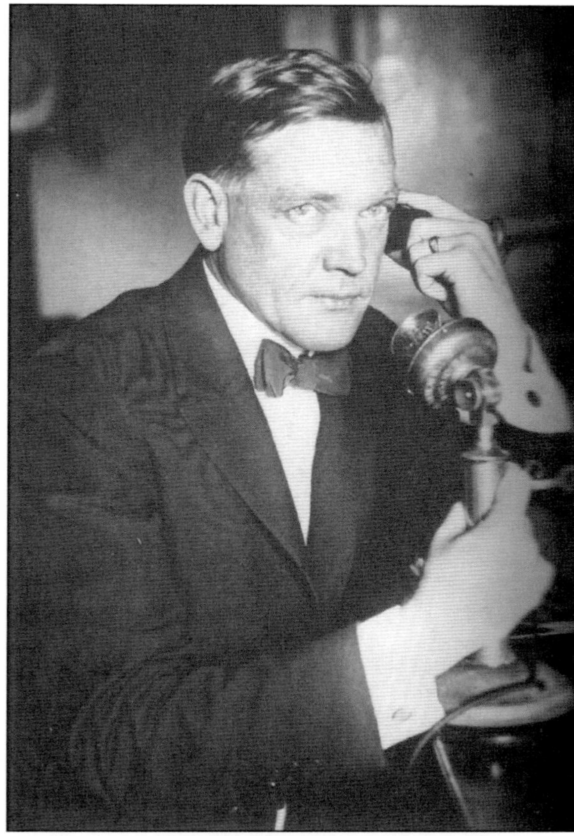

Senator McNary returned home to vote at the Chemawa precinct polls in 1940. McNary was Wendell Wilkie's vice-presidential running mate in that election. He was warmly greeted on the campaign trail in his home state, with signs declaring him "Oregon's own son!" He awaited the verdict in the comfort of his home, Fir Cone, but the senator had few illusions about their chances against FDR. (SPL: Maxwell.)

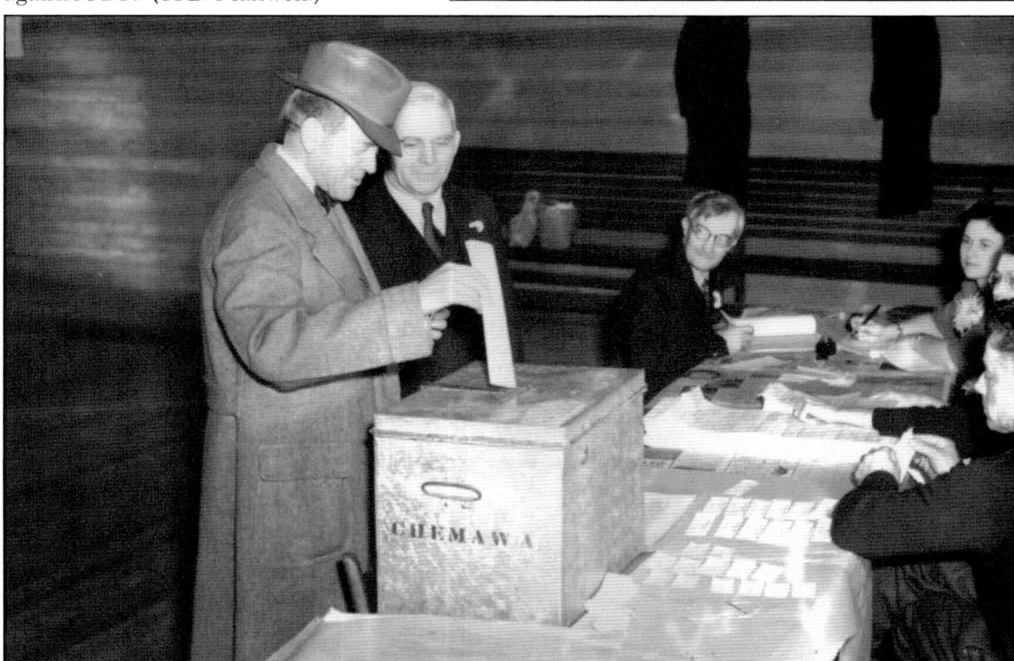

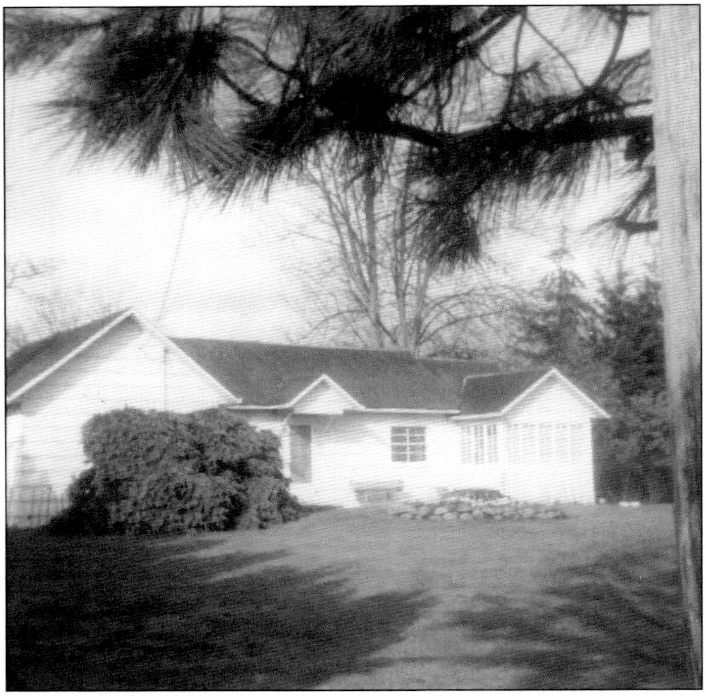

This home is located on the site of the original McNary family buildings, on the hill to the south of McNary Golf Club. The property was owned by H. Thomas and E. Bess (McNary) Bruce, then by C.A. and Alice Harold. It was later purchased by Raymond and Josephine Jungwirth. On the ridge, the house, garage, and barns now stand sadly abandoned and overgrown with vegetation. (KHM.)

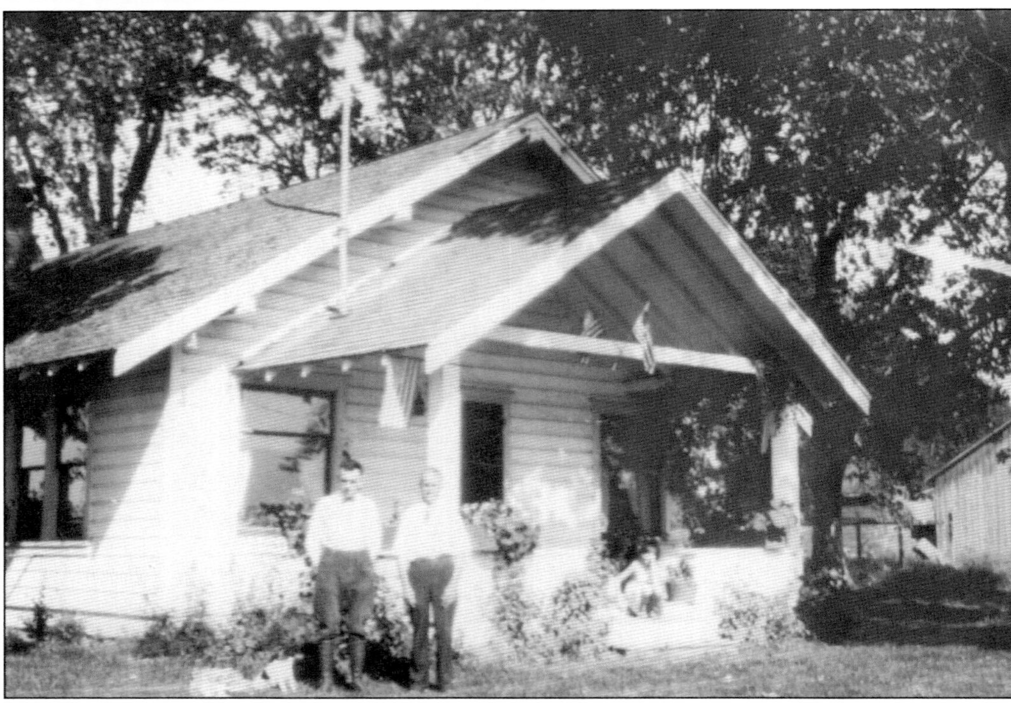

Ben and Mabel Claggett built their home on Verda Lane in 1920. Shown here around 1925 are, from left to right, Ben, his brother Doc, and his daughter Sally. The Claggetts raised grain, corn, and strawberries, and they had a filbert orchard against Chemawa Road, with sprouts from Senator McNary, a cousin of Ben. (Claggett.)

Ray Clark (pictured), son of Theodore J. Clark, farmed in southwest Keizer near some of the Weeks family's farm tracks. Bill Newmyer recalled a fruit inspector coming to their family farm in 1905 and digging up two large strawberry plants to take to the International Exposition in Portland. The huge plants were of the Wilson variety, with 100 berries on them. This photograph is from T.J. Clark's granddaughter Maxine Clark Dugger. (KHM.)

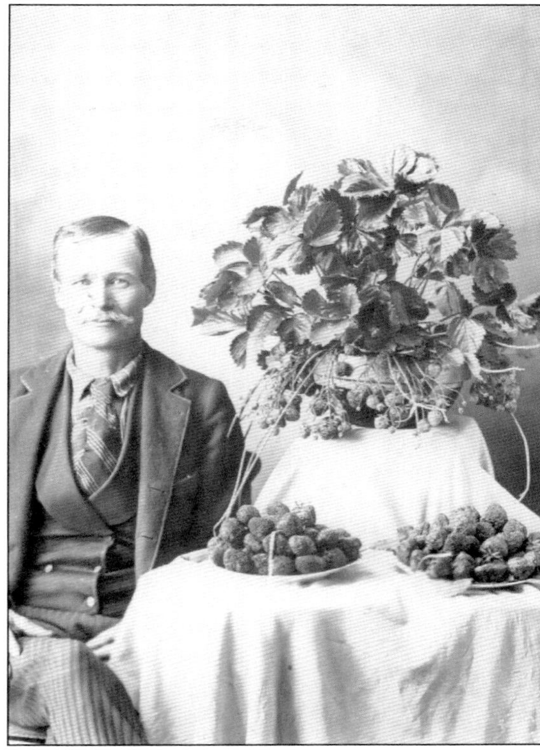

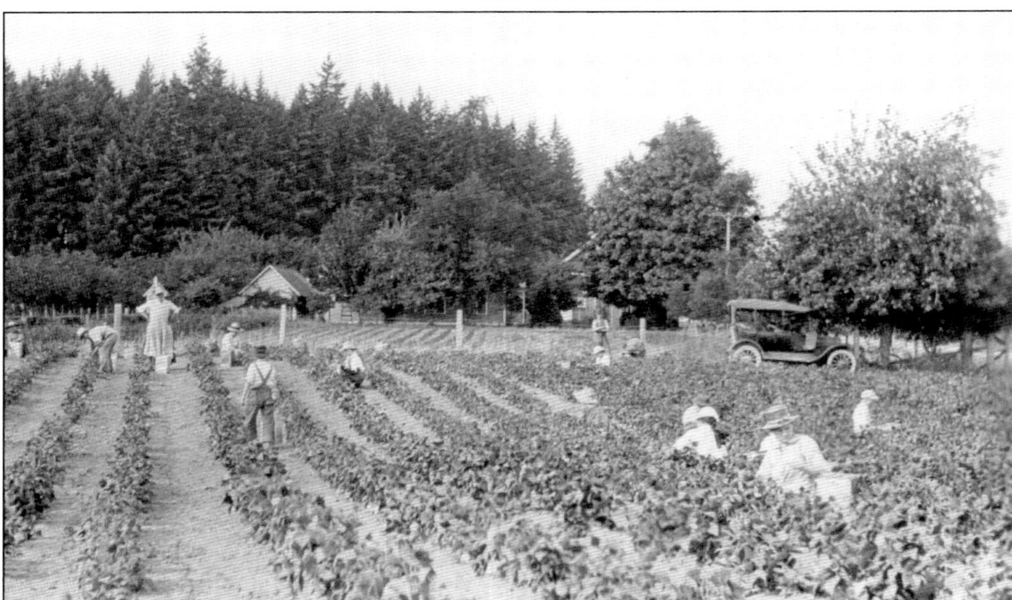

Workers pick strawberries on Theodore Clark's farm in 1906 or 1907. The farm was located in the southwestern area of Keizer, just north of the Salem city limits on the old P.C. Keizur donation land claim, near the Marion County Poor Farm. Standing in the center is the field boss, Blanche Knox; in front of the car is Hattie Given and Nellie Knox (Maxine Clark Dugger's grandmother). (KHM: Dugger.)

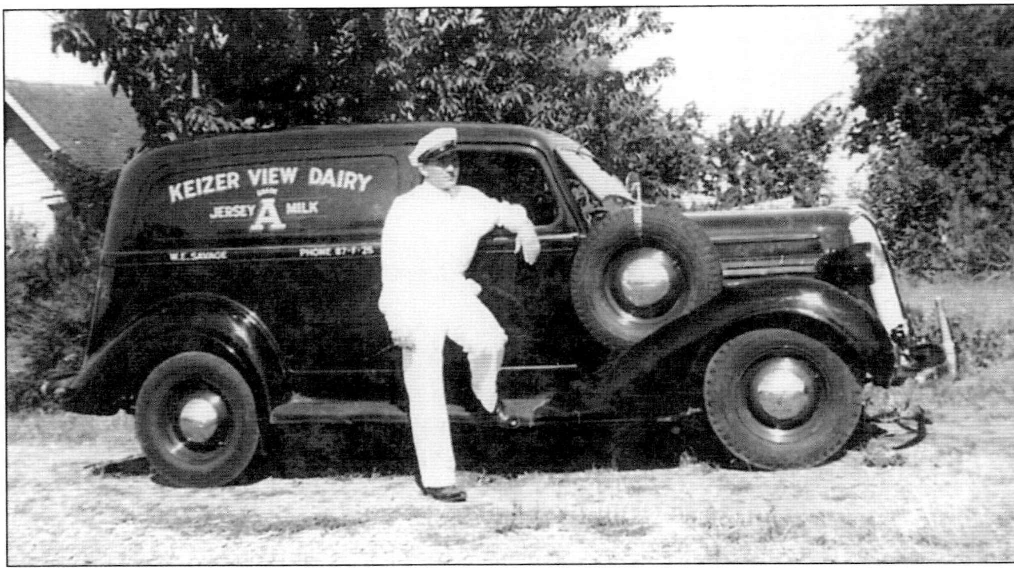

The Keizer View Dairy, owned by the Savage family, raised Jersey cattle and bottled rich, raw milk that they then delivered by horse and wagon. Beginning about 1925, milk was delivered by the family automobile, first a 1923 Star, then a 1929 Chevrolet van. Shown here is Willard "Bob" Savage in 1932. (KHM: Savage.)

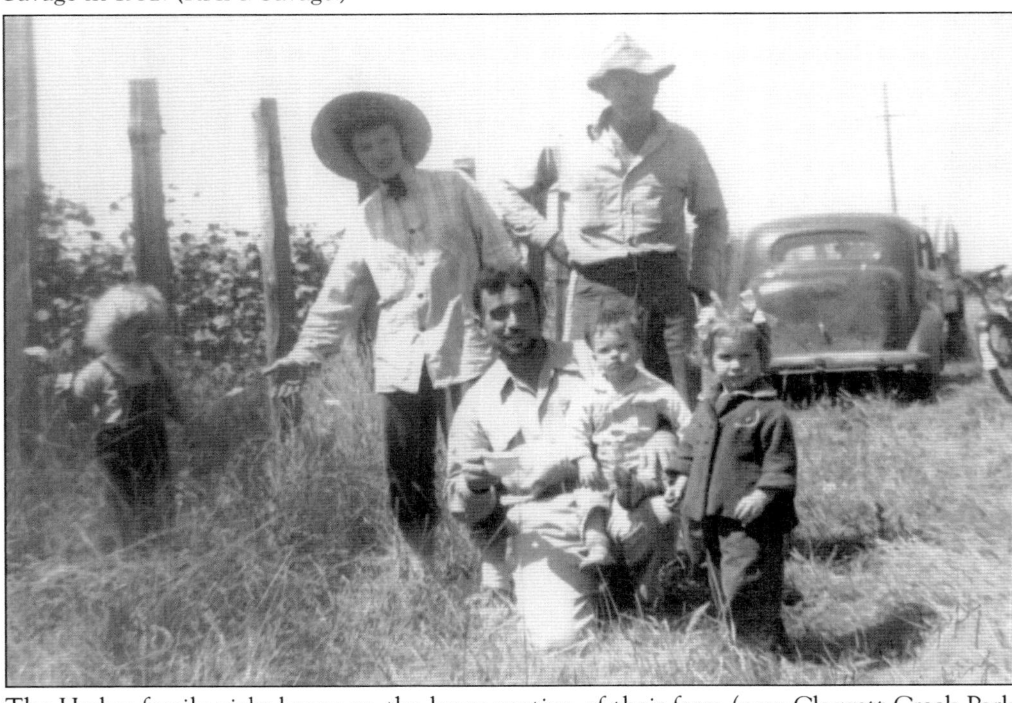
The Herber family picks beans on the lower portion of their farm (now Claggett Creek Park) in the late 1940s. From left to right are Judy, Rosalie, Joe, Joey, and Tyrene. In back is Rosalie's brother-in-law, Ralf Oldenkamp. Their property is the original land claim of John and Sally (Claggett) Pugh. The Herbers moved to the historic home in 1943 and purchased the farm from the Savages in 1948. (Herber.)

Three

SCHOOLS

Multiple accounts mention the early one-room log schoolhouse that the Claggett and McNary children attended on the knoll at the northern crossroads (where the apartments now sit between Wheatland and River Roads). As recorded in Charles McNary's biography by Steve Neal, young Charlie started attending classes there at age six and would carry "his lunch in a tin pail and cut across his grandfather Claggett's meadow, through some brush, and along a dusty path. One of his first teachers was a man named Royal with a reputation as a strict disciplinarian." Ann Lossner documented the following: "In 1866 Hugh McNary brought his wife, the former Margaret Claggett, and his family from Linn County back to the Keizer area, presumably to the Claggett farm. He became the school's teacher and preacher in the little schoolhouse."

Also noted is an early Keizer family pioneer school on the T.D. Keizur property. Keizur and Force children attended this school, closer to their farms. A 1935 newspaper article by R.J. Hendricks recalled the school.

In 1878, John and Sally Pugh donated one-and-a-half acres at Keizer Corners (now Schoolhouse Square), and a frame one-room school was immediately built. It was furnished with the handmade desks and benches from the old Claggett School. The first teacher was Nina McNary, a daughter of Hugh and Margaret McNary. John Pugh's brother, William P., was Marion County's first school superintendent, then known as "school commissioner," serving from 1851 to 1857. The following are the Keizur-area schools and their year of construction: Keizur family pioneer school (pre-1878), Claggett-McNary School (pre-1878), Keizer one-room schoolhouse (1878), Clear Lake School (originally a separate community from Keizer) (1892), Keizer School (four rooms and a basement, now Keizer Heritage Center) (1916), Cummings Elementary (J.B. Keizur donation land claim) (1953), Salem Private School on Chemawa Road (became city hall building) (1962), Kennedy Elementary (1964), McNary High School (also housed Whiteaker Junior High students) (1965), Whiteaker Junior High School (1968), Gubser Elementary (Nolan property, Zieber donation land claim) (1977), Keizer Elementary (new school) (1987), Clear Lake Elementary (new school) (1994), Claggett Creek Middle School (2001), Weddle Elementary (2001), and Forest Ridge Elementary (2002).

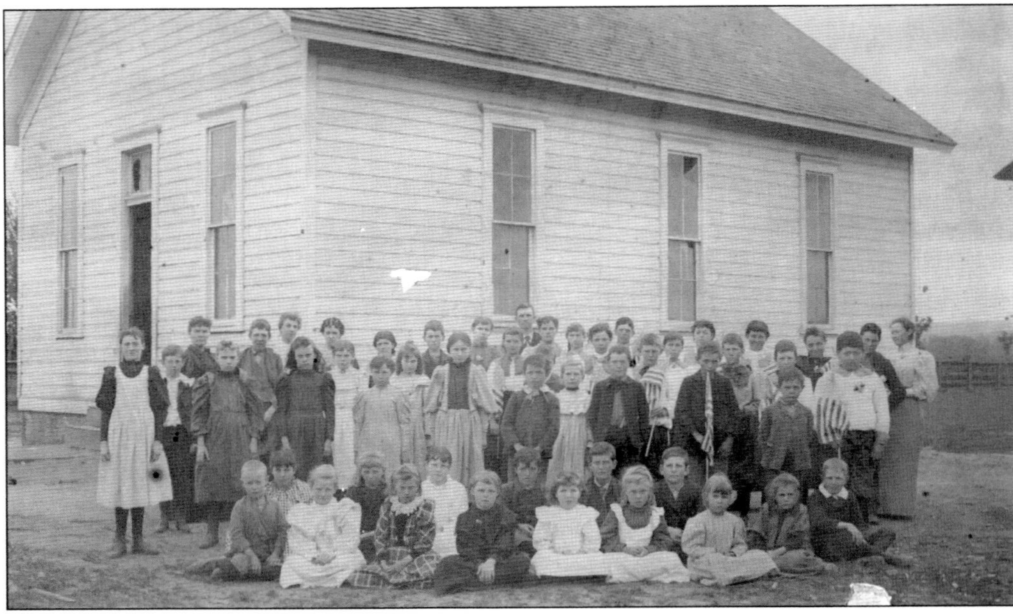

This photograph, taken in 1896, is the oldest known of the one-room Keizer School. The Keizer Corners property was in the lower elevation, closer to the river, and was known as Keizer Bottom. Among those most likely pictured here are Elsie Pearmine, Roy Clemens, Lottie Clark, Lena McIntire, Edna Hoffman, Maude Hoffman, Ora Goodrich, and Olive Howe. John Jackson is one of the teachers represented. Note the broken windows. (Pearmine.)

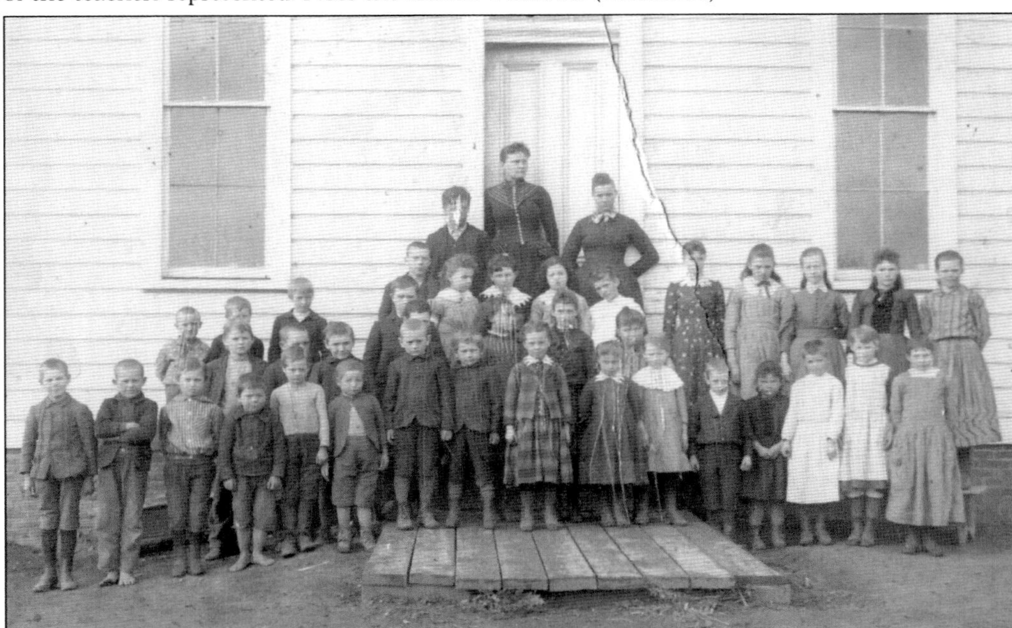

This 1899 photograph was featured in a 1940 *Statesman* article. Note that some students are barefoot. Former students recorded memories of eating nut-grass tubers on the playground; they are said to be tasty! A field on the west side of the school had previously been planted with turnips. At recess and lunch, kids would dig them up and eat them, mud and all! (KHM.)

This 1900 souvenir card neatly lists the pupils in three columns on the back. The listed surnames are Achilles, Beardsley, Bolten, Cardwell, Clemens, Etter, Goodrich, Hall, Huffman, Keizer, MacIntire, McLeod, Nelson, Nye, Osterman, Pearmine, Ryan, Smith, and White. (Donated to KHM by Hall descendant Jo Uecker.)

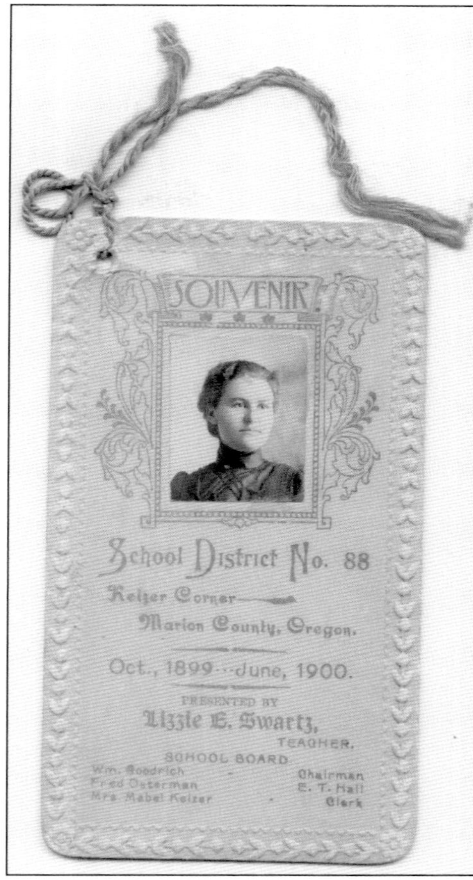

The admired bike riders have a prominent position in this 1901–1902 Keizer School photograph. School District No. 88 was established in 1878, when John and Sally (Claggett) Pugh donated one-and-a-half acres for a school in the centrally positioned crossroads. The new one-room school was located on the original John and Reeda (Keizur) Ford land claim, of which the Pughs purchased a portion in 1877. (KHM.)

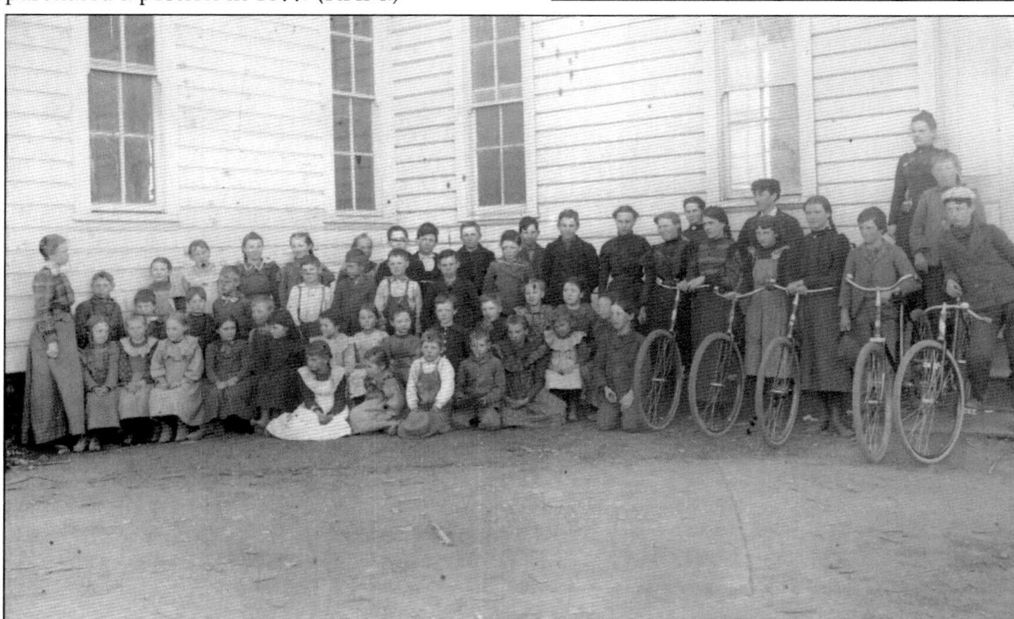

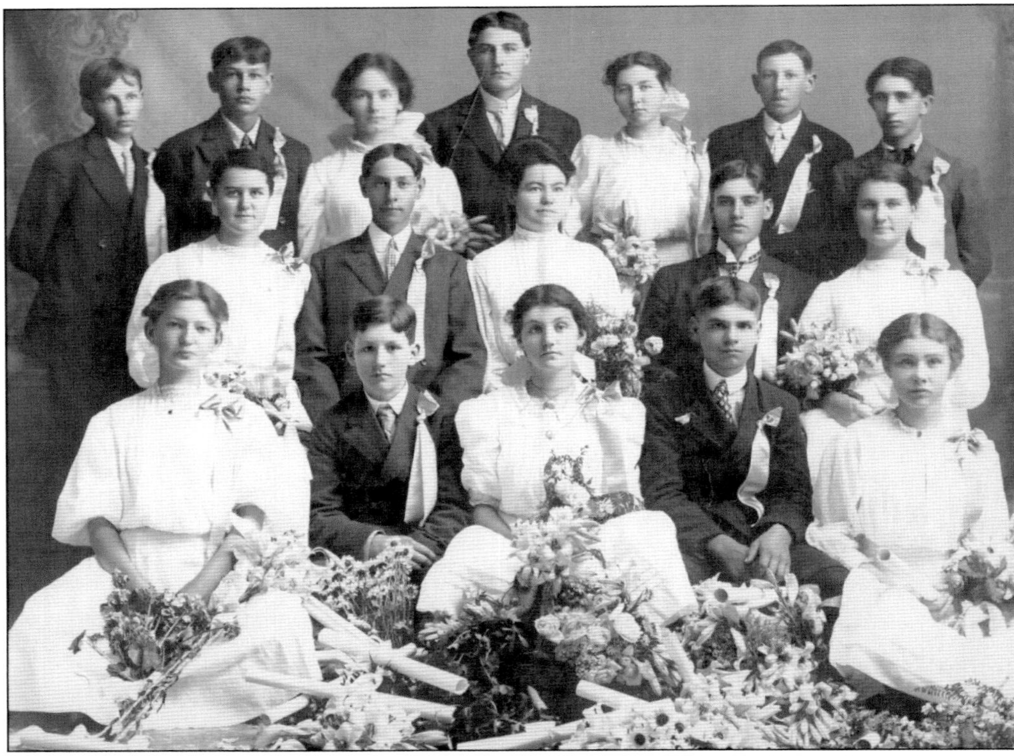

The 1906 graduates shown here are, from left to right, (first row) Ella Keizer, Lester Pearmine, Clarissa Pearmine, Ralph Hess, and Alice Blake; (second row) Alta Hall, Glenn Goodrich, Miss Holst (teacher), Roy Wesley, and Mary Hall; (third row) Harry Keefer, Ben Hall, Murray Keefer, Bernice Williams, Iva Williams, Carl Alleman, and Obed Frogley. The *Statesman* printed this in 1940 and listed the teacher as Anna Lindgren. The identification of names was provided by Edna Frogley. (Pearmine.)

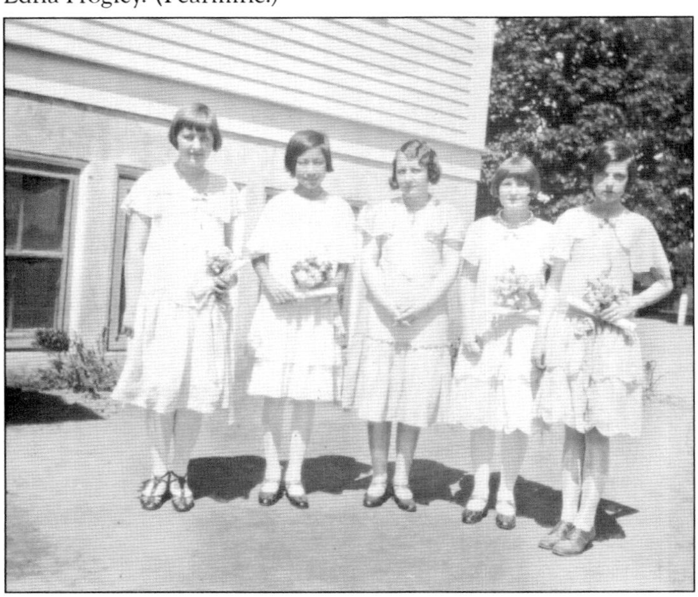

Keizer School eighth-grade graduates and their teacher pose in 1930. They are, from left to right, Dorothy Rulifson, Martha Okuda, Beryl Porter (teacher), LaVaun Gardner, and Ruth Melson. Porter was a well-liked teacher who shared stories about teaching in one-room schools, where she was in charge of building the fire every morning. (KHM: Blanche Betzer Pinneo.)

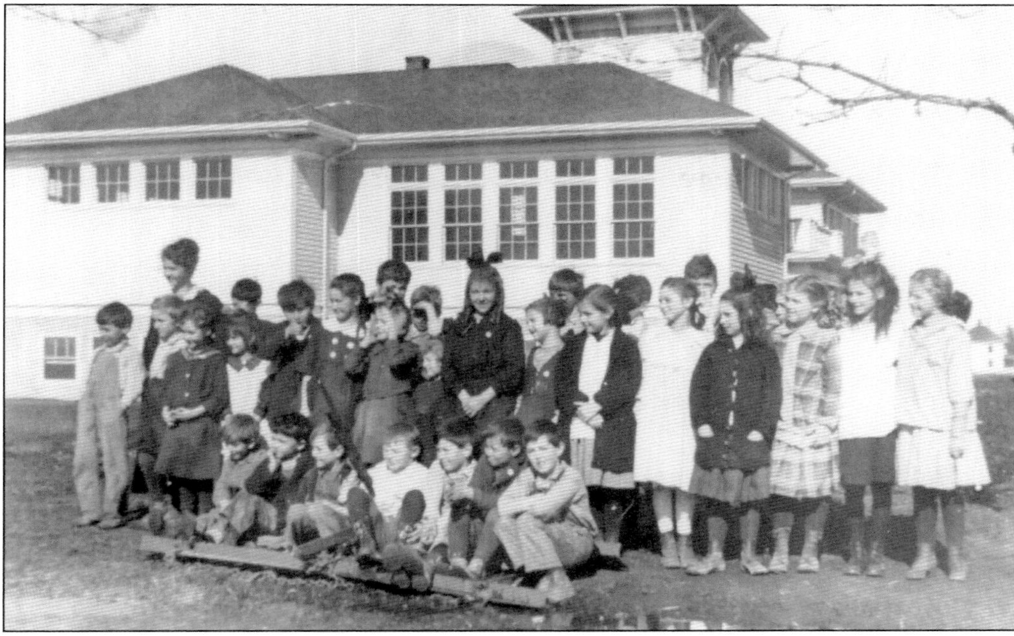

Keizer School's younger students are shown in this 1917 class photograph with teacher Ann Lindgren (Myers), pictured at left in the back. Posing in front of the 1916 school building, they display the dress and hairstyles of the day. The playground in the entrance area invited students each morning for a day of learning and play. (Blake.)

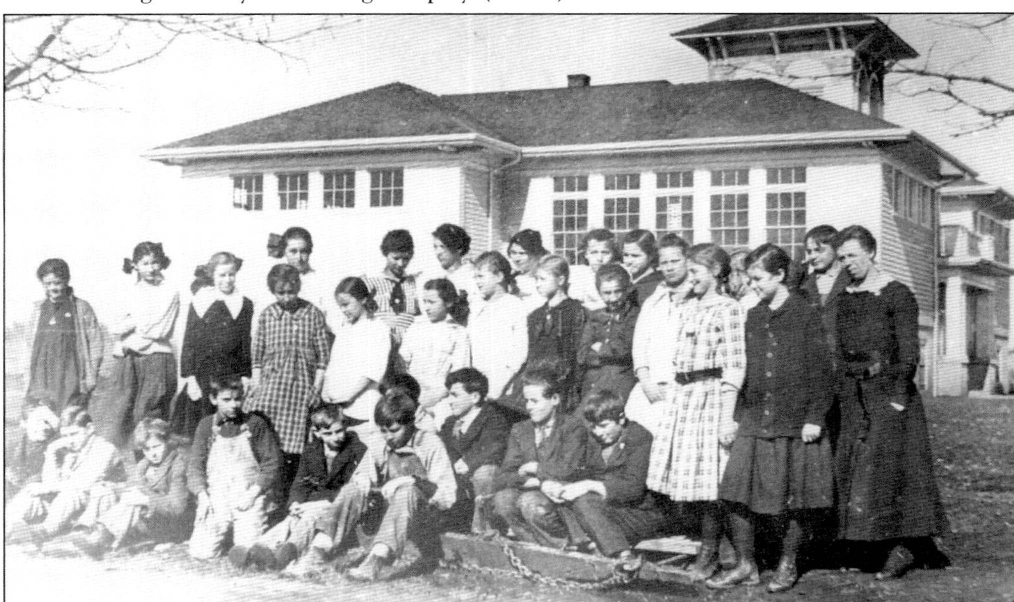

This 1917 class photograph shows older students and teacher Cora Miller (Beardsley Clark, at far right) in front of the 1916 building. The dress of the era is on display here. All girls wore dresses with bloomers underneath to school. The first two teachers in the new building were Miss Miller, who taught the four upper grades, and Anna Lindgren (Myers), who instructed the younger pupils. Cora Clark celebrated her 100th birthday in 1987. (KHM.)

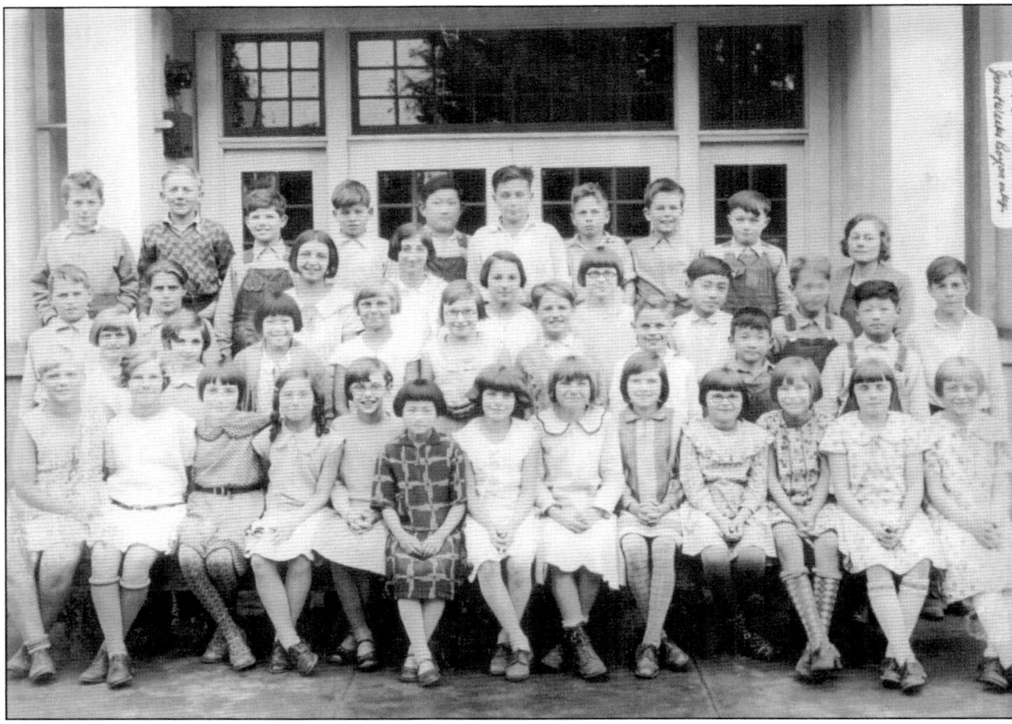

Girls with short hair and stylish socks are among Eva Kelso's 1930 fifth- and sixth-grade classes. Shown are, from left to right, (first row) Bartruff, McGinty, Russell, Addison, Claggett, Wong, Sanford, Varbel, Klubundy, Holden, Miller, Frogley, and Harold; (second row) VanCleave, McCall, Sun, Melson, Smith, Gardner, Evans, unidentified, and Furukawa; (third row) Rulifson, Donor, Miller, McClay, Weeks, Downey, Fukuda, Larry ?, and Donor; (fourth row) unidentified, Harold, Bliven, unidentified, Sugai, Blake, Keeney, Miller, and Weathers. (KHM: Terri Thompson-Hoag.)

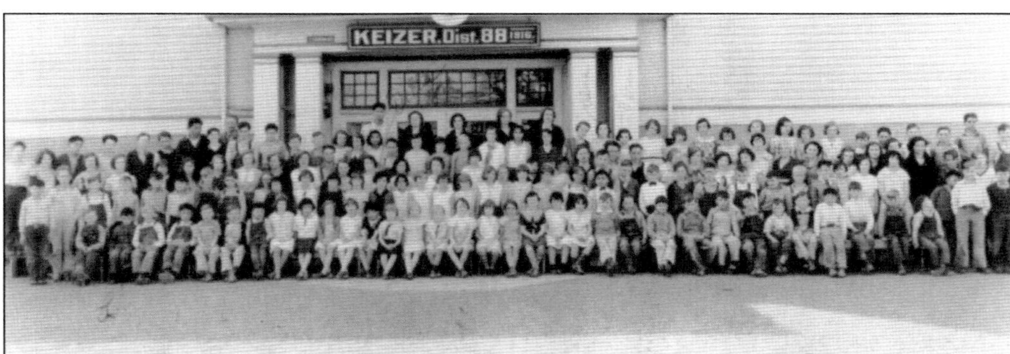

The entire Keizer School student body is represented in this 1933 panoramic photograph. There were about 200 students in attendance at that time. By 1952, Keizer would be designated as the largest school in all of Marion County. To relieve crowding, a bond was passed, and the new Cummings Elementary opened in 1953. On July 1, 1955, Keizer School District No. 88 consolidated with Salem School District 24JC. (KHM.)

This north-facing photograph of Keizer School includes Shattuc's Keizer Corner Store (left). Note the narrow, tree-lined River Road at right. Nancy Veal Marnell remembers: "Mr. Mickey McClure was a popular, but strict teacher. Sometimes he would say, 'Pack a lunch tomorrow; we are walking to the river.' We were all well-behaved and would walk single file with Mr. McClure leading us down Chemawa Road to the Willamette River." This photograph was taken in 1939 or 1940. (KHM.)

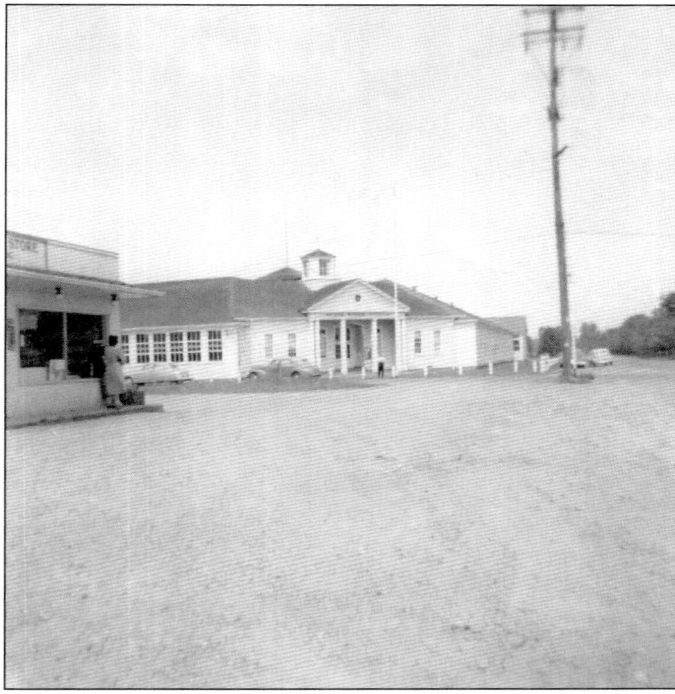

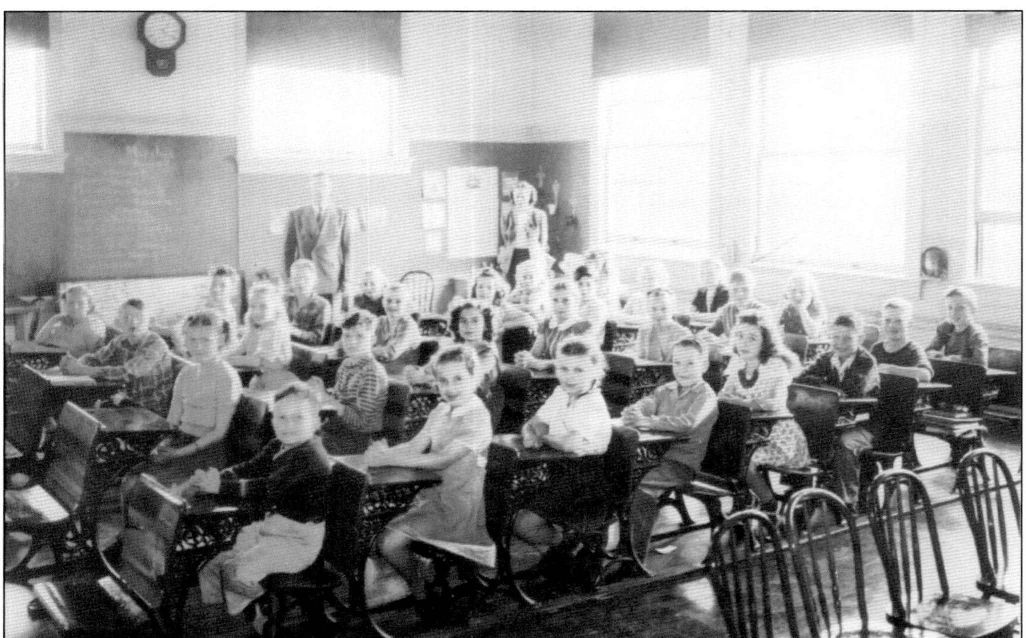

"We're all in our places with bright, shining faces." This is a 1940s classroom at Keizer School. Student jobs are listed on the chalkboard. In this era, student enrollment continued to grow. In 1939, a large wing was added containing four classrooms, health room, teachers' lounge, kitchen, auditorium, and principal's office. (Donated to KHM by Vivian Cannoy from the Roderick J. Cannoy family.)

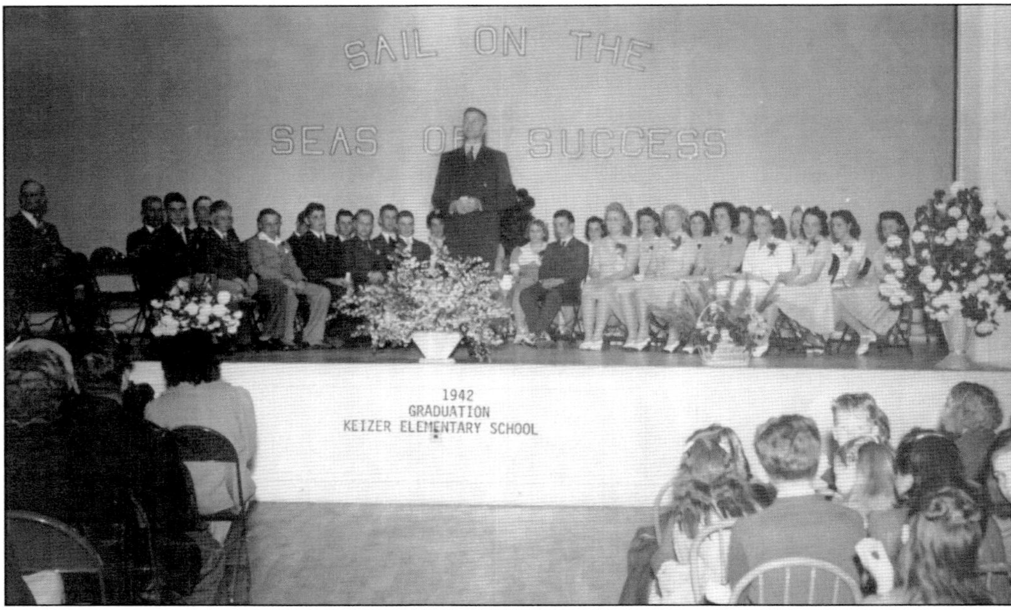

The graduating class of eighth graders enjoy this milestone event at Keizer School in 1942. The girls all received corsages, and the boys were given boutonnieres for the ceremony. In later years, older students would attend Parrish and Waldo Junior High Schools. Beginning in the early 1930s, McClean's bus service transported students to the junior and high schools. (KHM: Barbara Baldwin Knight.)

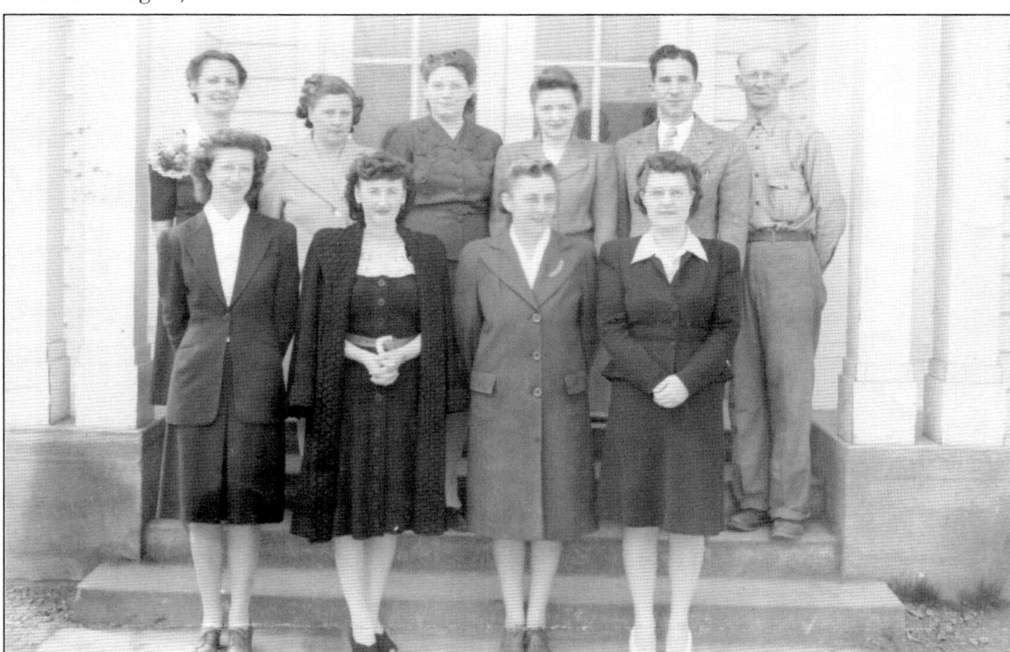

The 1944–1945 Keizer School faculty are, from left to right, (first row) Nellie Yung, Elda Bradfield, Elizabeth Folston, and LaVaun Gardner; (second row) Freida ?, Leona Beck, Hazel Rolboke, Ruth Weatherby, Vincent Johnson, and Mr. Olson. (KHM: LaVaun Gardner White Buck.)

Teacher Elizabeth Folston stands with her 1948 fourth-grade class. An orchard is in view out the windows. The sturdy school desks are all in a row, with iron feet screwed to wooden rails. The desks had ornate sides of cast iron and wooden seats that folded up. The wooden desktops had inkwell holes, pencil slots, and a shelf underneath for supplies. (KHM: Fred Gast Jr.)

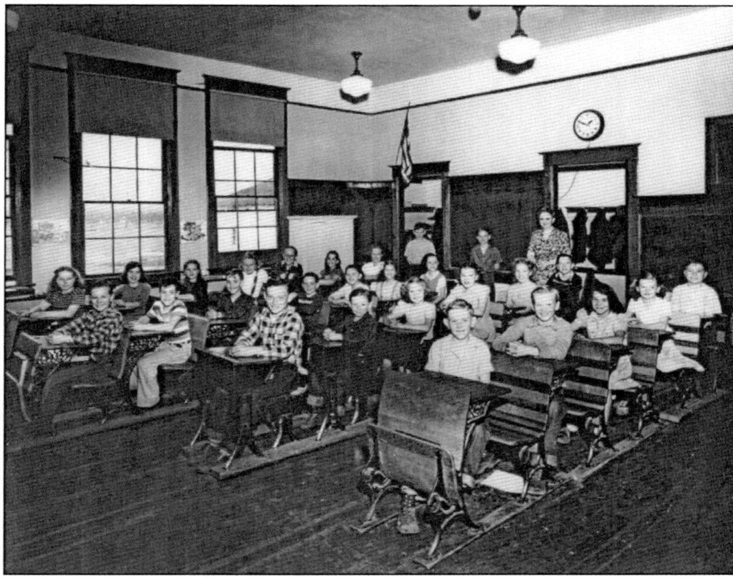

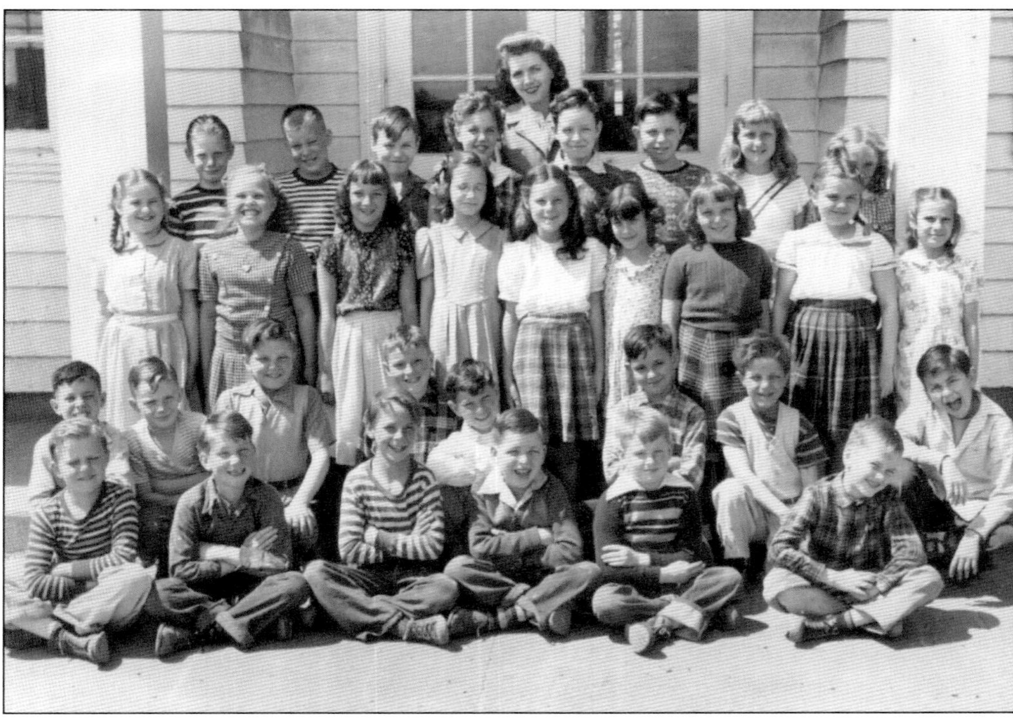

This class of fun-loving fifth graders surround their pretty teacher (unidentified) in 1949–1950 at Keizer School. Girls were required to wear dresses at that time (with bloomers underneath). The boys are wearing jeans. Most students walked to school, and parents were involved with the Parent Teachers Association. (KHM: Jeanette Shattuc Pont.)

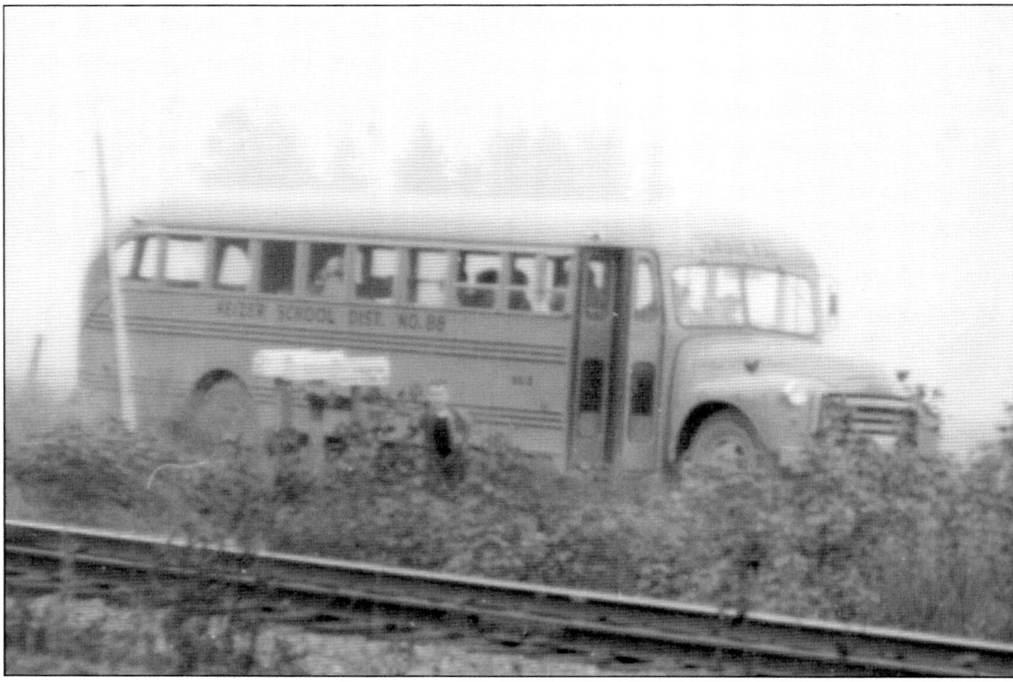

John Sangster's mother, Katherine (Barry) Sangster, snapped this photograph of him getting off the school bus at their Ridge Drive home in 1953. The Keizer School bus transported students to parochial school as well. This is the only District No. 88 bus photograph that has been found. (Hersch Sangster.)

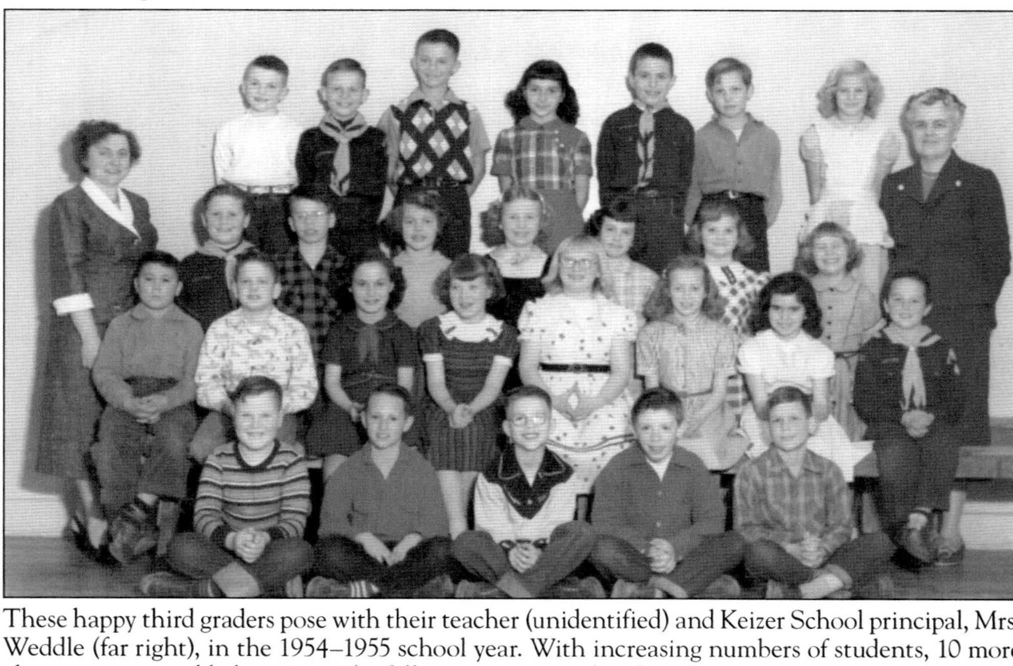

These happy third graders pose with their teacher (unidentified) and Keizer School principal, Mrs. Weddle (far right), in the 1954–1955 school year. With increasing numbers of students, 10 more classrooms were added in 1948. The following year, another five classrooms and other rooms were constructed. The original basement was put to use as a music room and library. (KHM.)

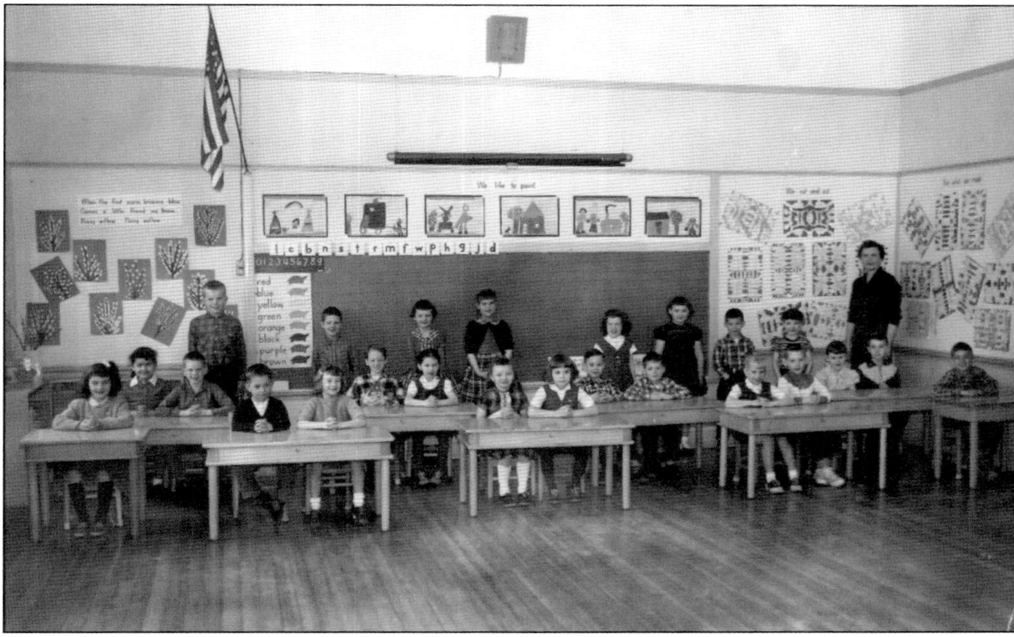

This is Mrs. Carl's first-grade class in 1959–1960 at Keizer School. Some of the seated students are, from left to right, Mary Herber (1), Julia O'Connor (2), Terry Baldwin (3), Bruce Sirnio (4), Diane Sullivan (6), Randy Miller (7), Debbie Peacock (9), Merita "Sue" Nelson (10), Wes Luke (13), Karen Johnson (17), Mary Beth Rice (19), David Graft (20), and Eddie Hopkins (24). (Diane Sullivan Taylor.)

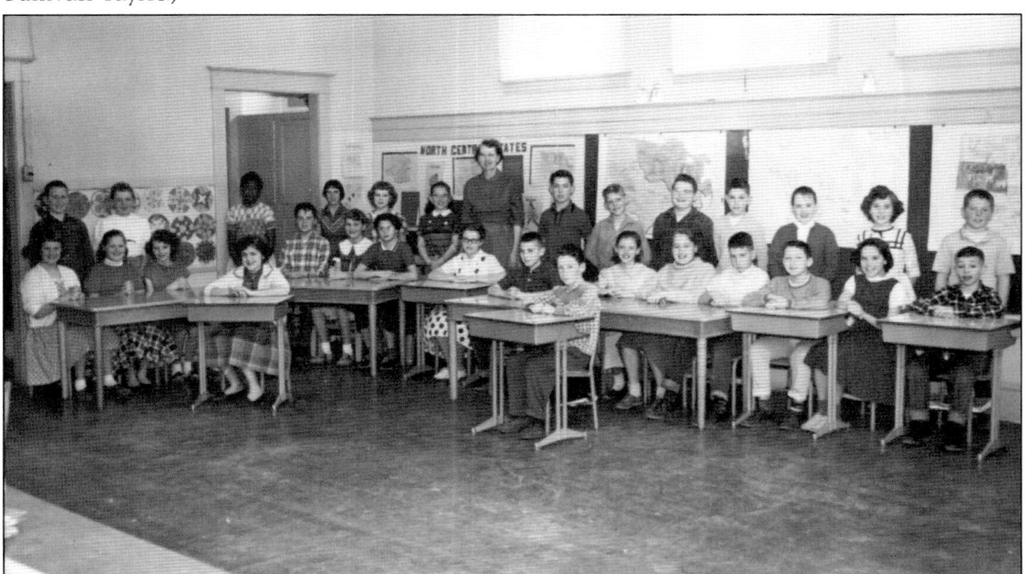

Mrs. Wilson's 1959–1960 fifth-grade class at Keizer School gathers for a photograph. Identified by surname, they are, from left to right, (seated) Blaschko, Sinsel, Wilkinson, Culps, Wilmschen, Dougall, Smith, Camp, Leffingwell, Hoover, Ries, Mackey, Paris, and Karn; (standing) Lakie, Wiesner, Dumond, Boeringer, Mrs. Wilson, Spangler, Boyd, Pfau, Barker, and Humphrey. (Susan Hoover Bevens Ramsdell.)

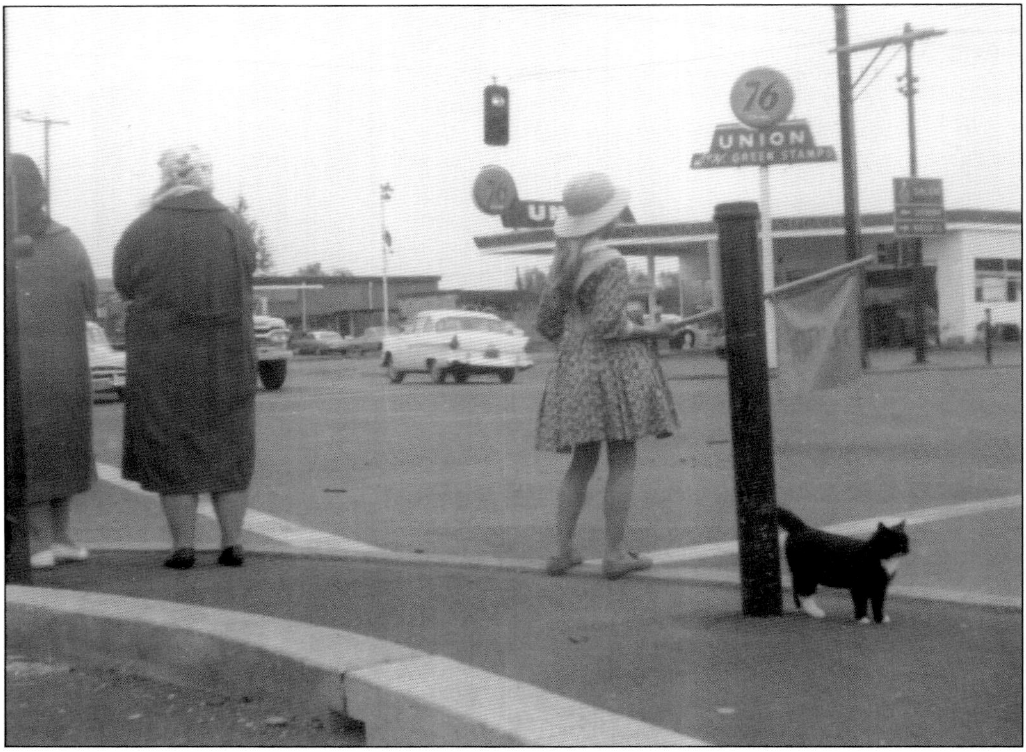

Standing at Keizer Corner in 1962 is Genese Franz, volunteer crossing guard for fellow students. As the city grew, the once-quiet dirt roads were paved and became filled with traffic. In the bustle of the day, a cat comes to greet the pedestrians. (Evelyn Melson Franz.)

THE KEIZER BELL

Since 1904 the Keizer School Bell has been a significant symbol of education to many of the remaining pioneer families. It is assumed that the Bell was initially used in the first one-room school. By 1914 the one-room school became the four-room schoolhouse which still remains the center of the present Keizer School.

The Bell could be heard for miles as it called students to the school each morning and throughout the day. The Bell was housed above the "cloakroom" in the northeast corner of the building where the 4th and 5th grade students were housed. Different students were appointed by the teacher to ring the Bell, which was considered to be a great honor and privilege. The rope hung down into the cloakroom and was knotted at the end, enabling the "puller" to get a good grip. Five pulls of the Keizer Bell were sufficient to summon the students in the morning to line up in front of the building. The students lined up according to size, the boys in the North "boys basement" and the girls in the South "girls basement". As they marched into the school, they were accompanied by a Keizer student playing various piano selections. Thus, another day would begin for the early-day Keizer students.

The traditional school bell was replaced with electronic sounds. This beautifully scripted prose is a reminder of years past. The new shopping center at the school's former location was named Schoolhouse Square in honor of the property. Its sign, as well as its structural design, incorporates a bell tower. A new Keizer Elementary School was built in 1987. (KHM.)

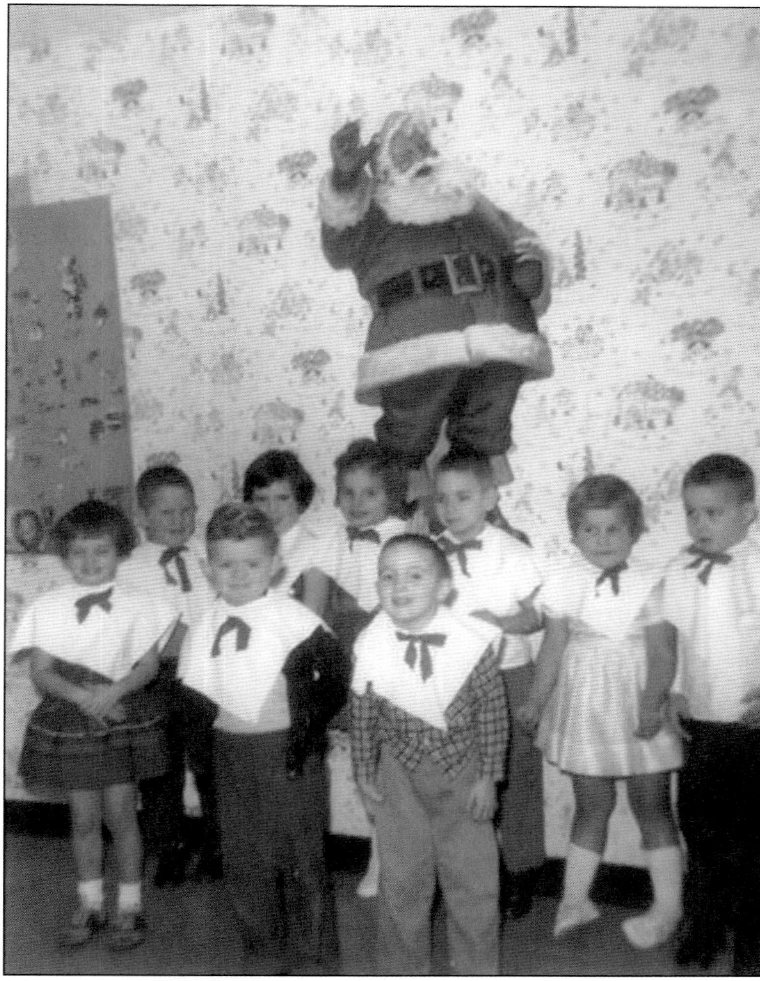

The private Keizer Kindergarten was located north of Keizer School, now the site of the Rose Park Apartments. The building was constructed by men from the Rose and Jones families. The main teacher was LaVaun White, assisted by her sister Cora Rose and a neighbor, Mrs. Koons. This c. 1961 photograph of a Christmas program shows students Mark Jones (first row, second from left), Robin Largent (second row, second from right), and Aniko Lengell (second row, third from left), among others. A small fee paid for the morning or afternoon class. (Jones.)

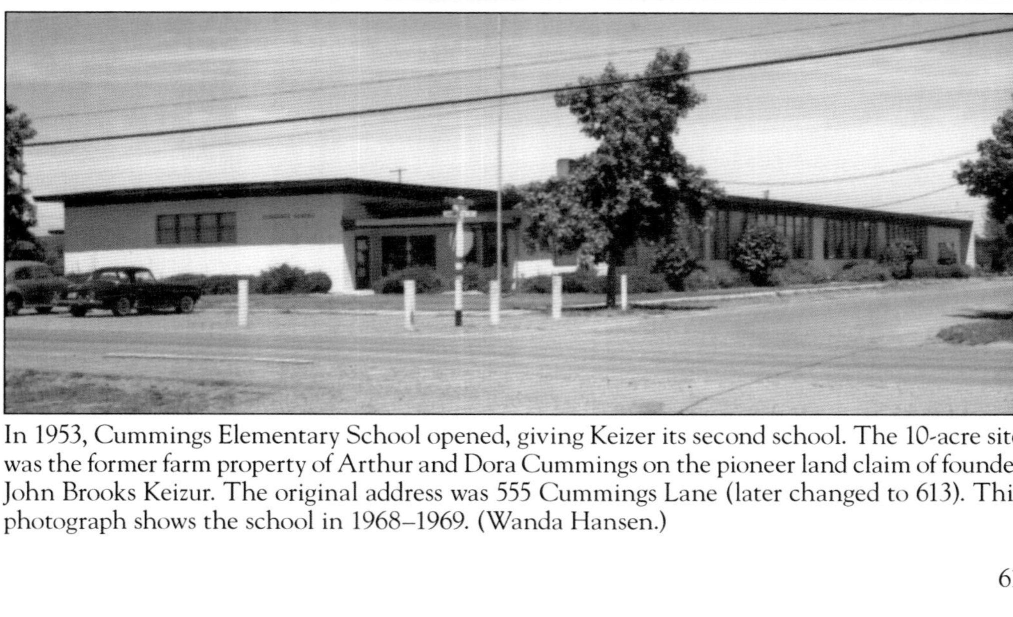

In 1953, Cummings Elementary School opened, giving Keizer its second school. The 10-acre site was the former farm property of Arthur and Dora Cummings on the pioneer land claim of founder John Brooks Keizur. The original address was 555 Cummings Lane (later changed to 613). This photograph shows the school in 1968–1969. (Wanda Hansen.)

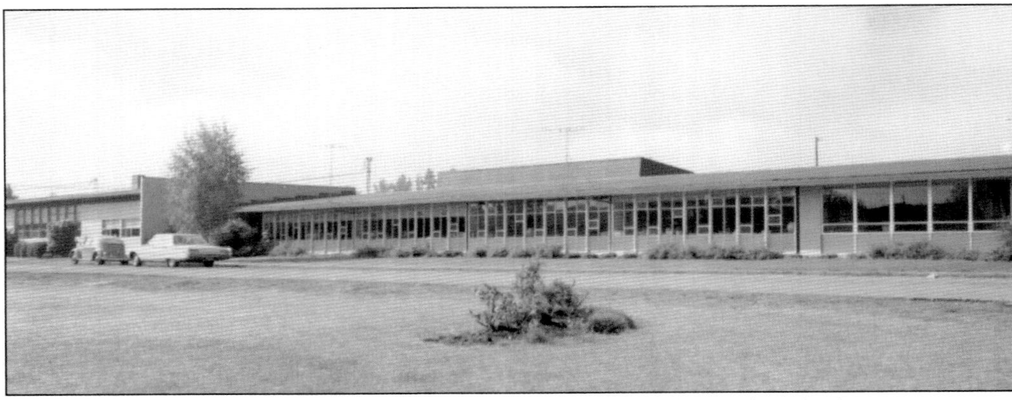

Cummings Elementary, seen here in 1969–1970 with its sleek, modern look, was a contrast from the older Keizer School. Enrollment in the opening year of 1954 was about 215 students, a result of continued growth from the fast-growing area in and around Manbrin Gardens. (Wanda Hansen.)

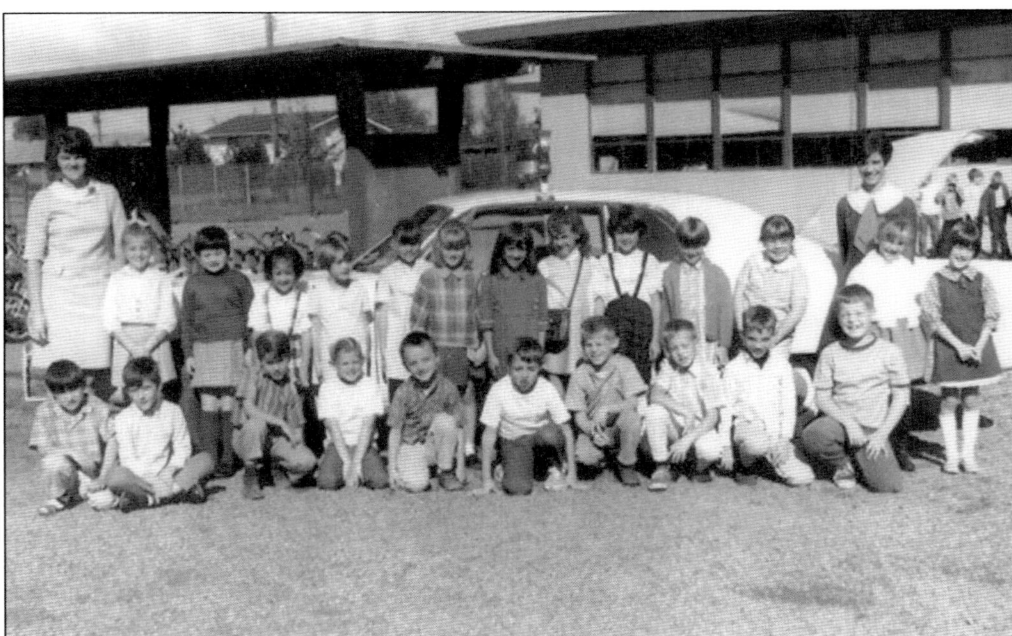

Second graders are visited by a police officer in 1969–1970. From left to right are (kneeling) Jesse Rodriquez, Brett Morgan, Greg Nairns, Randy Strickfaden, Charley Worth, Bobby Gallagher, Lindsay Guenther, Jeff Bell, Todd Winnings, and David Tookey; (standing) Mrs. Hansen, Riona Thompson, Julie Hoevet, Jackie Lowe, Vickie Ness, Vickie Burt, Michelle Wentzell, Susan Matthys, Marcia Jorgenson, Michelle Stovin, Kippy Keppinger, Amy Dungey, Lorrisa Underwood, Marlene Stanley, and Miss Rathbone. (Bob Gallagher.)

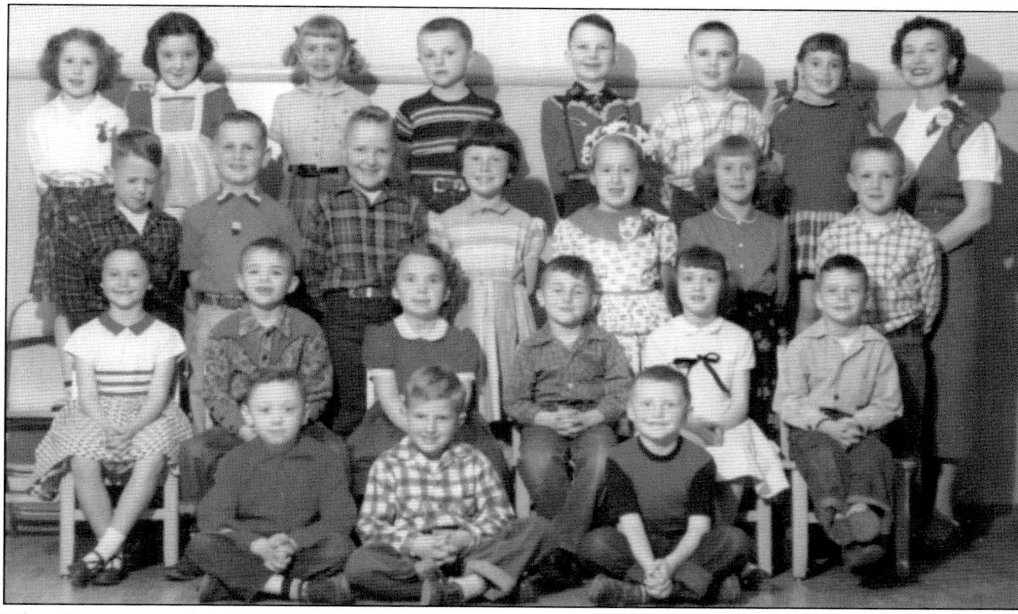

The Cummings first graders in Mrs. Bergman's 1955–1956 class are, from left to right, (first row) Michael Lappin, John Mason, and Bruce Moffitt; (second row) Diane Amy, Dana Dunlap, Rebecca Sawyer, Joseph Hopkins, Sandra Olson, and Michael Green; (third row) Danny Jensen, Don Chapman, Tommy Baker, Linda Ewing, Susan Hoover, Lori Gardner, and Joe Henry; (fourth row) Patty Olson, Patricia Church, Linda Reagan, Jay Richter, Dana Rappe, Charles Wilson, and Marilyn Butte. (Susan Hoover Bevens Ramsdell.)

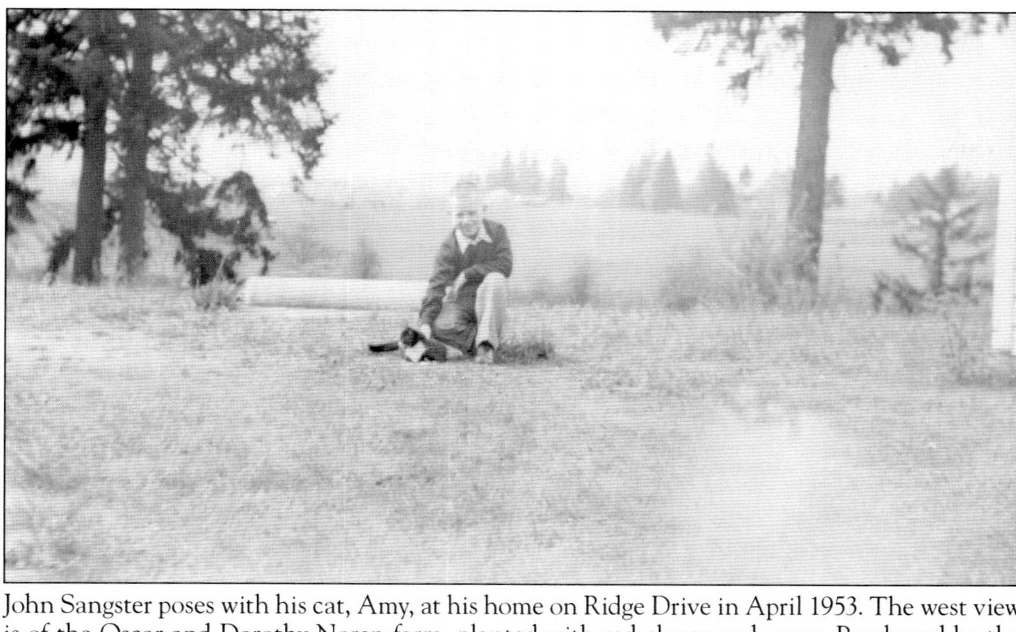

John Sangster poses with his cat, Amy, at his home on Ridge Drive in April 1953. The west view is of the Oscar and Dorothy Noren farm, planted with red clover and pears. Purchased by the Salem School District for $15,000 in 1959, the farm would become the site of Kennedy Elementary School, built in 1963. (Hersch Sangster.)

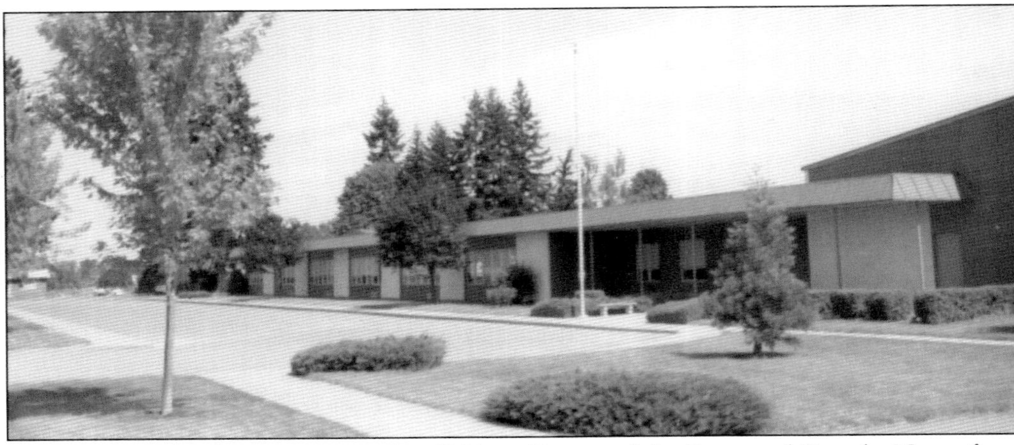

Keizer's third school was constructed in 1964 on 10 acres of the Oscar and Dorothy Noren farm. (Oscar's sister, Mabel Noren Claggett, lived nearby on Verda Lane.) Among the names considered for the school were East Keizer, Claggett, and Claggett Creek. But, due to the death of Pres. John F. Kennedy in November 1963, it was named in his honor. Kennedy Elementary opened its doors to more than 270 students. (Bob Wild.)

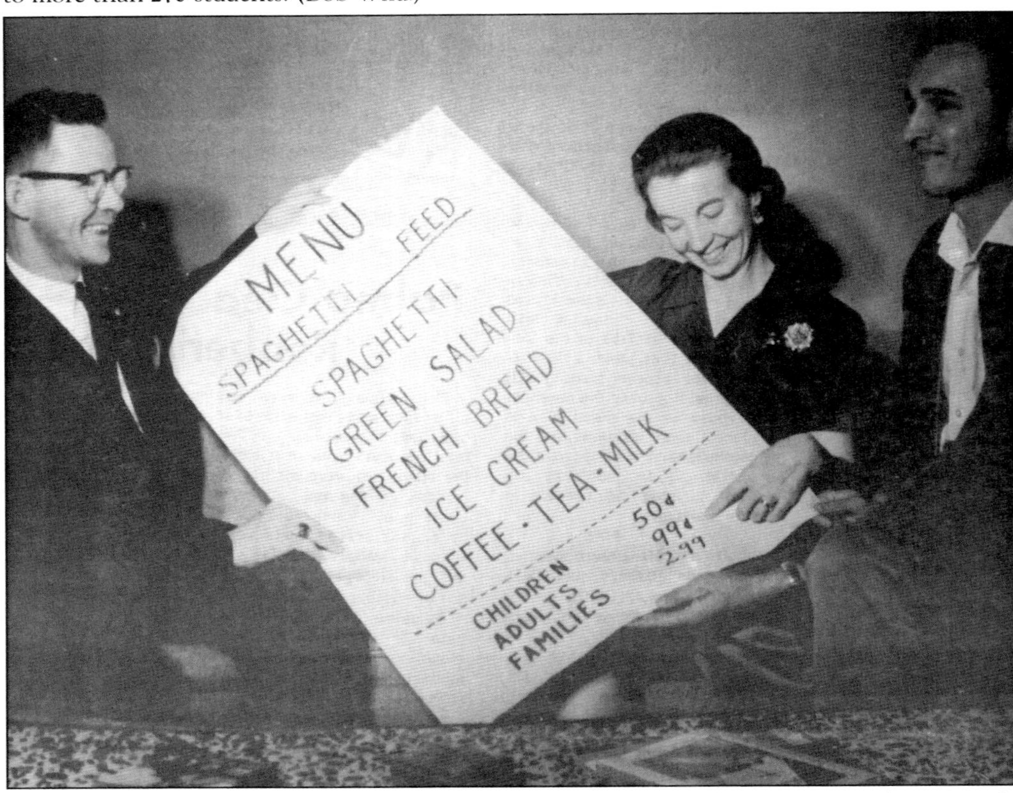

Kennedy had an active parents' club, which organized a spaghetti fundraiser in December 1964. The *Keizer News* highlighted this event, aimed at raising money to purchase a television set for the school. Ed Warmoth, Barbara Lucky, and Jim Fisher are seen as they prepare for the event. Funds were also raised for landscape plants. Carmalite Weddle, the principal, appointed a shrubbery committee. She was previously the principal at Keizer School. (*Keizer News*: Kennedy scrapbook.)

It was an exciting experience for students and staff alike, as Gov. Tom McCall served ice cream at an event promoting keeping Oregon "Green, Clean and Beautiful" at Kennedy Elementary School in Keizer. Living near the capital city offers advantages to students; field trips and choir concerts at the Oregon State Capitol building in Salem are common. (Photograph by Gerry Lewin; *Statesman Journal*.)

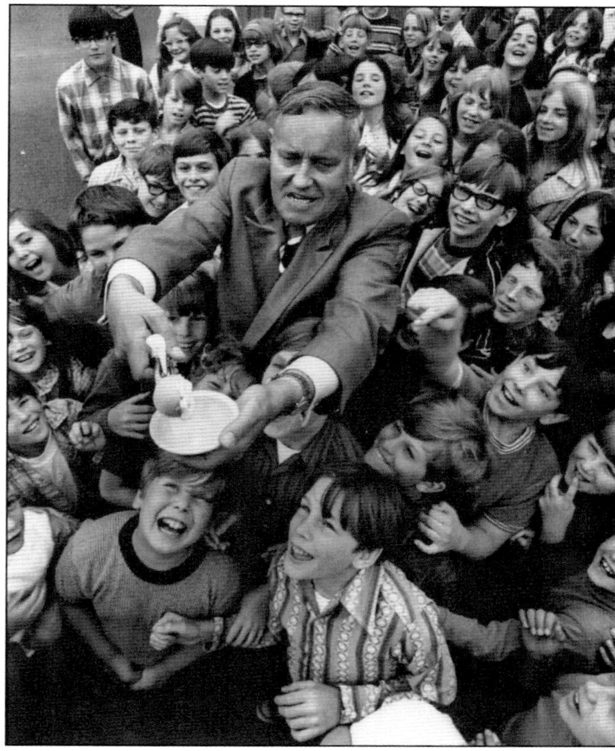

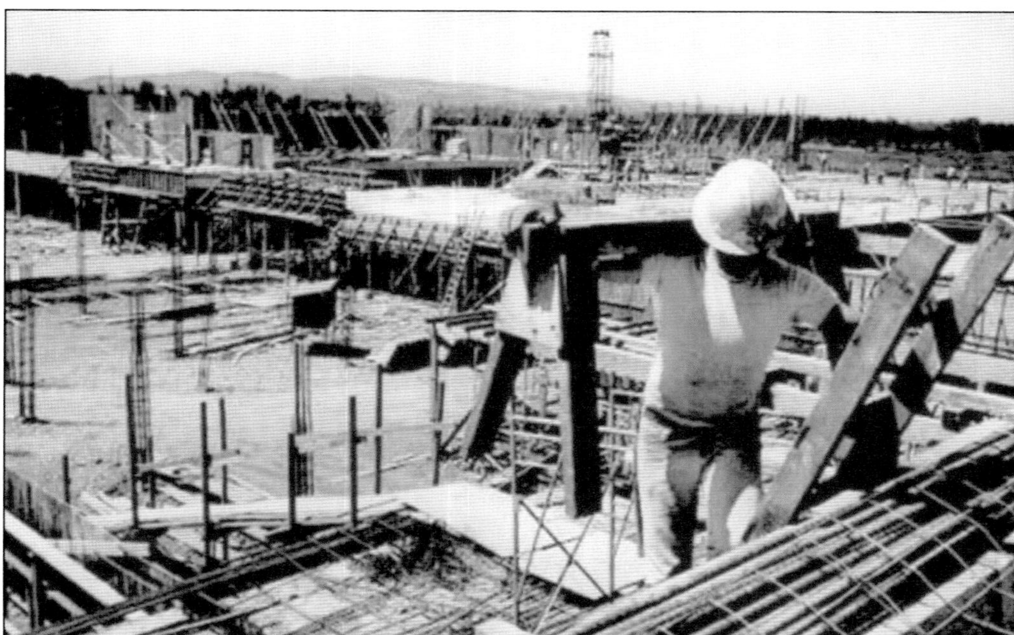

Shown here is the construction of McNary High School in Salem. The northwest-facing photograph of the campus shows the cafeteria and the gym. In the foreground, a worker climbs a ladder with a sawhorse over his shoulder. McNary was completed in 1965. (SPL: SJ.)

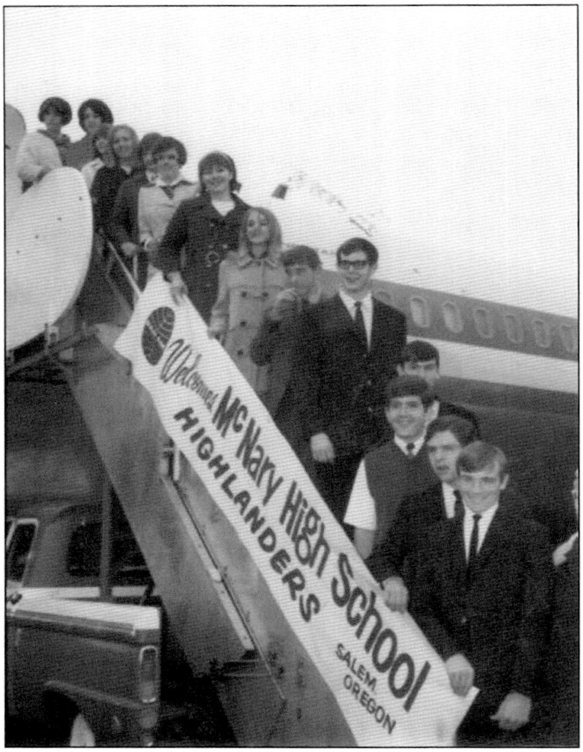

This 1968 promotion with Pam Am Airlines created excitement and helped with the many fundraising events for the McNary Highlanders and their 1970 spring break choir trip to Hawaii. Alice (Rose) Jones was the first choir teacher at the high school, continuing in that capacity until her retirement in 1985. Some of the students pictured here are Corie Jones, Pam Piesker, Gary Lindgren, and Rex Yoder (far right, at bottom). (Jones.)

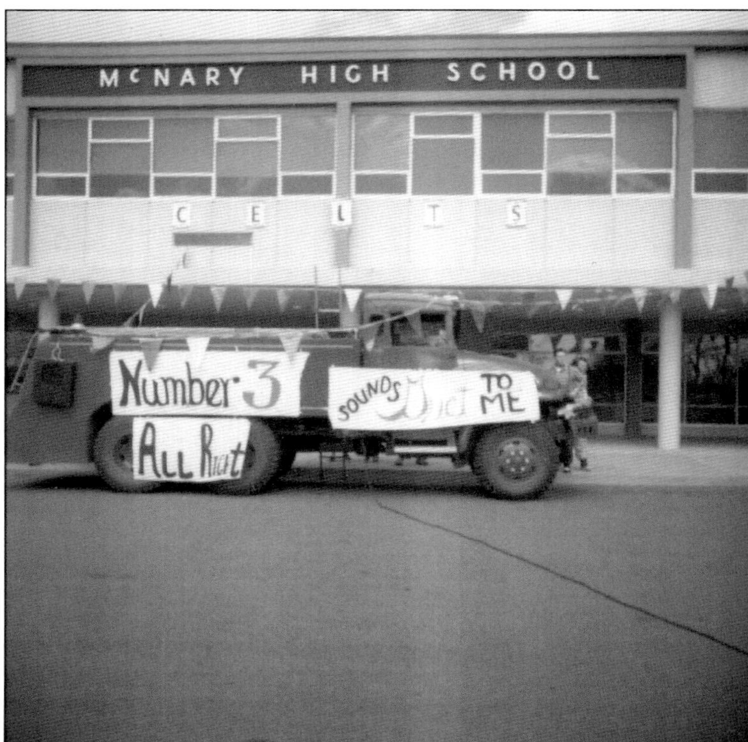

The Keizer Fire District has been a vital part of the community since 1948. The fire engines added to the celebration for the basketball team's first state championship placement. The 1968–1969 McNary team earned third place. "Number 3 All Right, Sounds 'Guet' to me" is painted on the banners. (Corie Jones.)

The Keizer Fire District created a water archway as the town celebrated the new high school's first state championship participation. The 1968–69 McNary basketball team earned third place. The former address for McNary High School was 505 Sandy Drive. (Photograph donated to KHM by Corie Jones. Photograph by Gerry Lewin; *Statesman Journal*, used with permission.)

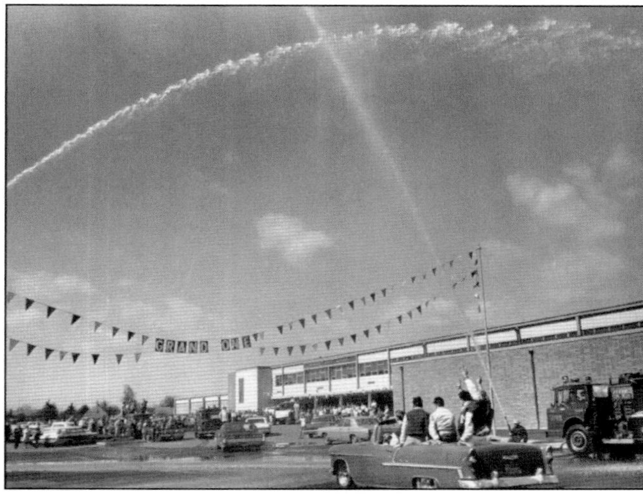

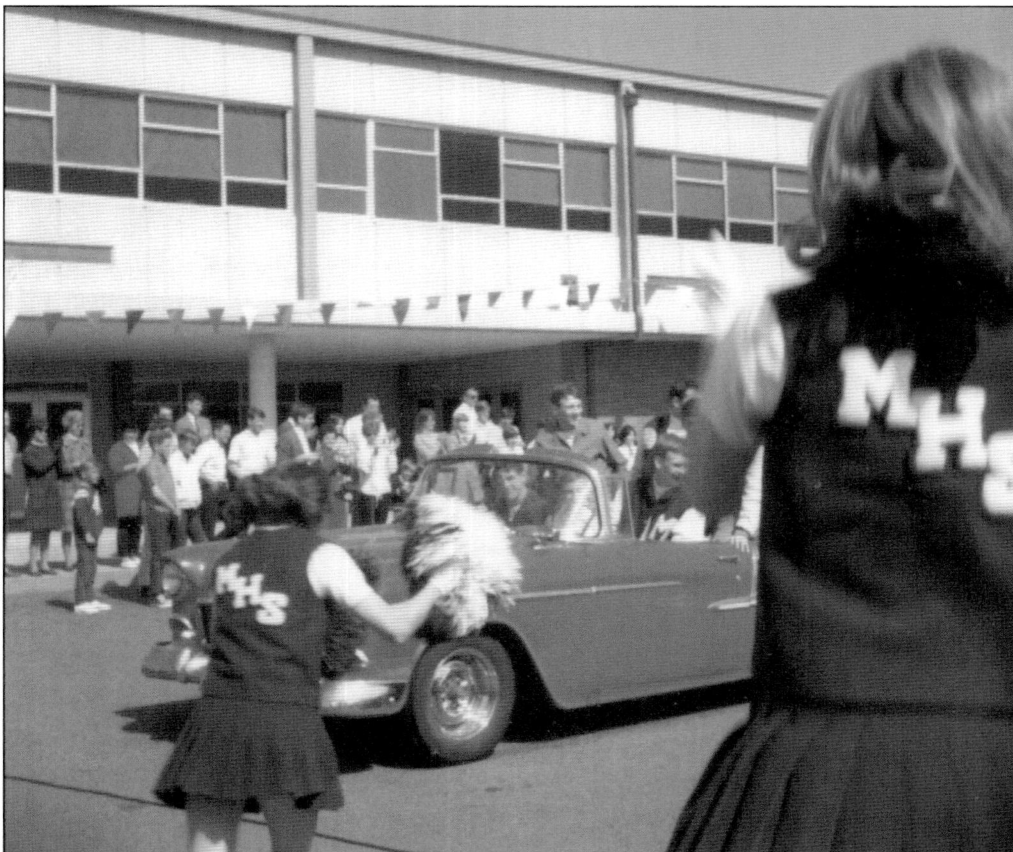

Cheered on by McNary cheerleaders, parents, students, and Keizer residents, the 1968–1969 McNary basketball team celebrates its third-place showing at the state championships. This was a big achievement for Keizer's first high school, built in 1965. Community involvement has been vital since the beginning, and it continues today. Many of the high school's sports complexes have been constructed by service clubs. (Corie Jones.)

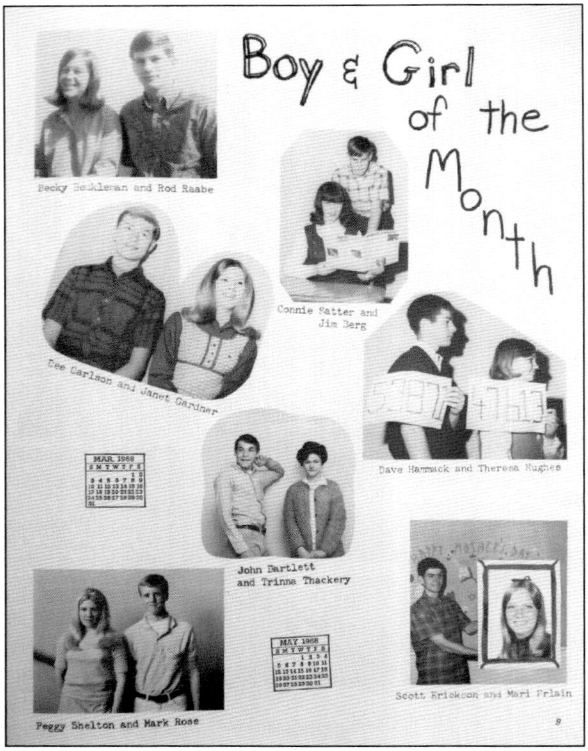

Whiteaker Junior High School was housed at McNary High School until the fall of 1968. This page from the 1967–1968 yearbook features the "Boy and Girl of the Month" for the school year. The first students would continue on at McNary as high schoolers, while the younger students moved to the new school. (Whiteaker Junior High yearbook.)

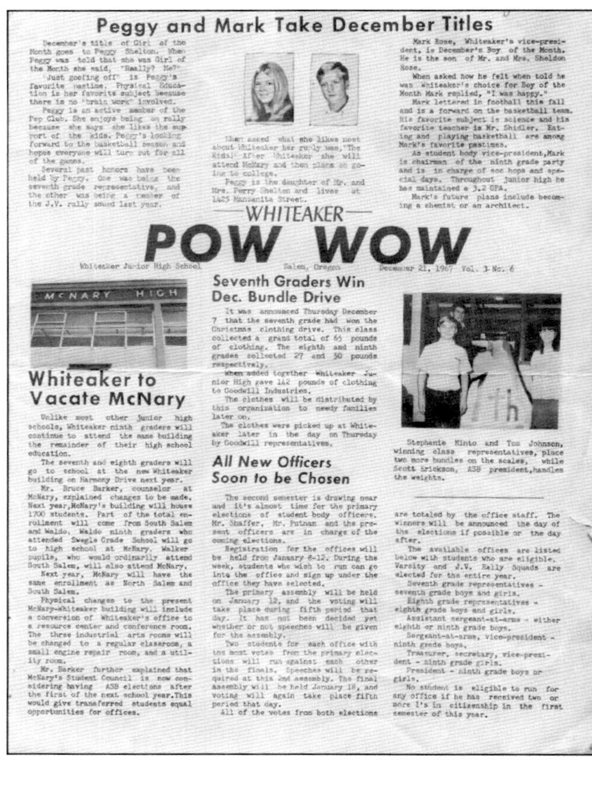

Peggy and Mark Take December Titles

December's title of Girl of the Month goes to Peggy Shelton. When Peggy was told that she was Girl of the Month she said, "Really? Me?"

"Just goofing off" is Peggy's favorite pastime. Physical Education is her favorite subject because there is no "brain work" involved.

Peggy is an active member of the Pep Club. She enjoys being on rally because she says she likes the support of the kids. Peggy's looking forward to the basketball season and hopes everyone will turn out for all of the games.

Several past honors have been held by Peggy. One was being the seventh grade representative, and the other was being a member of the J.V. rally squad last year.

When asked what she likes most about Whiteaker her reply was, "The Kids!" After Whiteaker she will attend McNary and then plans on going to college.

Peggy is the daughter of Mr. and Mrs. Perry Shelton and lives at 1425 Manzanita Street.

Mark Rose, Whiteaker's vice-president, is December's Boy of the Month. He is the son of Mr. and Mrs. Sheldon Rose.

When asked how he felt when told he was Whiteaker's choice for Boy of the Month Mark replied, "I was happy."

Mark lettered in football this fall and is a forward on the basketball team. His favorite subject is science and his favorite teacher is Mr. Shidler. Eating and playing basketball are among Mark's favorite pastimes.

As student body vice-president, Mark is chairman of the ninth grade party and is in charge of soc hops and special days. Throughout junior high he has maintained a 3.2 GPA.

Mark's future plans include becoming a chemist or an architect.

—WHITEAKER—

POW WOW

Whiteaker Junior High School Salem, Oregon December 21, 1967 Vol. 3 No. 6

MCNARY HIGH

Whiteaker to Vacate McNary

Unlike most other junior high schools, Whiteaker ninth graders will continue to attend the same building the remainder of their high school education.

The seventh and eighth graders will go to school at the new Whiteaker building on Harmony Drive next year.

Mr. Bruce Barker, counselor at McNary, explained changes to be made. Next year, McNary's building will house 1700 students. Part of the total enrollment will come from South Salem and Waldo. Waldo ninth graders who attended Swegle Grade School will go to high school at McNary. Walker pupils, who would ordinarily attend South Salem, will also attend McNary.

Next year, McNary will have the same enrollment as North Salem and South Salem.

Physical changes to the present McNary-Whiteaker building will include a conversion of Whiteaker's office to a resource center and conference room. The three industrial arts rooms will be changed to a regular classroom, a small engine repair room, and a utility room.

Mr. Barker further explained that McNary's Student Council is now considering having ASB elections after the first of the next school year. This would give transferred students equal opportunities for offices.

Seventh Graders Win Dec. Bundle Drive

It was announced Thursday December 7 that the seventh grade had won the Christmas clothing drive. This class collected a grand total of 65 pounds of clothing. The eighth and ninth grades collected 27 and 50 pounds respectively.

When added together Whiteaker Junior High gave 142 pounds of clothing to Goodwill Industries.

The clothes will be distributed by this organization to needy families later on.

The clothes were picked up at Whiteaker later in the day on Thursday by Goodwill representatives.

Stephanie Minto and Tom Johnson, winning class representatives, place two more bundles on the scales, while Scott Erickson, ASB president, handles the weights.

All New Officers Soon to be Chosen

The second semester is drawing near and it's almost time for the primary elections of student body officers. Mr. Shaffer, Mr. Putnam and the present officers are in charge of the coming elections.

Registration for the offices will be held from January 8-12. During the week, students who wish to run can go into the office and sign up under the office they have selected.

The primary assembly will be held on January 12, and the voting will take place during fifth period that day. It has not been decided yet whether or not speeches will be given for the assembly.

Two students for each office with the most votes from the primary elections will run against each other in the finals. Speeches will be required at this 2nd assembly. The final assembly will be held January 18, and voting will again take place fifth period that day.

All of the votes from both elections are totaled by the office staff. The winners will be announced the day of the elections if possible or the day after.

The available offices are listed below with students who are eligible. Varsity and J.V. Rally Squads are elected for the entire year.

Seventh grade representatives - seventh grade boys and girls.

Eighth grade representatives - eighth grade boys and girls.

Assistant sergeant-at-arms - either eighth or ninth grade boys.

Sergeant-at-arms, vice-president - ninth grade boys.

Treasurer, secretary, vice-president - ninth grade girls.

President - ninth grade boys or girls.

No student is eligible to run for any office if he has received two or more I's in citizenship in the first semester of this year.

First housed in 1965 at the newly built McNary High School, Whiteaker Junior High students had a separate identity at the high school building. This December 1967 newsletter highlights student government, activities, and the move to the new Whiteaker building on Harmony Drive (now Lockhaven) in the fall. (Corie Jones.)

Four

Churches

Keizer pioneers who arrived via the Oregon Trail had a history of Christian roots and faithful church involvement. John Force of the 1842 Elijah White wagon train came west to support the Methodist Mission. Force gave a significant amount of money to erect a chapel at the Willamette Falls. The Jason Lee Mission house in north Salem was often listed as situated in "Wallace Prairie." William Pugh and his son John were ministers.

Schools were the first church meeting places outside of homes. From 1866, Hugh McNary preached in the Claggett log school, as did Rev. W.C. Kantner, a pioneer Evangelical preacher. Baptisms took place in the Willamette River at the steamboat landing near the Cummings' home and at Spong's Landing. Claggett Creek was also used for this ceremony.

Nearby Quinaby Park was founded by the United Evangelical Church in 1908. The site was used by Clear Lake Church. George Thompson, who lived in the big white house at the corner of Chemawa Road and Delight Street, ministered at the Clear Lake Evangelical Church. The Chemawa (Keizer) Grange was also used for early church meetings. Roger Hawley recorded Mary Hall Moore's memories. She recalled: "We had the Methodist church until people could get into town with their automobiles. Then that killed the church in the schoolhouse. Later, the American Sunday School Union was the only thing that held services on Sunday afternoon." Farmers donated property: Adam Stephens for Hayesville Baptist, at which many Keizer residents attended; Edna Bair for the Clear Lake Church; and Frank Evans donated two lots in his prune orchard and named the street Churchdale Avenue. As the population grew, local places of worship sprang up. Among the churches in the area have been the following (with year of establishment): Methodist Church, which met in Keizer School (1800s); Clear Lake Church, which met in Clear Lake School (1894); Keizer Community Church (1945); Church of Christ on Dearborn Avenue (1947); Faith Lutheran Church (1950); Keizer Open Gate Church of the Nazarene (1951); Salem Mennonite Church (1961); John Knox Presbyterian Church (1963); Keizer Christian Church (1963); St. Edward Catholic Church (1967); and Community Baptist Church (Dayspring Fellowship) (1970s).

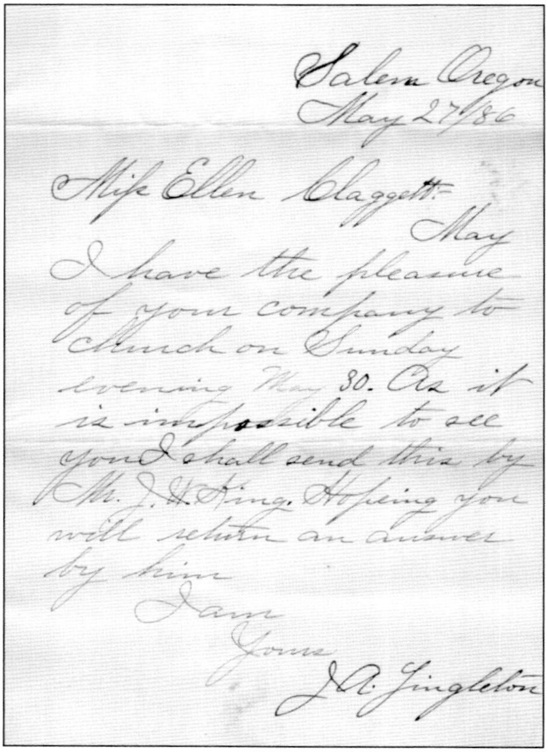

Salem Oregon
May 27/86

Miss Ellen Claggett—
May I have the pleasure of your company to church on Sunday evening May 30. As it is impossible to see you I shall send this by Mr. J.W. King. Hoping you will return an answer by him
I am
Yours
J.A. Lingleton

This 1886 letter to Ellen Claggett was delivered by the "kindness of Mr. King," as noted on the envelope. The invitation reads, "May I have the pleasure of your company to church on Sunday evening May 30. As it is impossible to see you, I shall send this by Mr. J.W. King. Hoping you will return an answer by him. I am yours, J.A. Lingleton." (Claggett.)

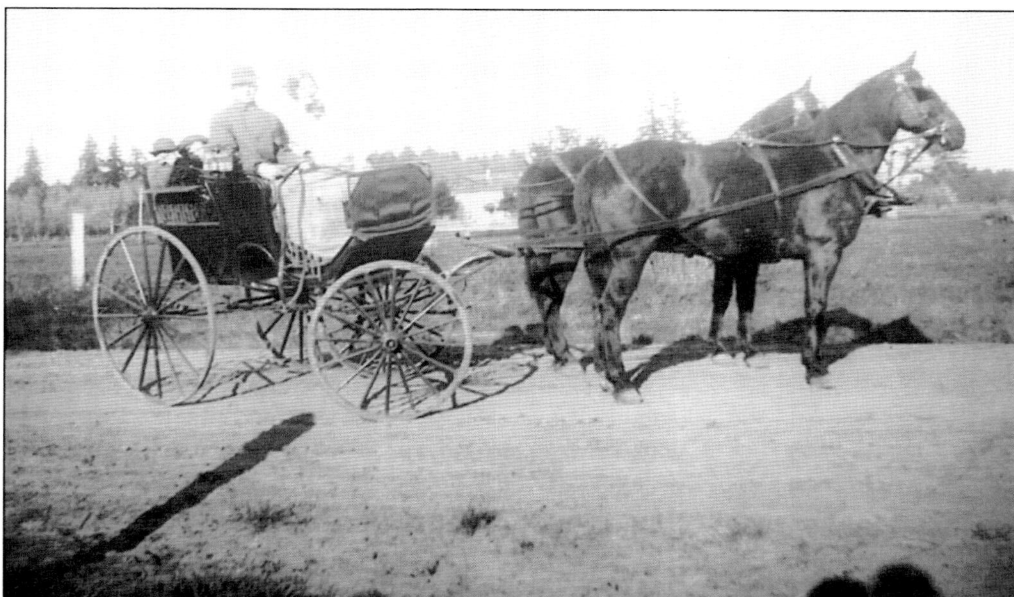

Ernest and Alwilda Savage are out with their sons Gilbert, Willard, and Glen in 1912. Their home is seen in the background. Years later, son Ernie recalled coming home with his family in a horse and buggy from Sunday school at Keizer School. It was a time of high water, when Claggett Creek was washing over the bridge on Chemawa Road. Shortly after the family crossed the bridge, it was washed out completely. (KHM: Savage.)

The Claggett siblings pictured here wearing their Sunday best are Boyd and Usona "Sally" on April 15, 1923. They are on their way to Sunday school. Ben and Mabel (Noren) Claggett's home, built in 1920, still stands on Verda Lane. Church services were conducted at Keizer School, a short walk down the hill on Chemawa Road. (Claggett.)

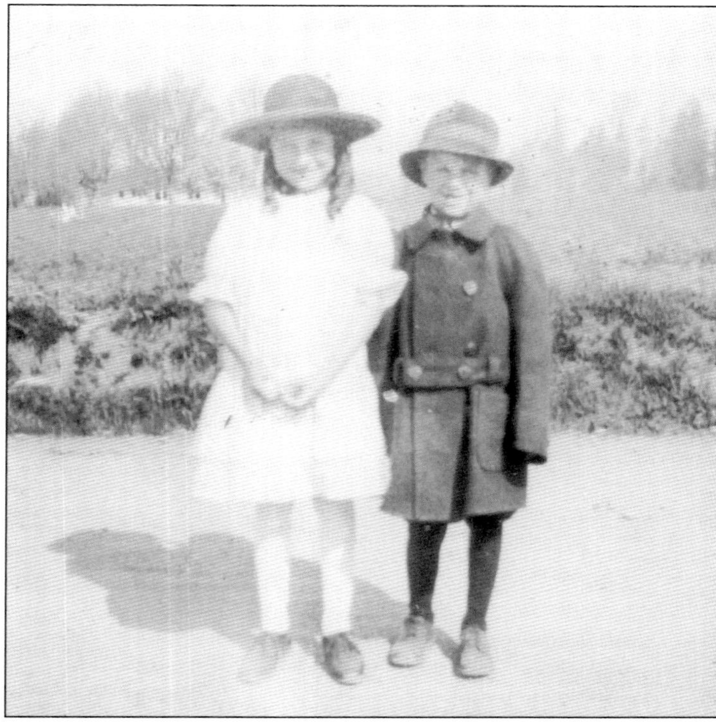

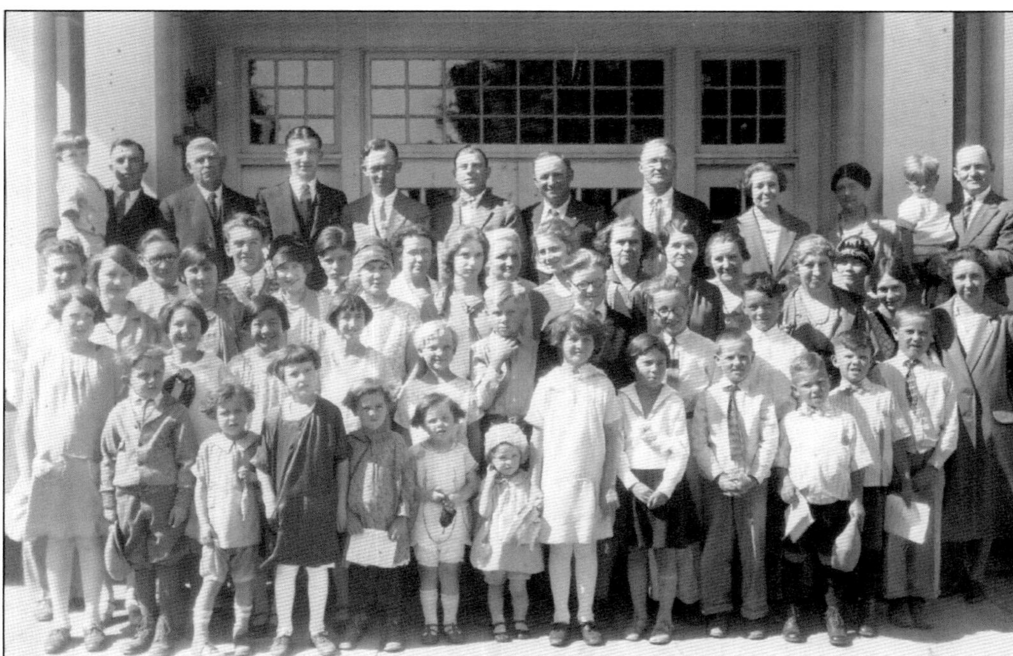

In 1926, the Methodist congregation met at Keizer School. The families shown here with Rev. Robert Witty are Gardner, Okuda, McClay, Bartruff, Cummings, Savage, Poole, Browning, Keefer, and Saucy. With the advent of automobiles, members began driving into Salem to attend services at the First Methodist Church. (KHM: Savage.)

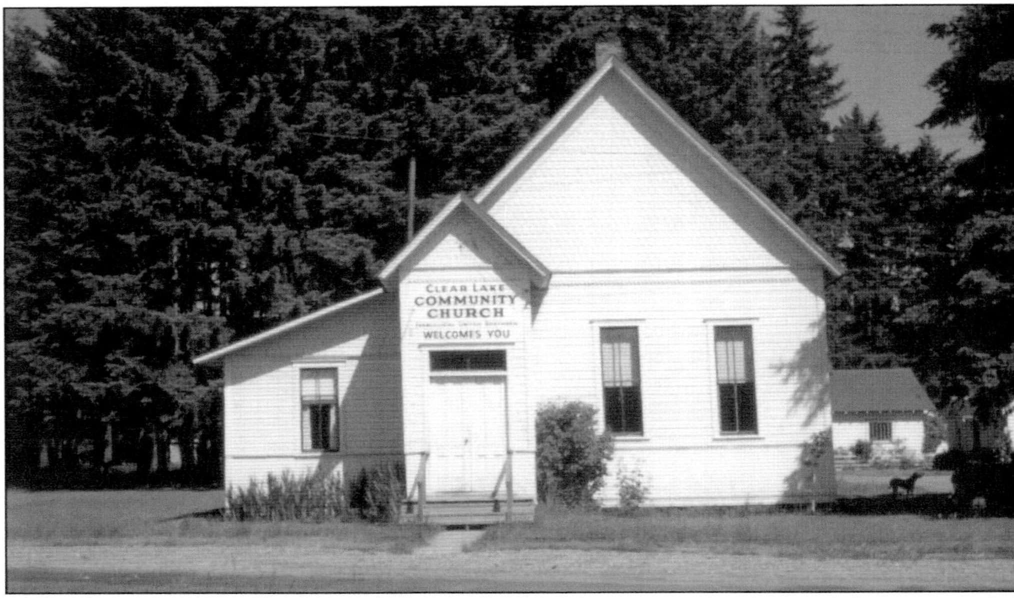

The first documented mention of the Clear Lake Church was in 1894. Reverend Pratt recorded: "The families were few and far between. There was no electricity, no flowers around the houses, and the road was narrow and full of ruts. Worshipers traveled by horse and buggy." The one-room church was built in 1900 on two acres of land offered by Edna Hollingsworth Bair. (Clear Lake United Methodist Church: Hohnbaum.)

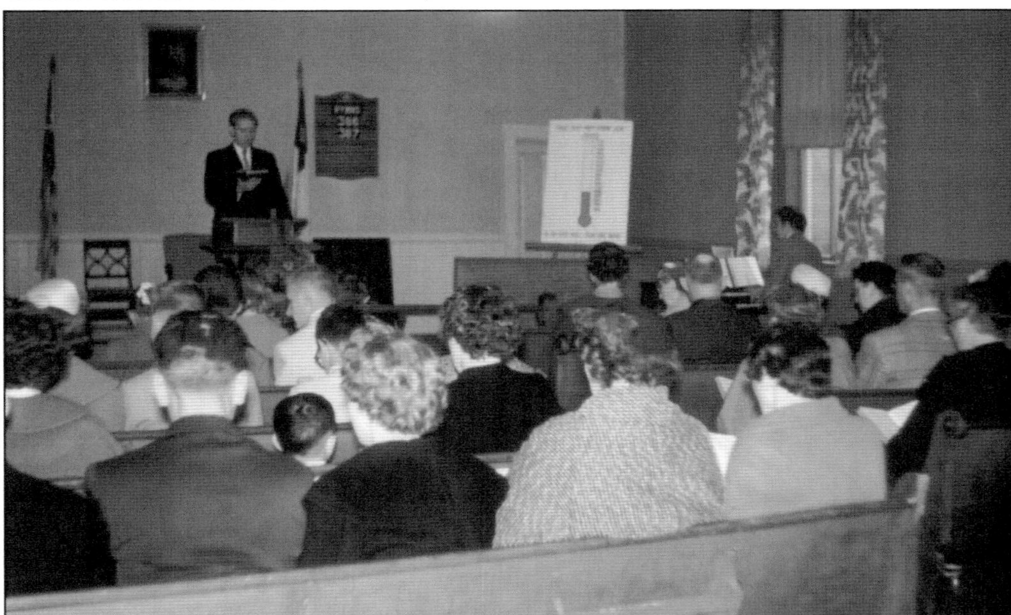

Charles Pugh cut trees from his farm for the church edifice. J.C. McFarland, a local schoolteacher, helped Pugh lay the foundation of the church, using rocks from the area. The foundation rocks now line the front of the present property along Wheatland Road. "It was always too warm near the stove and cold in the front of the church," recorded a church member. (Clear Lake United Methodist Church: Hohnbaum.)

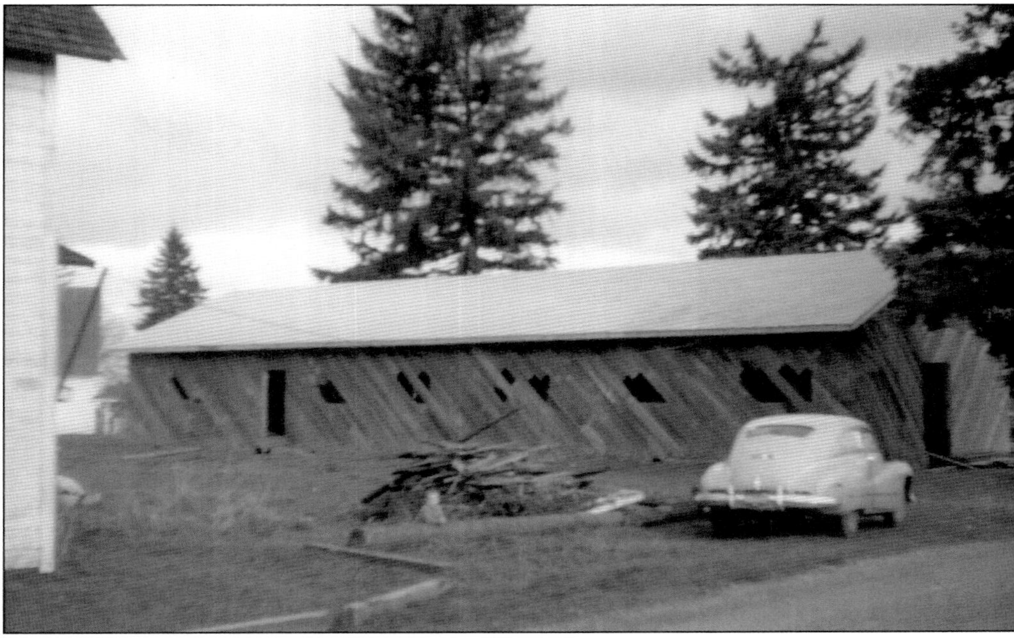

On February 19, 1957, the Clear Lake Church accepted an offer of a hop dryer by a Mr. Brown. Church members did the work, and in 1959, the lumber was used from the hop dryer shed to build the educational unit that is in use today. Before the new building, the church used the school next door for potlucks. (Clear Lake United Methodist Church: Hohnbaum.)

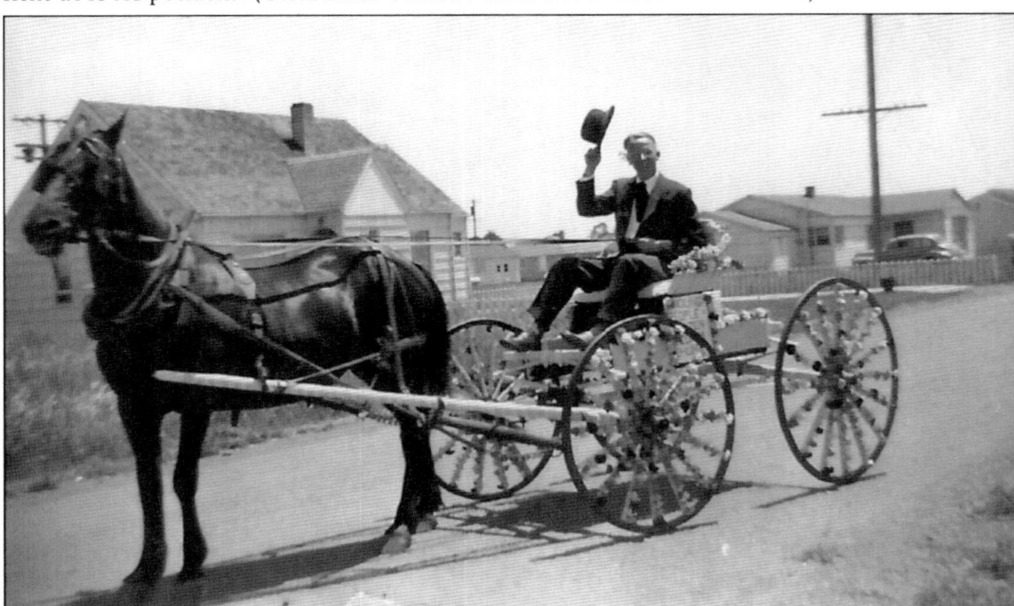

Hugh Adams rode in the 1951 Keizer Days Parade for the Keizer Community Church. The sign on the wagon states, "Young People Keizer Community Church." The Adamses were early members of the church, which first met at Keizer School from June 1937 to the fall of 1940. It was the first church in Keizer to have its own building. Its basement was completed in 1947. (Craig Williams.)

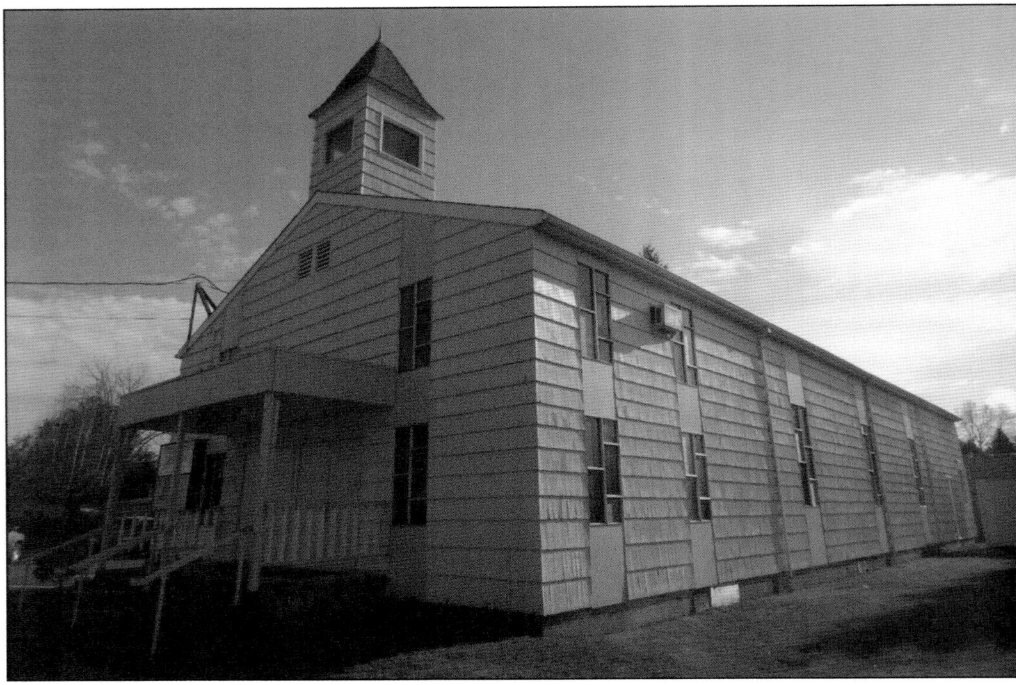

Built in 1940 and moved in 1947, the former Church of Christ building on Dearborn Avenue was relocated from Camp Adair, north of Corvallis. The structure was previously used as US Army barracks. Ownership has changed over the years, with various denominations using the historic building and educational wing. (Tammy Wild.)

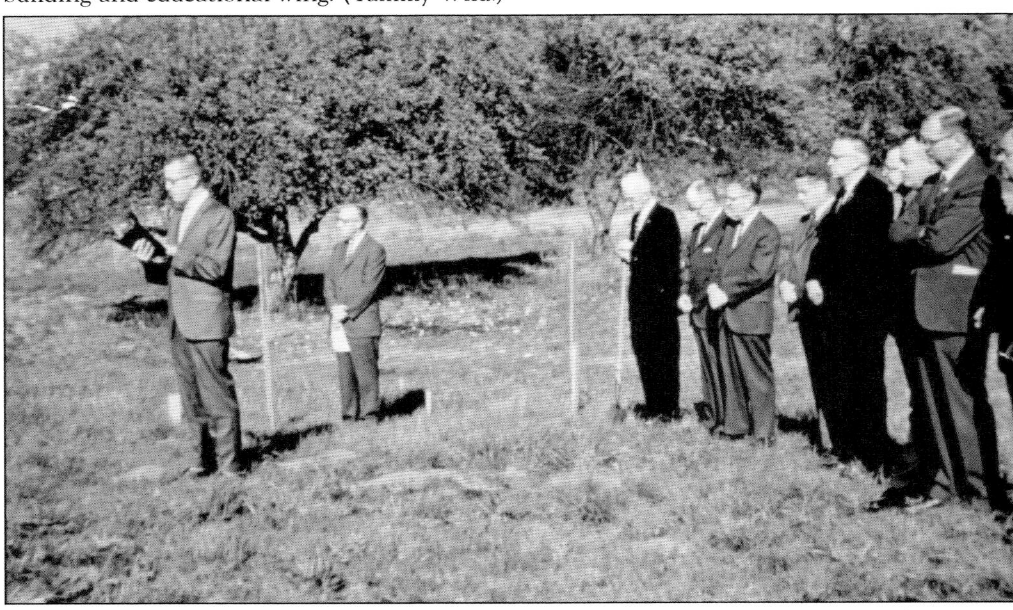

The first service of Keizer Christian Church (Disciples of Christ) was held in October 1963 at the Keizer Grange Hall. A ground-breaking dedication was held amid the orchards at the 5450 River Road site in October 1966. The new church building was completed in 1968. (Keizer Christian Church.)

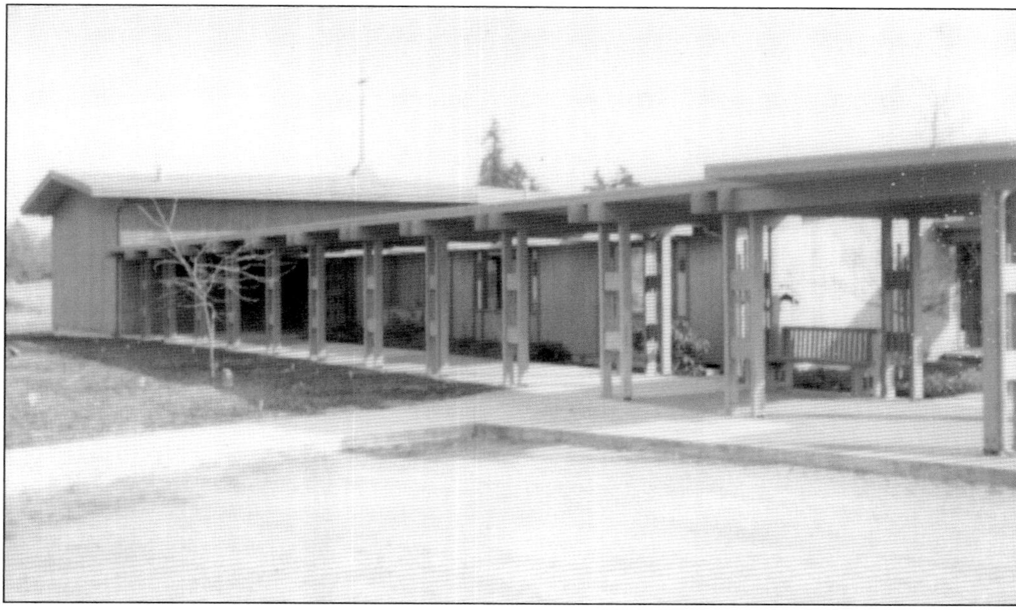

Noted as "the church on the move," the Keizer Christian Church's congregation first met at the Keizer Grange before the house of worship was constructed. In 1984, the church was moved from its River Road location when the property was purchased by Albertson's for its new store. The structure was moved up Wheatland Road to the new site at 6945 Wheatland Road. (Keizer Christian Church.)

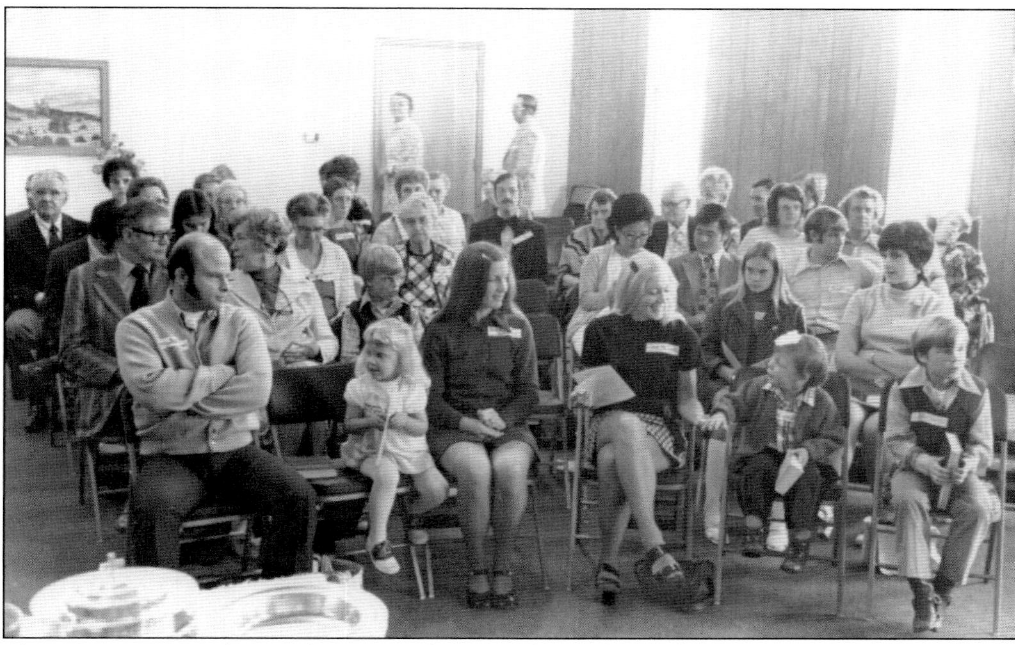

The congregation gathers at the Keizer Christian Church (Disciples of Christ). In 1984, the church physically moved from its 5450 River Road site to 6945 Wheatland Road. A new sanctuary was constructed, and the old building was split in two and reconfigured for classrooms and a large meeting area. (Keizer Christian Church.)

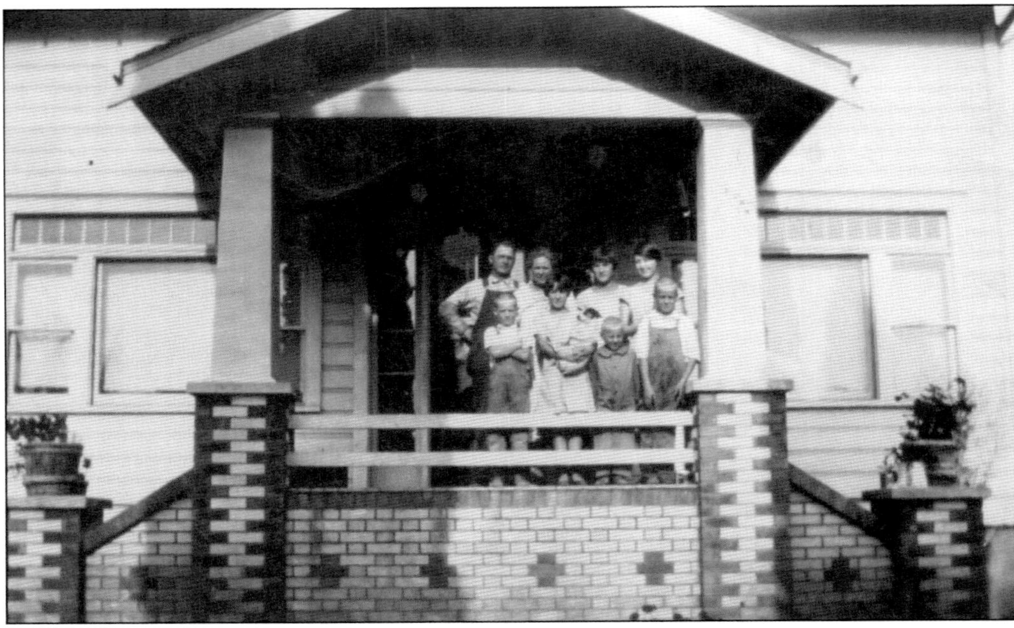

The John and Alice Gardner family are shown at their home on the corner of Cummings Lane and River Road. Faith Lutheran Church purchased the house in 1950. The first service with Pastor George Holmquist was attended by over 100 people. The house was later moved to Chemawa Road and used for the Chemawa Chapel. (KHM: LaVaun Gardner White Buck.)

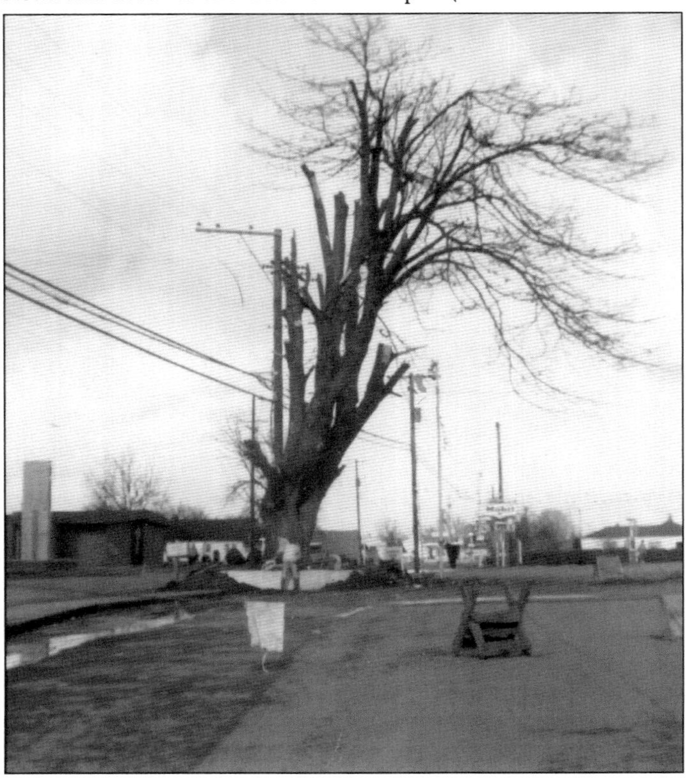

This April 1960 photograph of a tree removal looks north on River Road at the Cummings Lane intersection (near Cherry Avenue). It is the location of the old Berg's Market and the current site of Keizer Towne Square. Faith Lutheran Church is on the west side. The tree is thought to be a cornerstone marker for the John Force land claim. (Melson Franz.)

Five

Roads, River, and Railroads

The waterways of the valley make for rich farmland, and the long-winding Willamette River provides a mode of transportation as it flows northward. In the early 1800s, fur traders set up a fort along the banks that would be known as the Wallace House. In 1845, A.J. Doak settled in Polk County and started a ferry service. Alexander Spong arrived in 1851 and began a competing ferry about 1853 on the Marion County side of the Willamette River. Riverboats carrying freight and passengers made regular stops at the multiple landing sites from Portland downriver. Hop pickers would travel the river to Mission Bottom to harvest the crops. Various vessels used the river, including sternwheelers, steamboats, snagboats, and tugboats. Many old-timers recall the loud whistle of the paddle wheelers. The Oregon Electric Railway, with the assurance of year-round shipping and the improvement of country roads, caused river traffic to gradually decrease. Eventually, the colorful riverboats stopped coming to Spong's and Beardsley Landings. Spong's Landing, still a gathering spot for swimming and picnicking, is maintained by Marion County.

Lesser, but important, streams are Claggett Creek, previously known as Grierson Creek, and Ford Creek. There are also smaller creeks that run through Wilark Park and nearby Lake Labish Ditch. Willow Lake was called Bybee Lake.

From 1908 to 1933, the Oregon Electric Railway provided service from Portland to Salem, with nearby stops in Quinaby, Chemawa, Claxtar, and at the Deaf (Mute) School. The rail line was a convenient way to move people and goods. Many students rode the train to Salem High School. Farmers benefited from the proximity and reliable shipping.

The early dirt roads had multiple names over the years. Chemawa Road was known as Beardsley Lane and Spong's Landing Road. River Road was called Champoeg-Salem Road. Trail Avenue was an early path for the native Kalapuyas and later for settlers from the Oregon Trail.

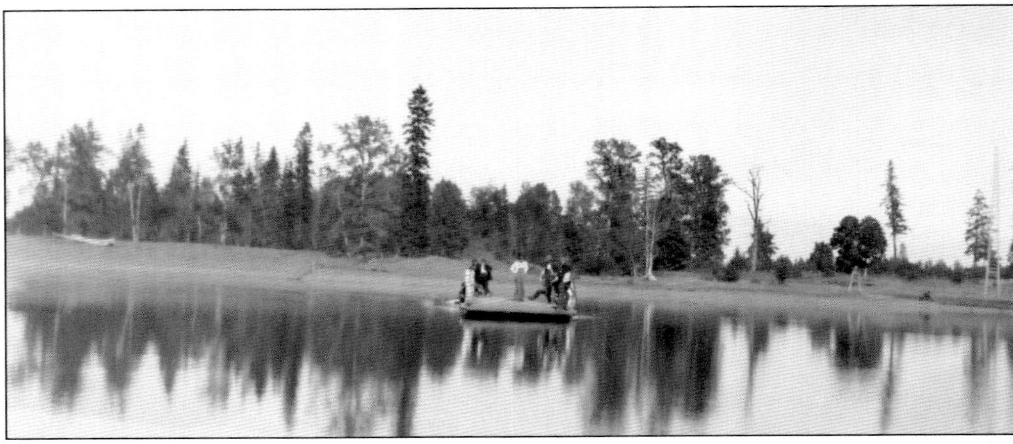

Alexander and Margaret Spong were 1851 pioneers who settled along the Willamette River. They operated a ferry from Spong's Landing to the town of Doak's Ferry (later renamed Lincoln) in Polk County. Several of their sons were stern-wheeler steamboat captains on the Willamette. The Spong family developed a park in 1913 and charged admission of 25¢ per car. Today, the park is operated by Marion County. (SPL: Ben Maxwell.)

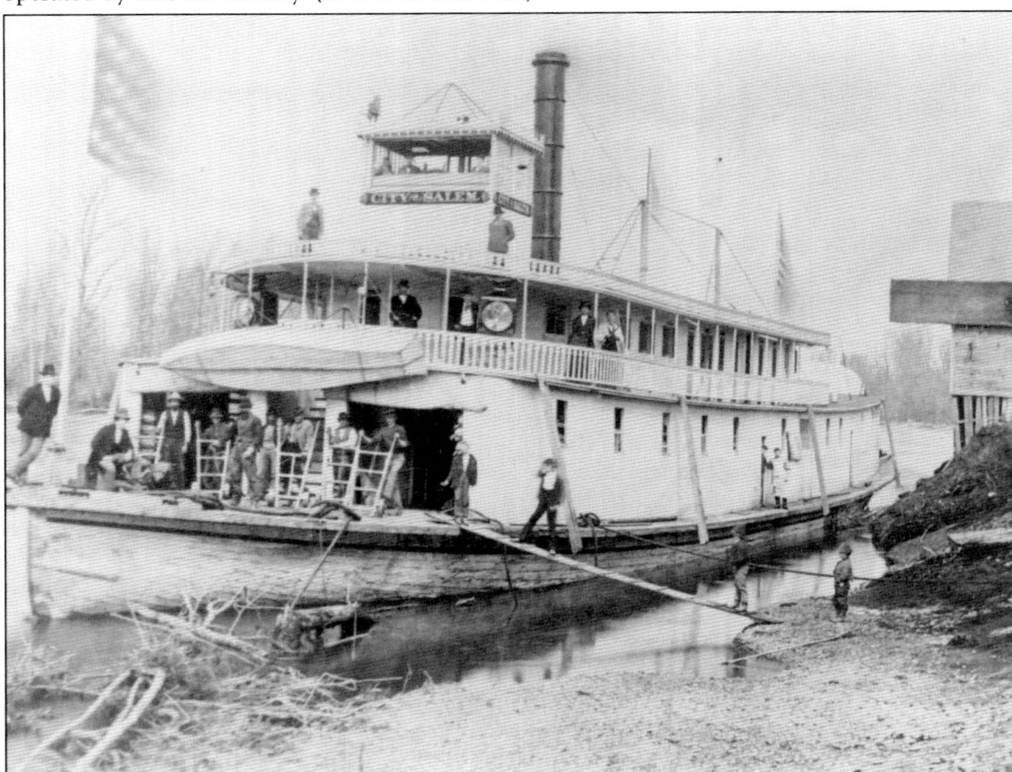

The stern-wheeler *City of Salem* was used on the Willamette River until 1895. The original photograph is from the collection of Captain Eckhart. The two locomotive headlights on the forward cabin deck permitted loading and unloading of freight at night. Jack Spong recalled the cargo they hauled of wheat, hops, and livestock, as well as the passengers. Snagboats kept the waterway free of debris and the channels clear for vessels. (SPL: Ben Maxwell.)

The cool waters of the Willamette River have also been a continual source of amusement. The Spong family developed a park in 1913 and charged admission of 25¢ per car and 5¢ for hikers and bikers. Today, the park is operated by Marion County. This c. 1920 photograph shows Violet Newton (Verda Lane family) and others enjoying a swim. (Vivian Heth Lloyd.)

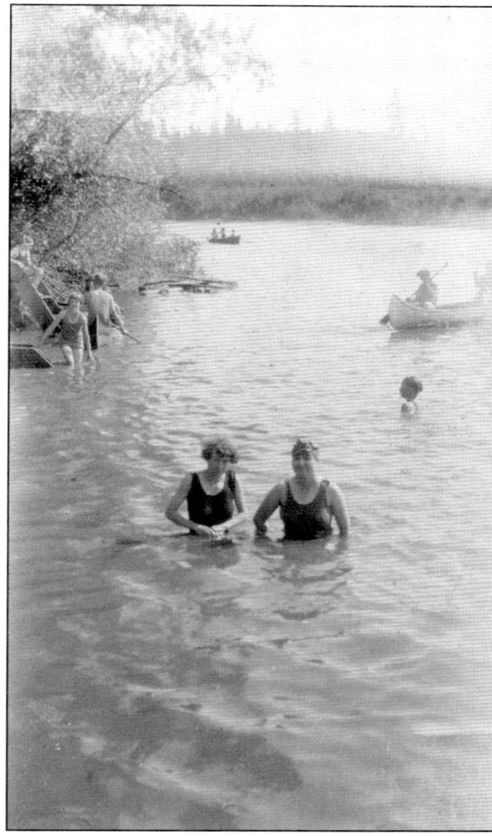

A steamship play structure at Spong's Landing Park reflects the historical significance of the area. It is a reminder of the time when Spong's, Keizer, and Beardsley Landings received steamboats. The whistle of the large vessels could be heard throughout the area. The park is still a popular riverfront location. (KHM.)

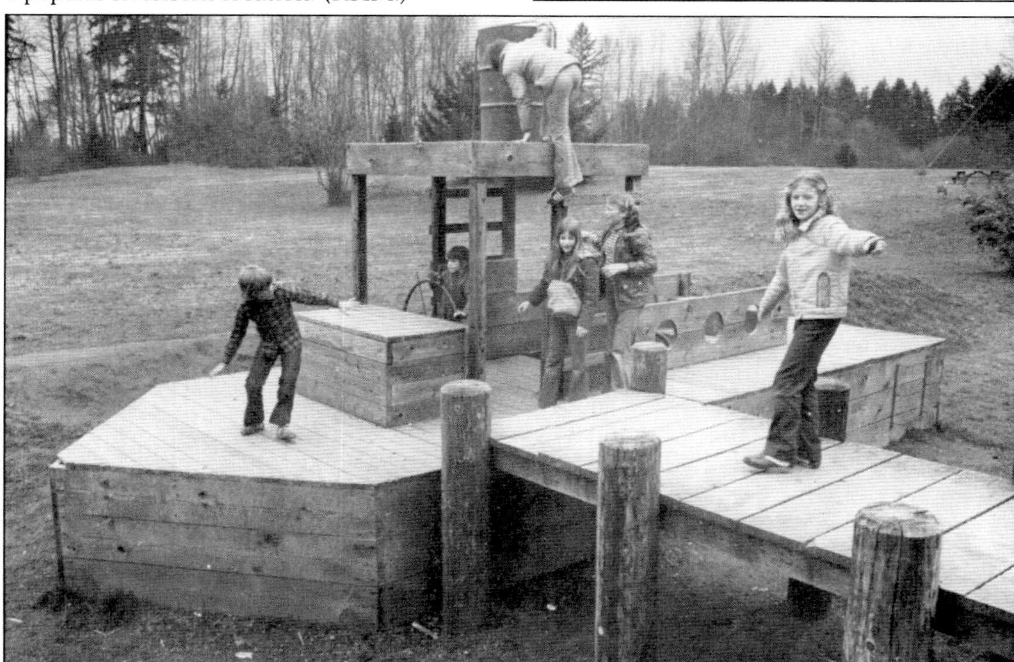

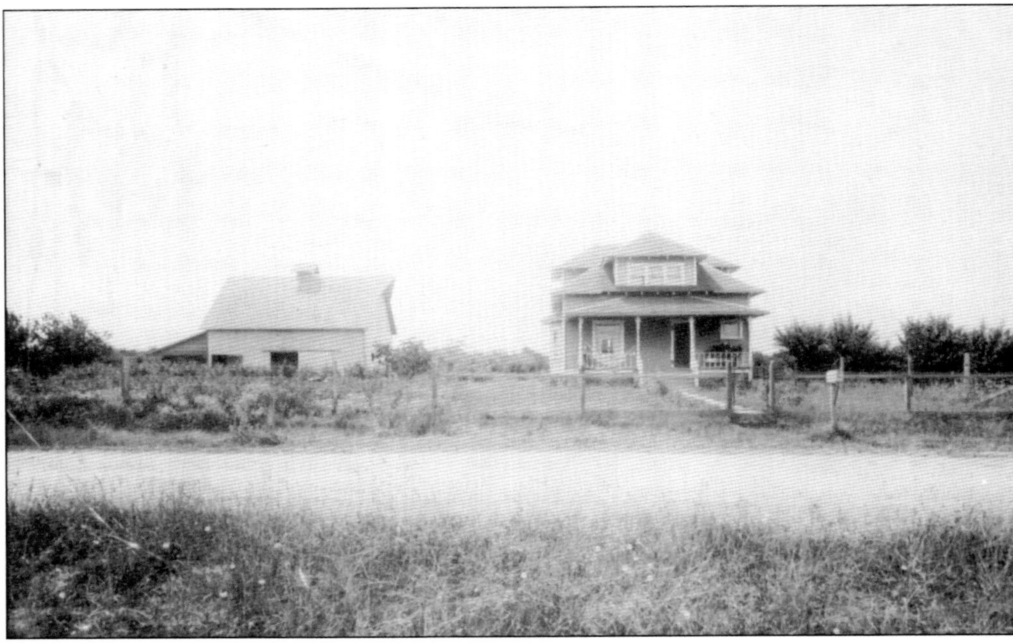

Frank and Elizabeth Evans owned fruit and walnut orchards along River Road. They purchased 40 acres, and their house was built around 1914. Frank Evans subdivided his property in the 1940s, and the resulting streets were named for his family. Delight Street is named after his daughter, and Elizabeth Street is named in honor of his wife. Evans donated two choice lots for Keizer Community Church in his prune orchard and named the access street Churchdale Avenue. (KHM.)

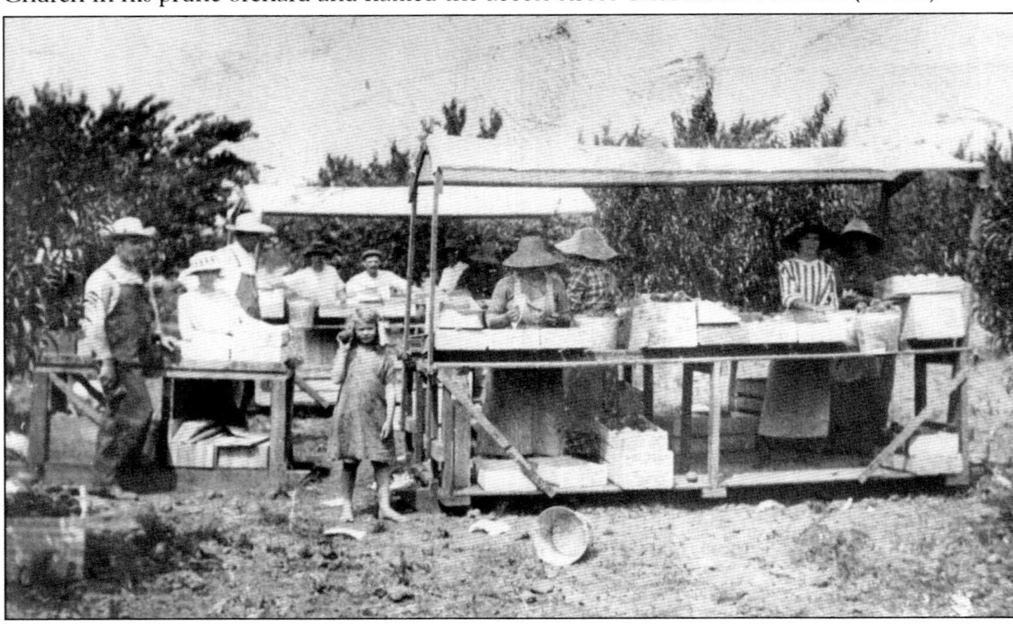

Packing peaches on the L.L. Ranch in this 1912 photograph are, from left to right, Grover Jones, a hired man, Mrs. Louis Lachmund, Harry Wilfred Bowden (ranch manager), and Violet Bowden (foreground). Others are seasonal helpers. Produce was often shipped by the Oregon Electric Railway to arrive in a timely manner. (KHM.)

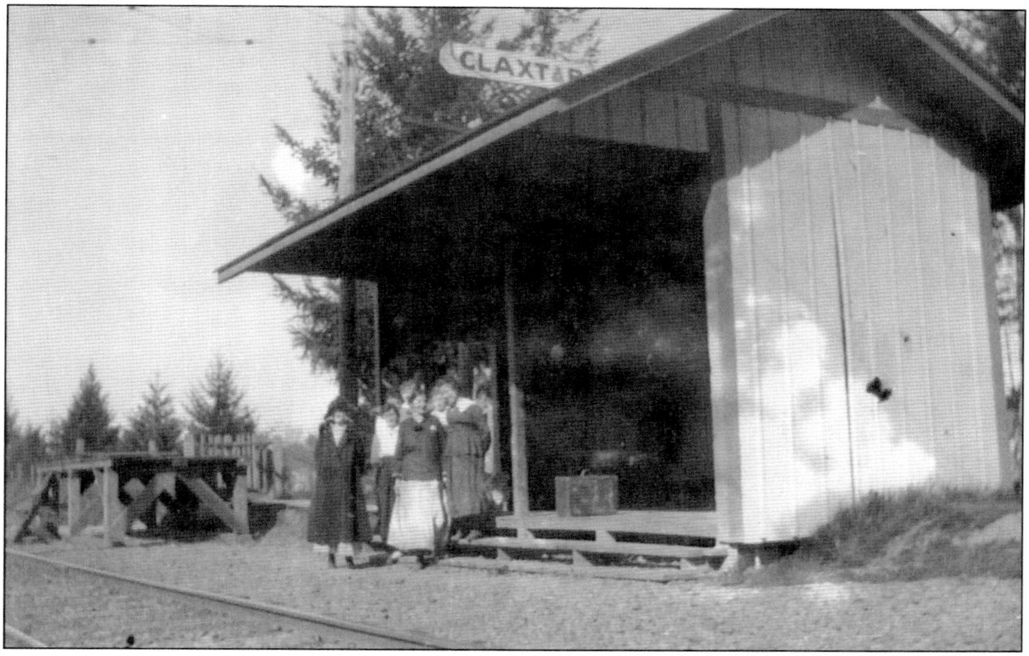

The Claxtar Station was a convenient point for Keizer and Hayesville residents to catch the Oregon Electric Railway. A 1916 article, "Claxtar Items," mentions that Gertrude Kelley of Claxtar went into Salem daily on the Oregon Electric car for her job as a bookkeeper and stenographer. A round-trip ticket to Portland cost $2.75. (Adam Stephens family photograph from Theresa Zielinski Haskins.)

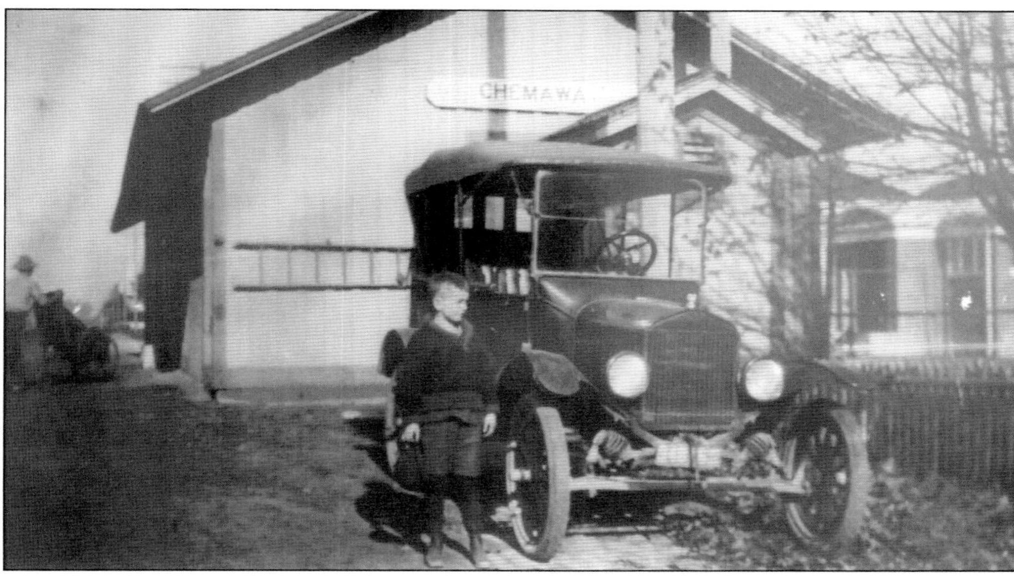

This 1920s photograph shows young Syd Jr. visiting his father, Sydney Hudson Francisco Sr., who worked for the Southern Pacific Railroad after World War I as the railroad agent at Chemawa Station. The family lived nearby on RFD No. 2, later called Ridge Drive by Nan Francisco, who petitioned Marion County for the street name. (Sydney "Syd" Francisco Jr.)

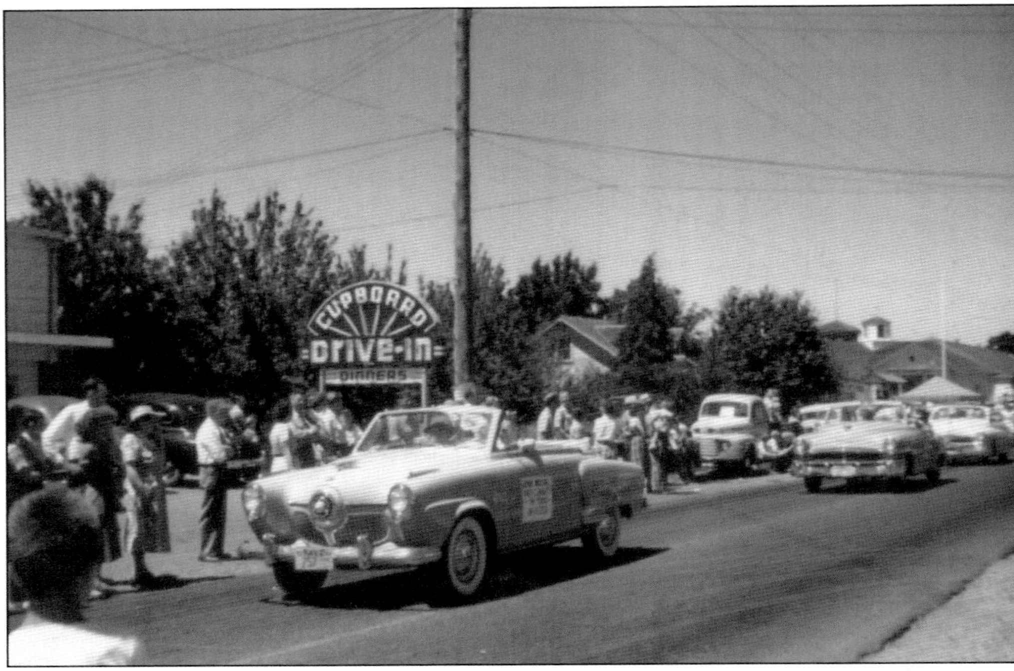

In 1951, River Road was a two-lane street lined with graveled driveways, businesses, homes, and orchards. For years, the Keizer Days Parade began at Keizer School and moved south. In later years, it proceeded in the reverse direction. Pete Pederson and his family lived above the two-story Cupboard Drive-In. (KHM.)

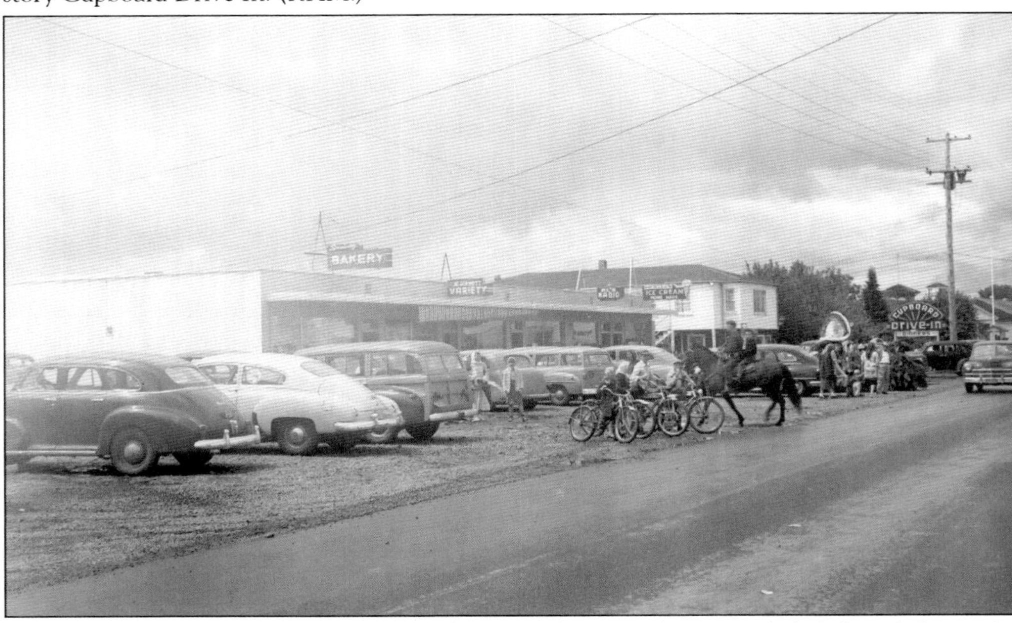

Businesses were built along River Road. The Keizer business district included, from left to right, Keizer Lockers (not shown), Teeter's Specialty Bakery, McDermott's Variety Store, Keizer Plumbing and Heating Co., Al's Radio, and Richlee's Ice Cream. This photograph was taken on the day of the 1951 Keizer Days Parade. (Craig and Sue Reiley.)

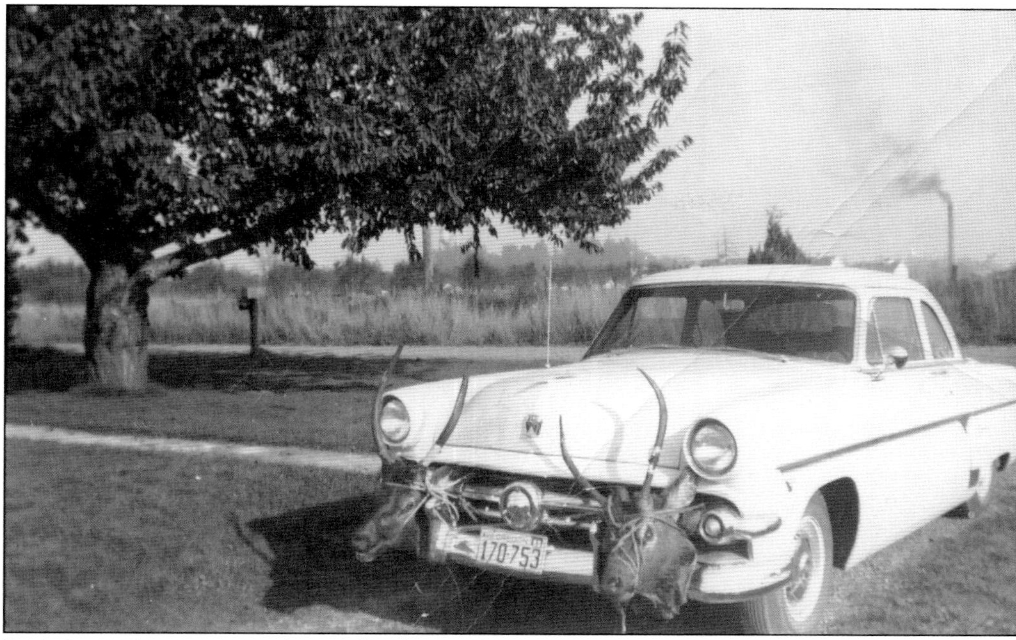

Back from a hunting trip, these folks show off the wild game on their car. This photograph, taken at the Sangster house on Ridge Drive, looks east toward Chemawa Indian School. Note the old smokestack. The farmland between would become Interstate 5. The house still stands and is owned by Pfeifer Roofing. (Hersch Sangster.)

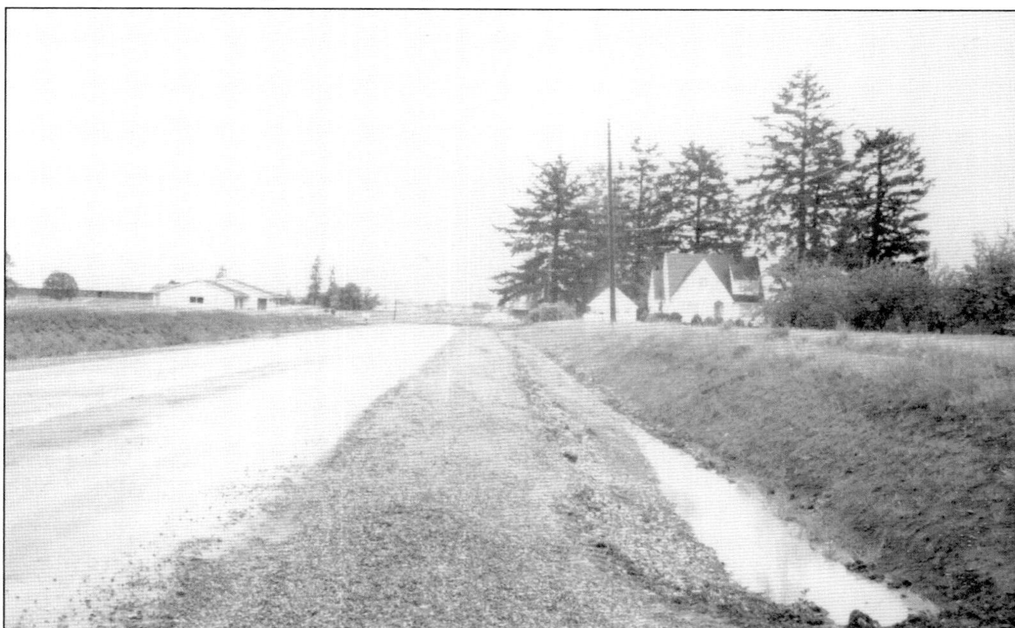

Shown here is preparation to install pipes along Lockhaven Drive by the Earle and Minturn houses in April 1969. The street leading to the Minturns' home was called Minturn Drive. Where Whiteaker Middle School is today was part of Harmony Drive before Lockhaven Drive went through the area. (Keizer City Hall photograph from Keizer Water District.)

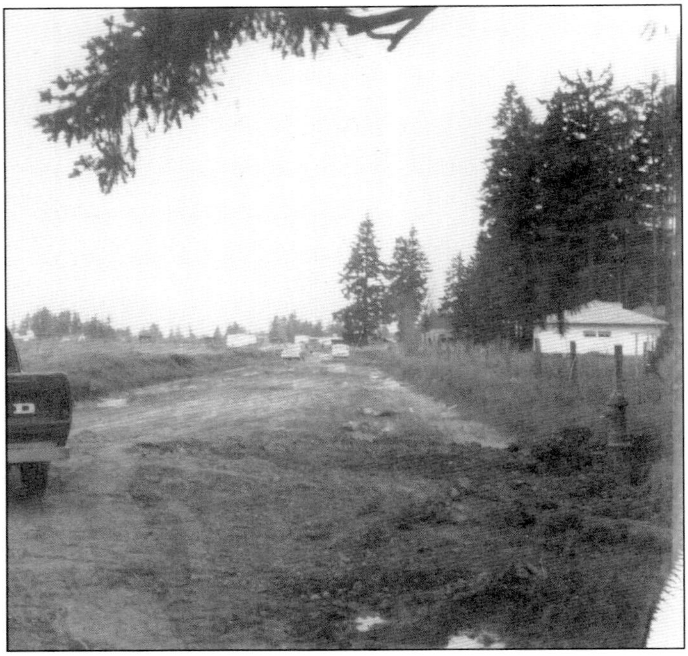

A new fire hydrant is installed along Nottingham Drive in 1969 at the construction of the Terrace Green neighborhood. A row of cedar trees would be planted to line the new throughway from River Road to Wheatland Road. The Clear Lake area was one of the later locales to be developed in Keizer. This photograph faces north. (Keizer City Hall photograph from Keizer Water District.)

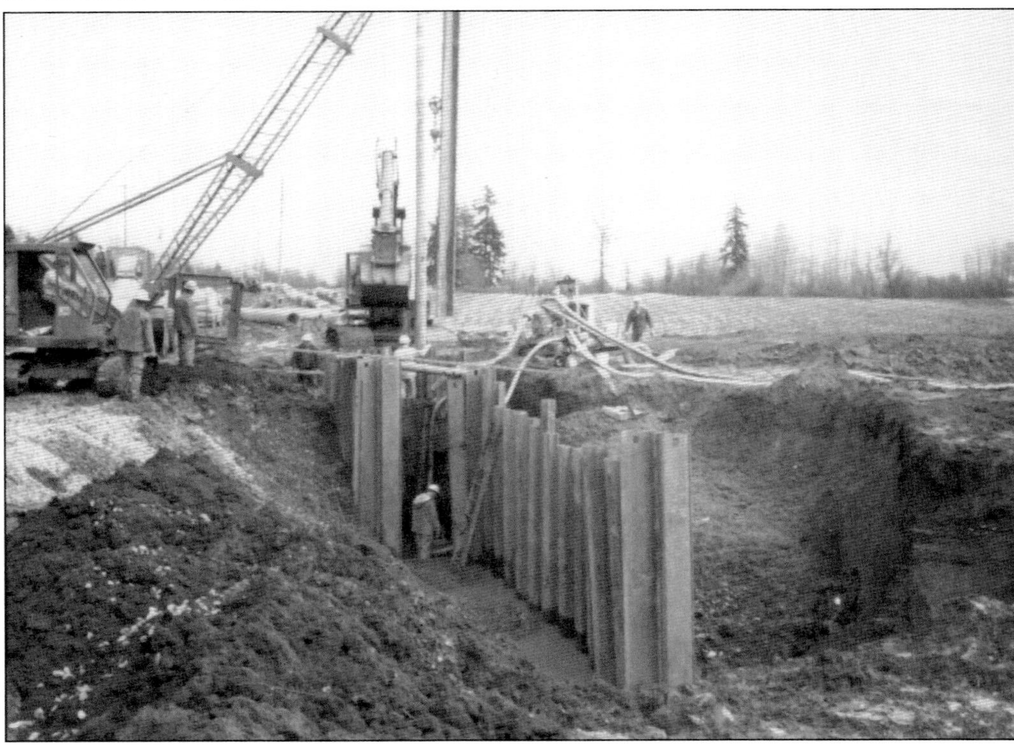

This 1972 photograph shows the installation of a 36-inch water main and construction at "River Bend Road" by Oregon Construction. River Road used to turn into what is now Trail Avenue and continue north. The road was straightened, and Trail Avenue was named for an old pioneer trail. (Keizer City Hall photograph from Keizer Water District.)

Six

Development and Disasters

Except for River and Chemawa Roads, there were no through streets in Keizer. These two roads were initially called County Roads North and East. The first streets were developed as access roads to farms. Many commented on how beautiful Keizer was, especially in the springtime, when the orchards were in bloom. Cherry Avenue was long called "Lovers' Lane," due to the solitude of the tree-lined road.

William Claggett filed a plat with the county in 1910 for the first subdivision, to be known as Claggett Fruit and Garden Tracts. Roads were dedicated for public use.

In the 1930s, permits did not have to be obtained for construction, and there were no restrictions. Many people put up a garage and lived in it as they built the adjoining house. There was no water or sewer system; every house had its own well and septic tank. Lots had to be large enough to accommodate the drain field. A shallow well of 20–22 feet would provide plenty of potable water.

In 1941, the Mankertzes and Brinkleys partnered to create Manbrin Gardens. The prune trees were replaced with 31 houses on either side of Sunset Avenue. The lots were large. At the end of the street, public access was provided to the Willamette River.

Upheaval came to some of these neighborhoods with the rising Willamette River in 1942, 1945–1946, 1948, and 1964–1965. Keizer Bottom has been subject to flooding throughout its history. One of the worst floods ever to hit the Willamette Valley devastated farmers in 1861. The construction of the Detroit Dam and dikes on the Willamette and its tributaries began to regulate the river to the extent that development began in earnest in the 1950s. This quiet country town was also disrupted by the Columbus Day storm of 1962 and earthquakes in 1949 and 1993.

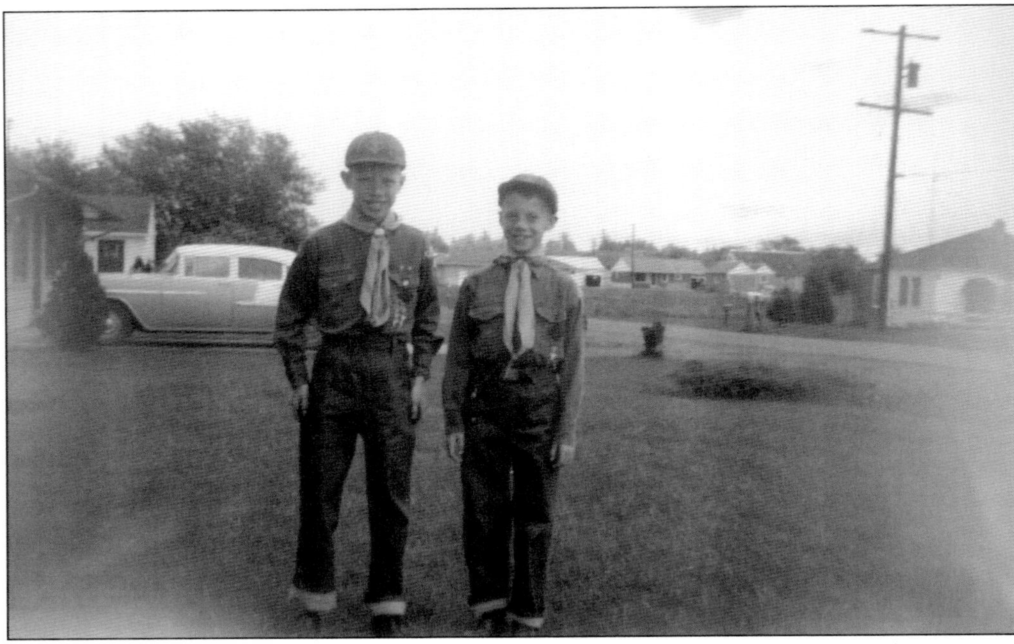

Tom and Doug McCarty stand in front of their house on Dietz Avenue, where the McCarty family lived from 1952 to 1961. During those years, the field in the background separated Dietz Avenue and Lawless Street. The car in the next-door neighbor's driveway is a 1955 Chevrolet Bel Air. (McCarty family collection.)

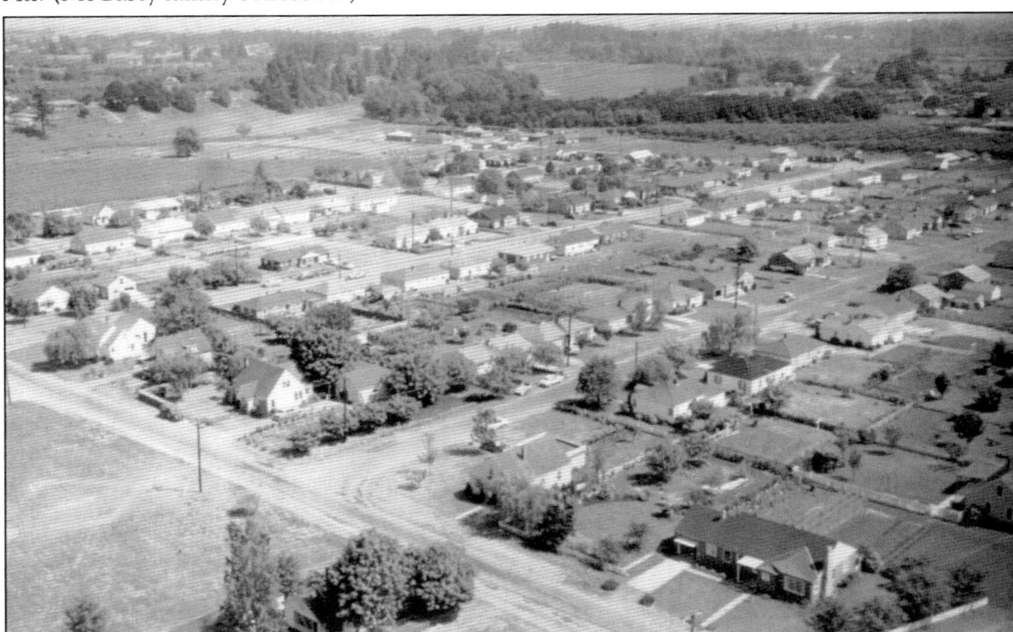

This 1950s aerial photograph of Carlhaven Subdivision from Dearborn Avenue looks southeast toward Claggett Creek. The avenues shown are Clark, Thorman, Lowell, and Harcourt. Originally part of the Wells farm, the Wells house, just west of Clark Avenue, was the first home on Dearborn Avenue. It still stands today. (KHM: Ann Lossner.)

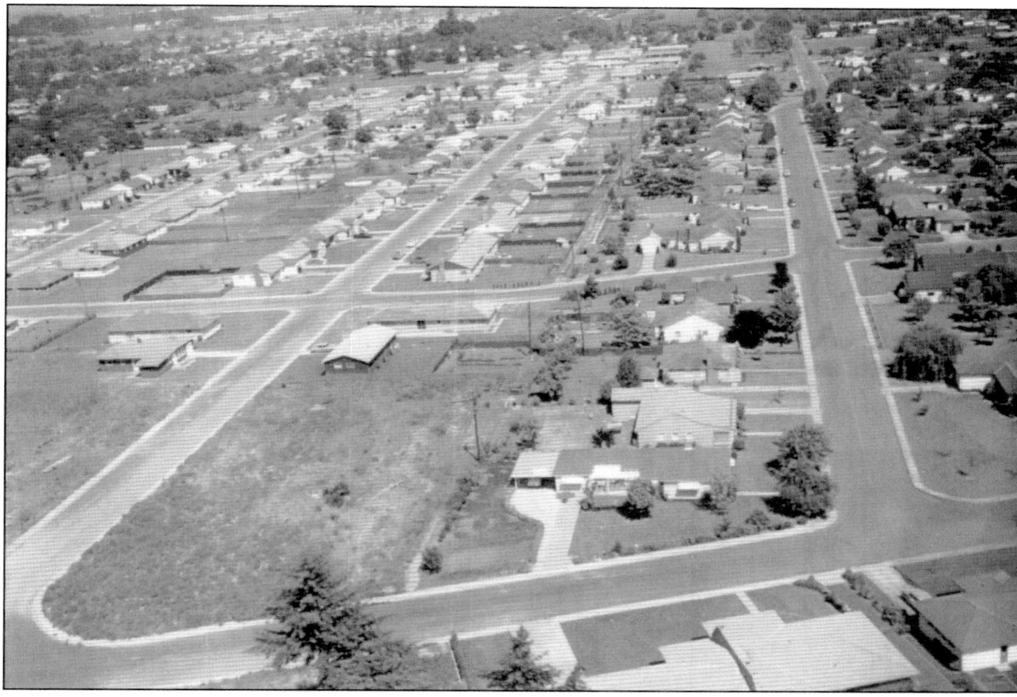

Looking east from the river down Manbrin Drive, this aerial photograph shows Manbrin Gardens and surrounding areas in the 1950s. The Mankertz and Brinkley families formed the name "Manbrin" and developed the subdivision in 1941. Replacing the prune trees were 31 houses on either side of Sunset Avenue. (KHM: Ann Lossner.)

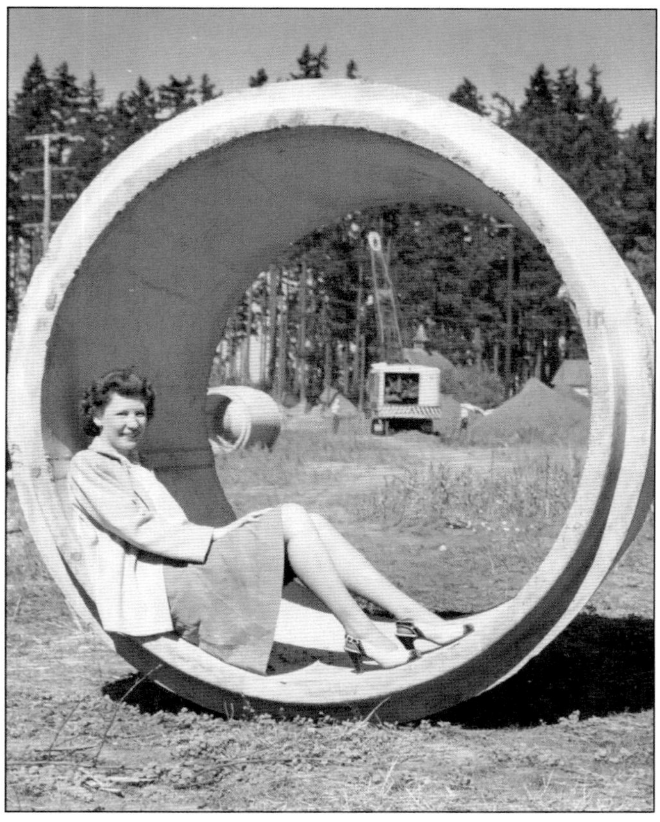

This entertaining photograph shows some of the Keizer sewer system in 1968. With new subdivisions and growth in the community came new infrastructure. Previously, there was no water or sewer system; every house had its own well and septic tank. Lots had to be large enough to accommodate the drain field. (Virginia Stone.)

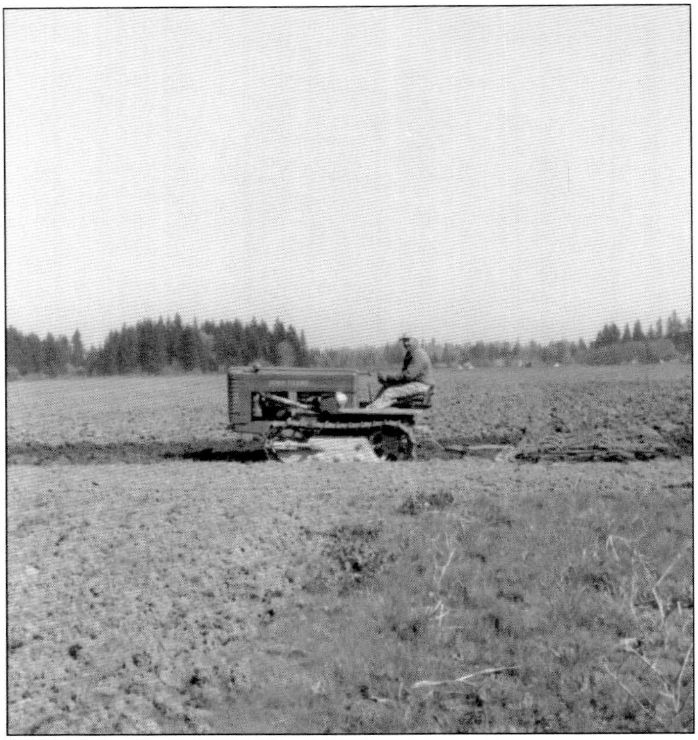

Leonard Schmaltz plows his field on the North River Road farm about 1959. Steve Ostrander took this photograph, which looks toward O'Neill Road. The Schmaltz farm became a new Clear Lake subdivision, The Meadows, in the 1990s. Meadow Park was created from three acres of the land. (Loreen Ostrander Wells.)

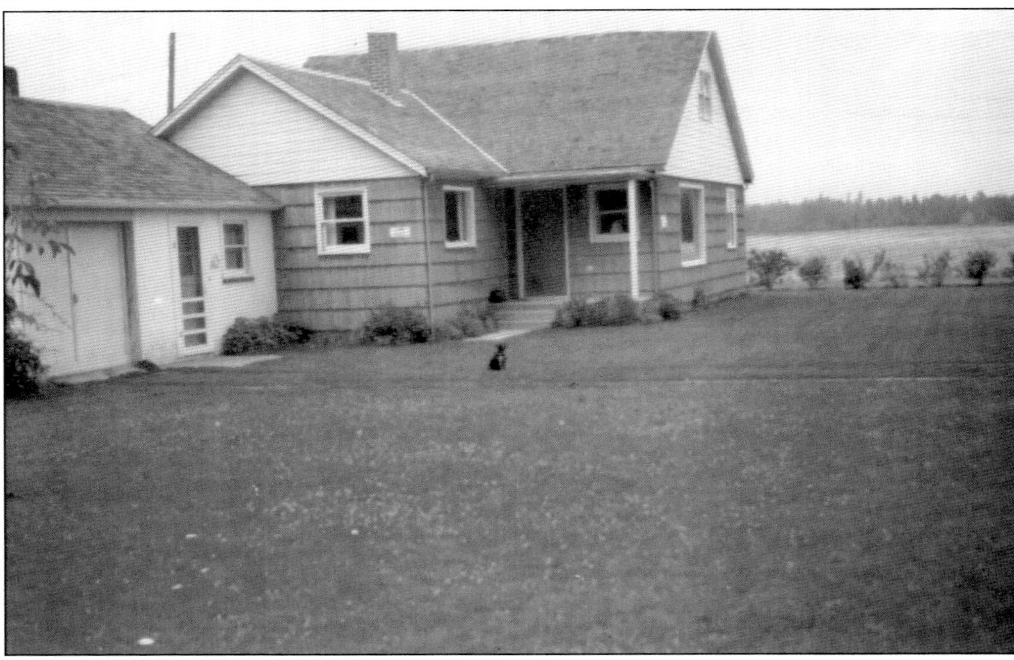

Shown here in 1952 is a house on the Leonard Schmaltz farm on North River Road. The Steve Ostrander family purchased the newer home and five acres of the Schmaltz farm. The property was a one-acre-wide side strip off the farm. The house still stands, and the land became a mobile-home park. The Schmaltz farm became a new subdivision, The Meadows. (Loreen Ostrander Wells.)

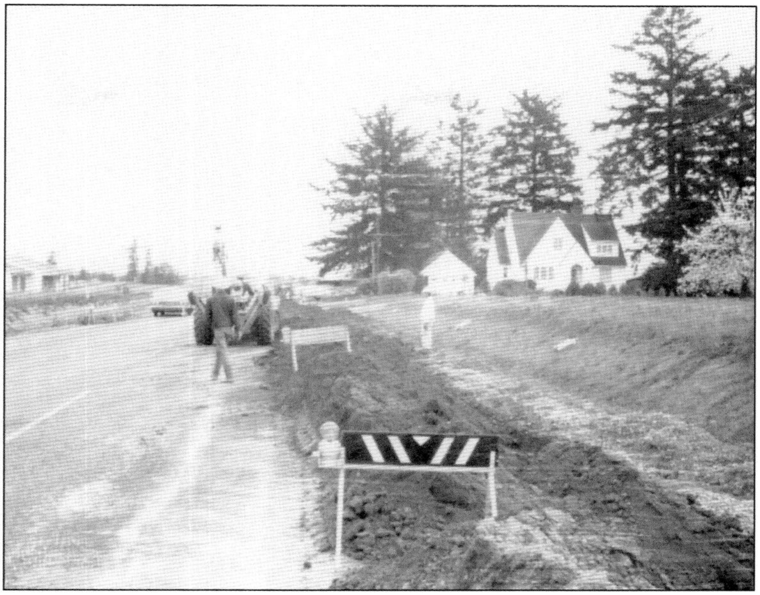

Pipes are being installed on Lockhaven Drive in 1969. Trail Avenue was an early path for the native Kalapuyas, and later, for the first settlers from the Oregon Trail. Chemawa Road was known as Beardsley Lane and Spong's Landing Road. River Road was called Champoeg-Salem Road. (Keizer City Hall photograph from Keizer Water District.)

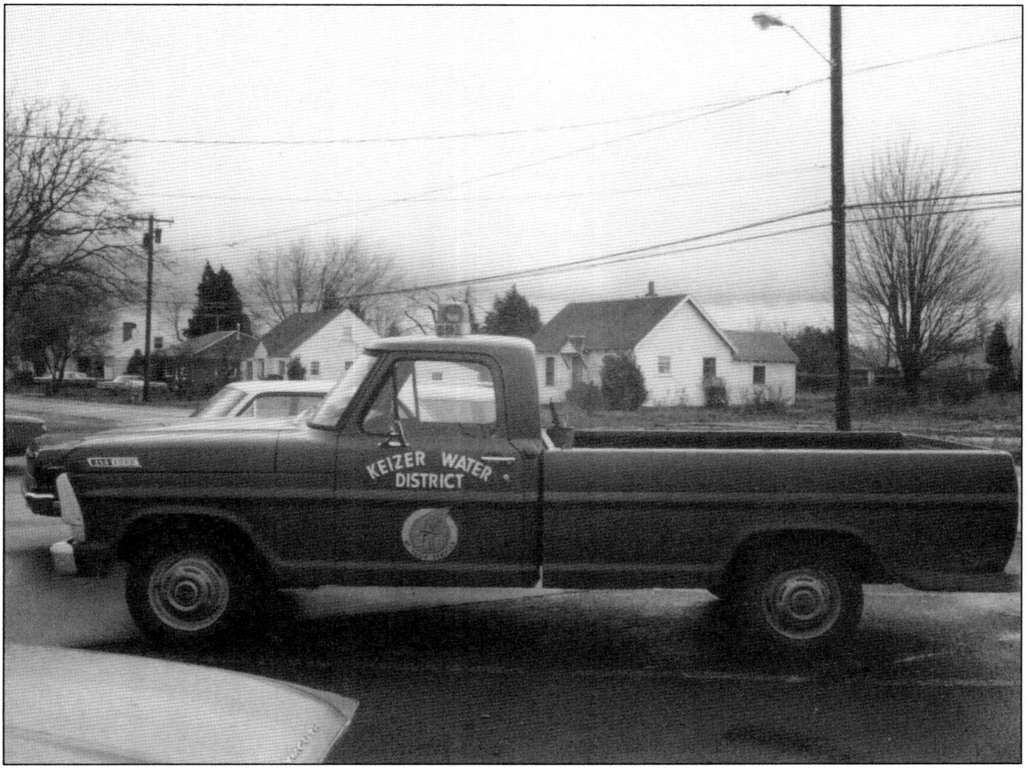

The Keizer Water District was formed in 1957. The board of commissioners was chaired by Sam Orcutt. The district's employees were James Nightengale, superintendent; Jean Snook, office manager; Harry Duncan, maintenance foreman, and Wally Mull, maintenance man. Equipment owned by the district included one backhoe-loader, one pickup, one van, and two scooters for meter reading. (Keizer City Hall photograph from Keizer Water District.)

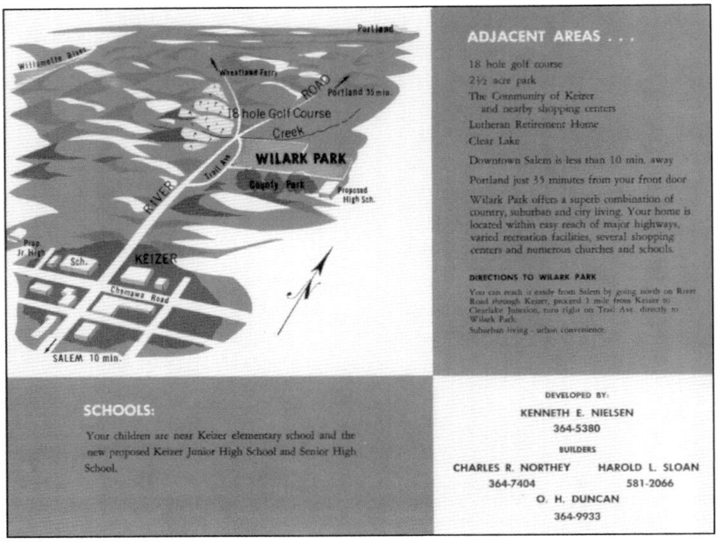

Ken Nielsen developed the 40-acre Wilark Park subdivision in the 1960s. According to daughter Julie Nielsen, it was named after Wilark Avenue in Linnton, Oregon, across the bridge from St. Johns. Ken's wife lived there when they met in 1968. He also developed the Wilark Trailer Park in Depoe Bay and Wilark Park West in west Salem. The name "Wilark" is derived from the Clark and Wilson Lumber Company in Linnton. (KHM.)

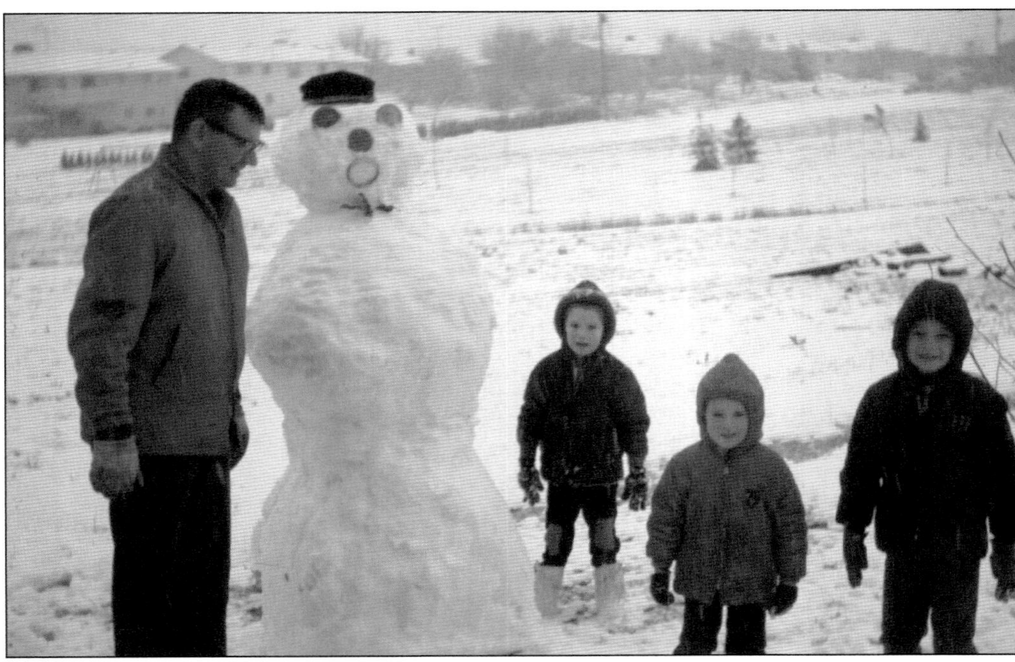

Bob Newton poses in January 1969 with his oldest sons, from left to right, Gregg, Jim, and Paul. They are enjoying the snowfall in their backyard at 6064 Twelfth Avenue Northeast, adjoining Wilark Park. The boys' mom, Marion Newton, took the photograph. Bob Newton was a longtime Keizer city councilor and served as mayor from 1999 to 2001. After his death, the park was renamed The Bob Newton Family Park in 2007. (Michael Newton.)

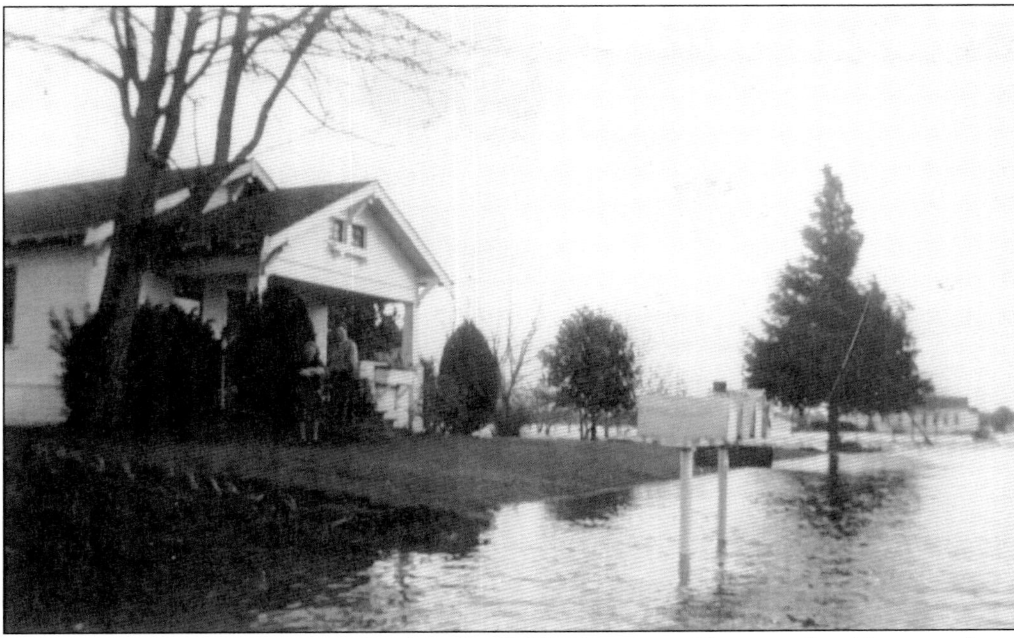

Shown here is the January 1943 flood at the Holden house on Chemawa Road between Jones Road and Keizer School. This view is looking east toward the school. In the greater Salem area, 400 homes were flooded and 10 people drowned as the river crested at 30.6 feet. This house still stands on Chemawa Road. (KHM: Hortense McRae.)

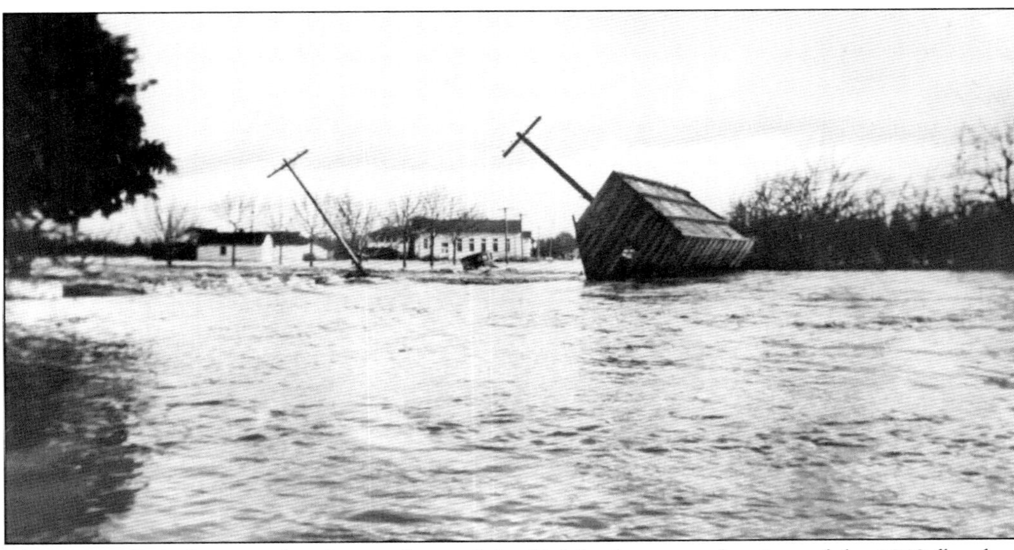

This is another photograph taken in front of the Holden house at the time of the 1943 flood on Chemawa Road near Keizer School. This view looks east toward the school. A barn is tipped upside down, and a car is stuck in the rising waters. At the time, the flood was the worst since the 1861 great flood, which eliminated the Champoeg community. (KHM: Hortense McRae.)

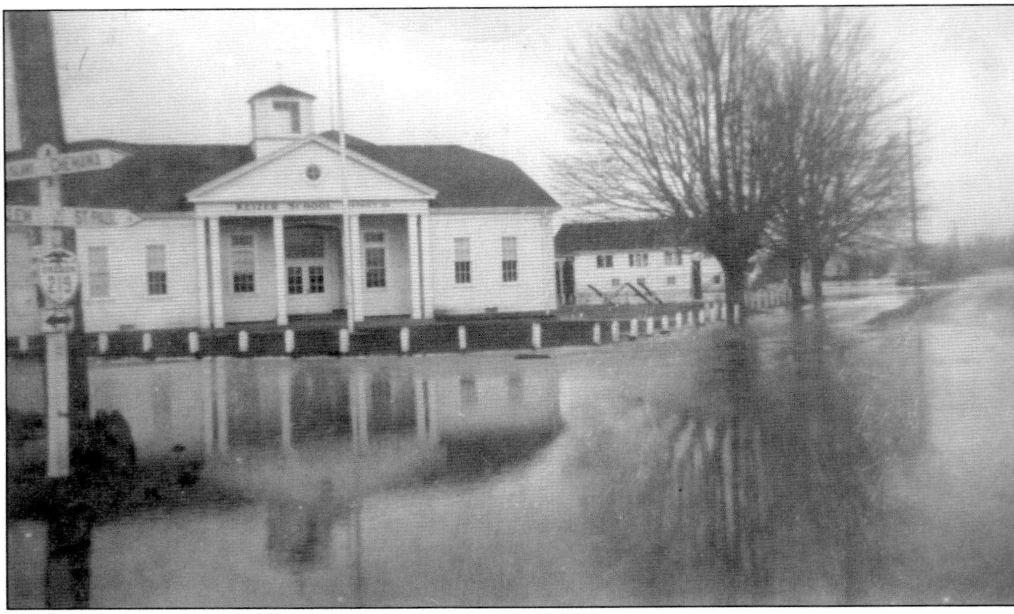

The Keizer School was spared from serious damage during the 1943 flood. Major flooding occurred again in 1945, 1946, and 1948. However, the dams being built on the Willamette River and its tributaries began to regulate the river to the extent that development began in earnest in the 1950s. (KHM: Hortense McRae.)

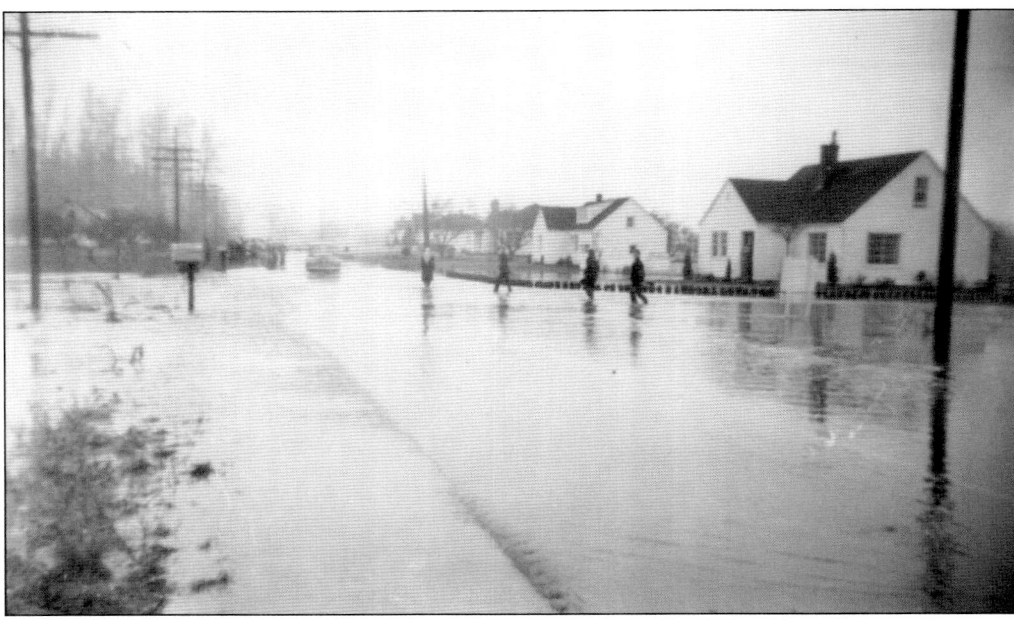

People walk on River Road at Manbrin Drive during the 1945 flood. Developers generally steered away from the Keizer area, especially after the major 1943 flood. The 1945 flood enabled a Coast Guard cutter to float onto the Rehfuss farm on Cherry Avenue through the draw, where the Keizer Elks lodge is situated. (Melson Franz.)

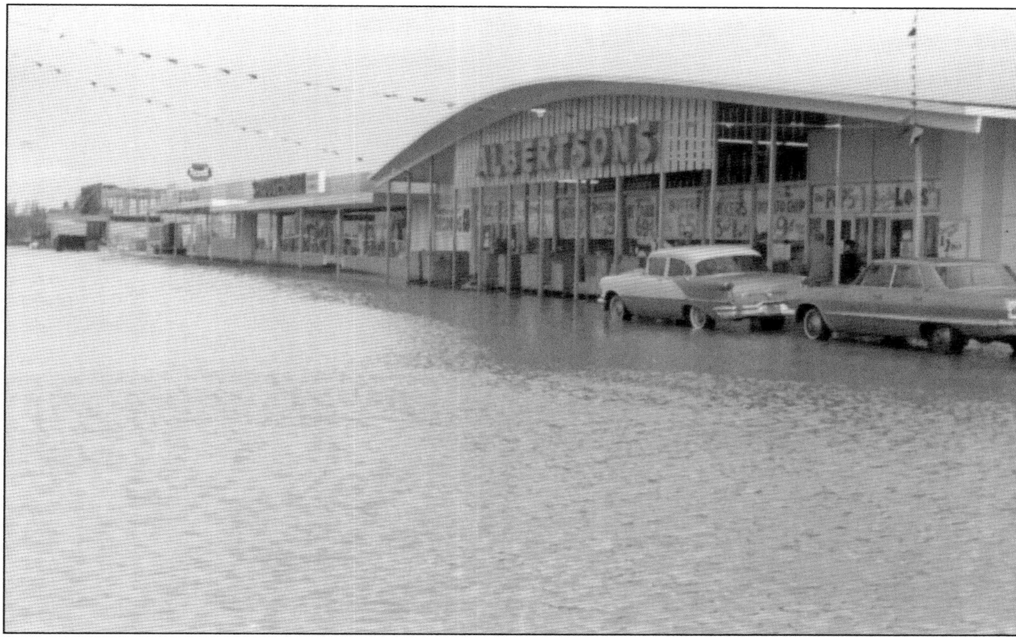

The 1964 flood is depicted here at the corner of River and Chemawa Roads. Businesses across from Keizer School are Albertson's, Sprouse Reitz, a drugstore, and the US Bank under construction. Carl Langeland, school custodian, used the fire department pumps and stayed across the street at the Keizer School to protect the furnaces. (Melson Franz.)

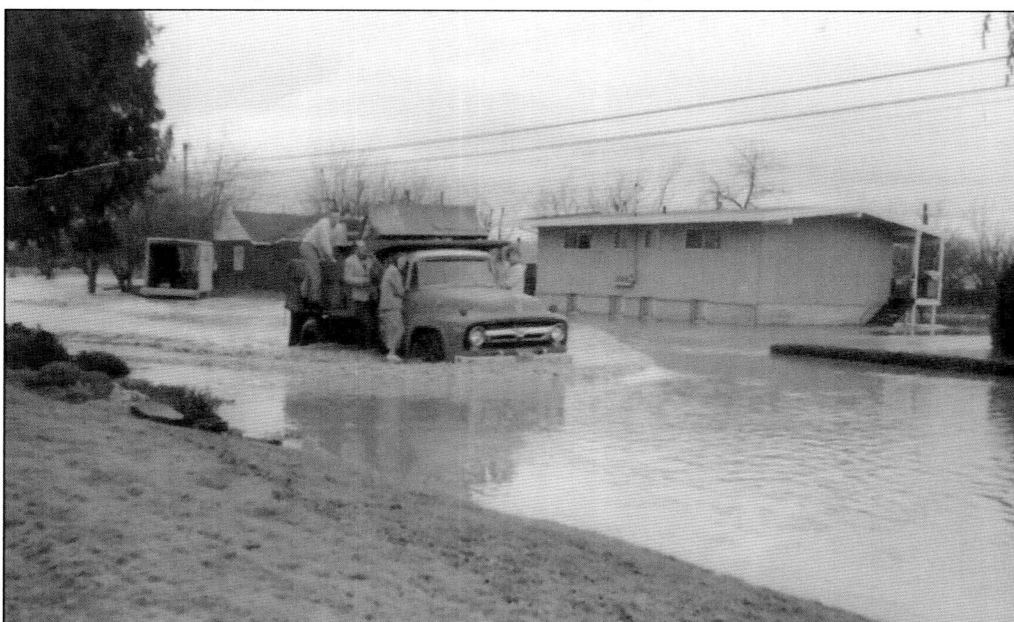

All types of trucks were pressed into service for evacuation of Palma Ciea on Christmas Day 1964. This view looks south from 431 Chemawa Road (Bear family home). Coast Guard helicopters landed in the field across from the fire hall to help with evacuation. The Willamette River crested nearly 10 feet above flood stage, and many other streams in Salem overflowed their banks. (KHM.)

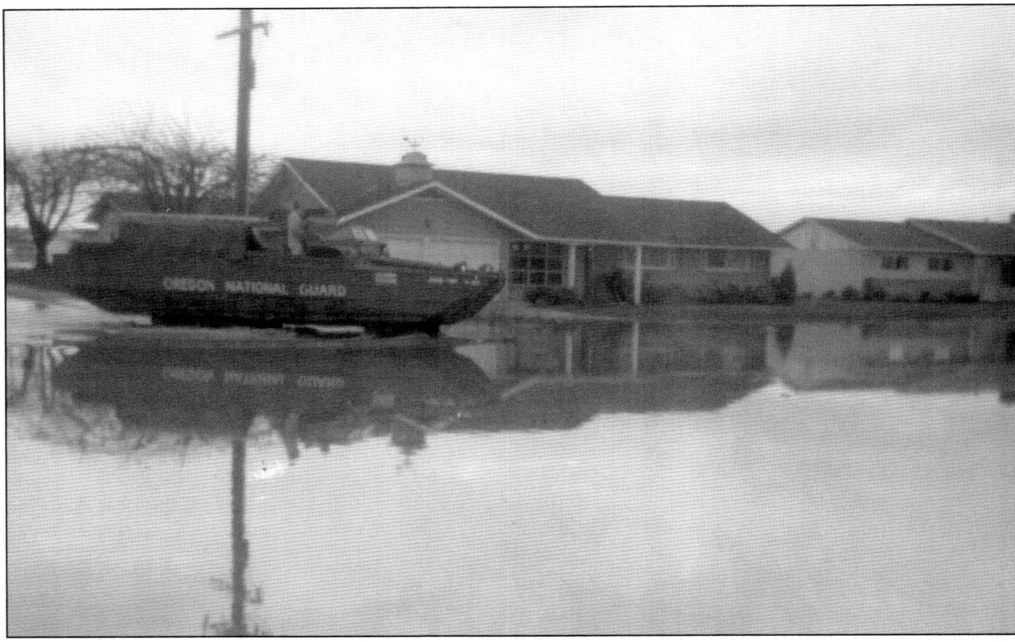

A National Guard amphibious "Duck" assists residents in the Palma Ciea neighborhood at the northwest corner of Shoreline Drive and Moneda Avenue during the 1964 flood. The valley saw two major floods, one in December 1964, and one in January 1965. The only floods larger than these occurred in 1861 and 1890. (Melson Franz.)

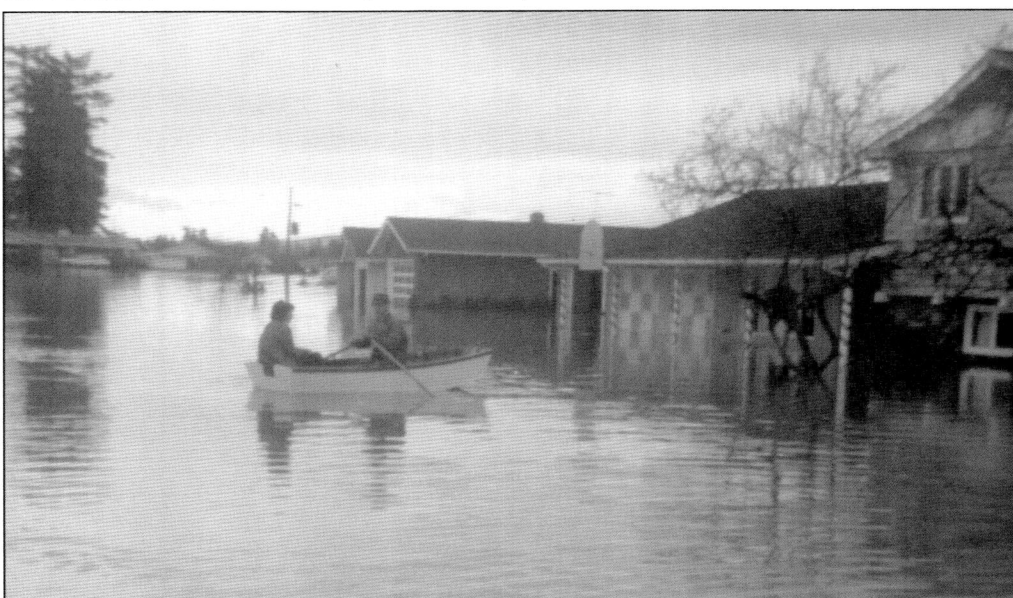

Residents are seen in a boat in the Palma Ciea neighborhood during the 1964 flood. This photograph looks west along the 900 block of Rafael Avenue. The candy-cane-striped support poles are decorated for Christmas. Damages to businesses, residences, and infrastructure were tremendous, and most of the residents were affected by the substantial impact on the transportation system, the loss of potable water, and the damage to personal property. (Melson Franz.)

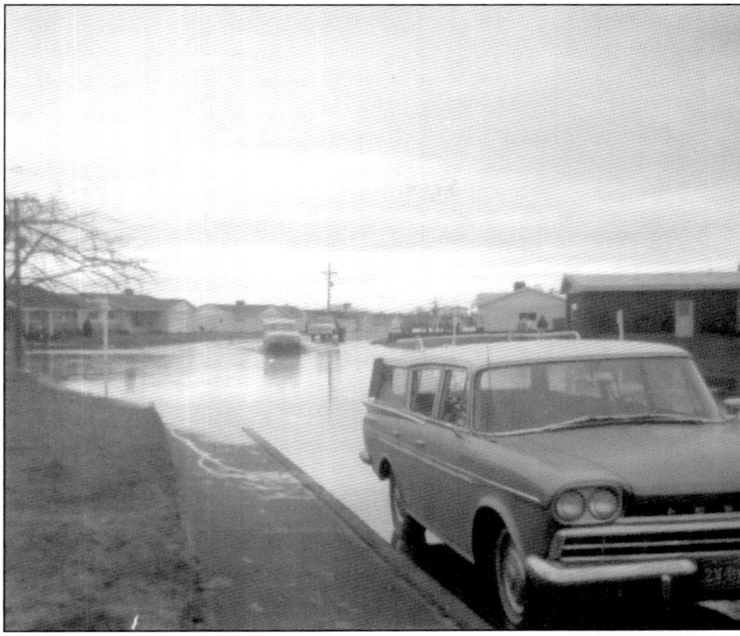

The Palma Ciea neighborhood is seen during the 1964 flood. The Christmas 1964 flood was rated "approximately a 100-year flood" by the Federal Emergency Management Agency and may be the most damaging in Oregon's history. It caused $157 million in damage, and 20 Oregonians lost their lives. Patients were evacuated from the Salem Memorial Hospital. (Melson Franz.)

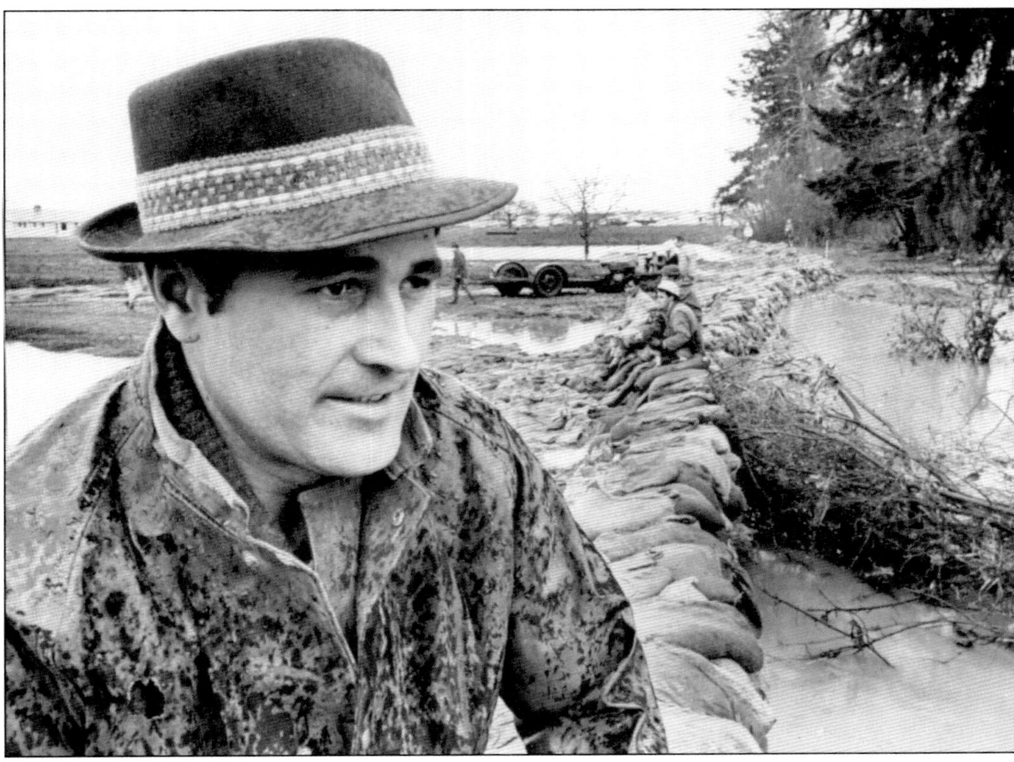

Frank Treml, of 4726 Carolina Avenue, looks over the sandbagging efforts to keep Willamette River floodwaters out of the area during the floods of December 1964 and January 1965. The dams did not guarantee freedom from flooding in the Willamette Valley. Every major tributary of the Willamette threatened to breech its banks. (SPL: SJ.)

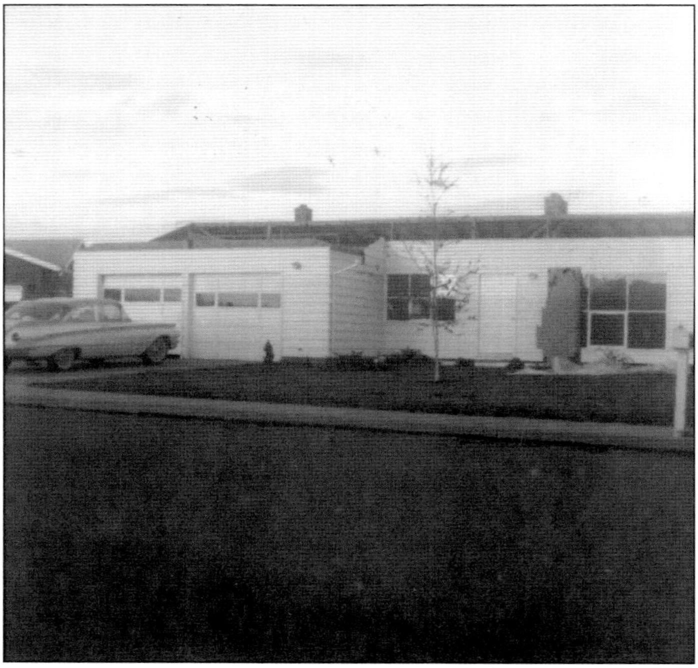

Winds from the 1962 Columbus Day storm hit this house at 4825 Ventura Loop North in the Palma Ciea neighborhood. The entire roof was blown off in one piece and landed in the backyard of Jim and Barbara Gallagher. Throughout the area, trees, power lines, and structures were damaged. Area wind gusts of up to 90 miles per hour were observed. (Gallagher.)

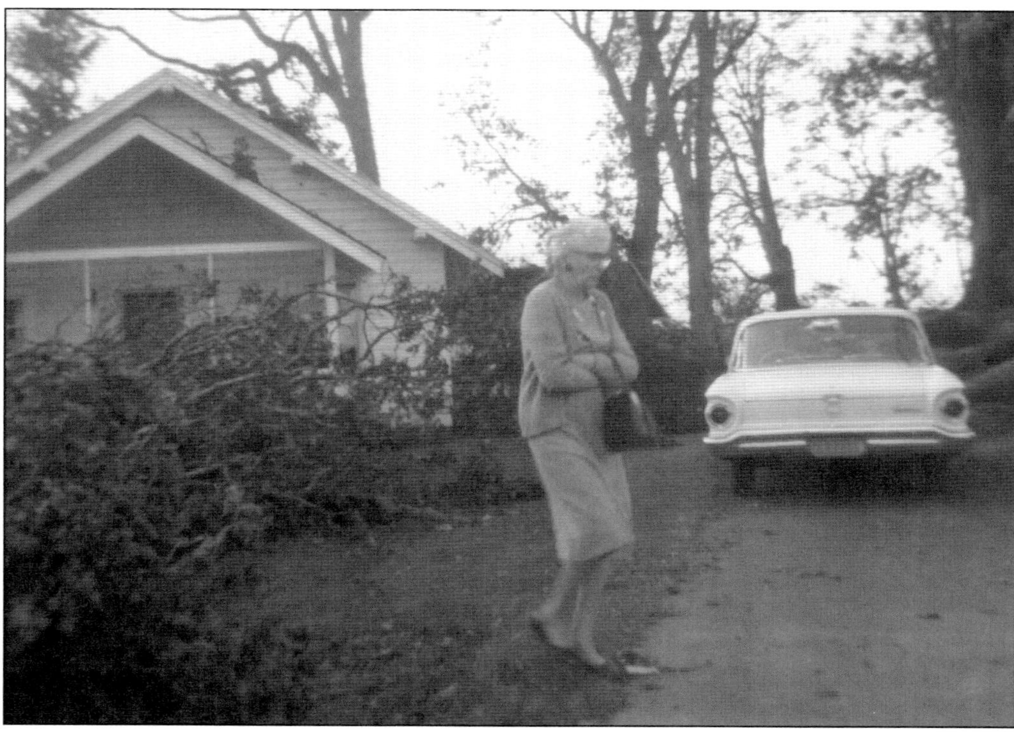

The old oaks surrounding Ben and Mabel Claggett's home on Verda Lane were wrecked by the powerful winds of the 1962 Columbus Day storm. The large oaks were there when the young couple built their home in 1920. One of the trees was blown over in the storm. Its rings were counted, establishing an age of 175 years. (Claggett.)

Seven

Community Life

The first multiuse building became a hub for school, church, and meetings. Roger Hawley's historical notes mention the Good Templars lodge (temperance society) at the Claggett school.

The oldest local fraternal lodge, Royal Neighbors of America Labish Camp No. 4148, was formed in 1907. Due to declining membership, the meeting hall at 7845 River Road was sold in 2004. Annie Beaty was a member of the Harmony Rebekah Lodge No. 75, Quinaby, and the Keizer Sewing Club (which began as the Ladies Aid in 1912). The Modern Woodmen of America met at a hall near the Indian School until a new building was completed in 1938. The Sewing Club also used the hall.

In 1931, the Chemawa Grange No. 785 was established. The national farmers' organization first met near the Indian School at the Woodmen of the World Hall. In 1938, it met at Keizer School until the new building was completed. In 1946, it became the Keizer Grange. Later, the grange was moved to Chemawa Road and remodeled in 1952. The Committee of Women's Activities and Keizer Community Club met at the grange. Dances were held at the grange as well. Saturday movies at Chemawa Indian School were enjoyed.

In 1948, the Keizer Rural Fire Protection District was organized. The fire engine was housed at the Keizer Food Lockers. Keizer Lions was formed in 1950. Its log meeting hall on Cherry Avenue was completed in 1957. Keizer Rotary Club was granted its charter in 1965. Keizer Masonic Lodge No. 219 merged with Salem in 2001. In 1968, the Keizer Seniors was established. The Fraternal Order of Eagles Aerie 3895 had its lodge until 2010. Keizer Elks Lodge No. 2472 was established in 1971. Garden clubs were popular as well.

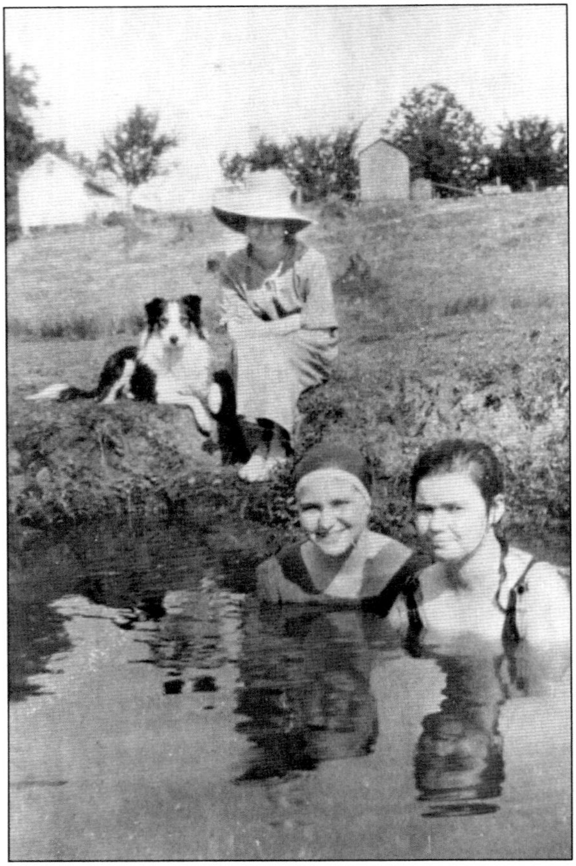

While neighbor Violet Newton sits creekside, the Hall sisters swim in Claggett Creek below the Hall farm on Claxter Road (now Verda Lane) around 1910. In the 1960s, four swimming pools offered classes and swim teams. (KHM: Thressa Hall Carlson.)

The 1930 Keizer School eighth-grade baseball team poses for a photograph. From left to right are (first row) Adrien Eichleberger, Fred Scott, Chris Bartruff, Robert McKnight, and Alvin Boyd Claggett; (second row) Ward Russell (coach), Warren Poole, Harold McCall, and Tommy Settlemeir; (third row) Herbert Harold, Robert McKnight, George Tekusaki, and Vernal Weathers. Coach Russell owned a gas station at Keizer Corner. The team members have been identified by Evelyn Melson Franz. (KHM: Russell.)

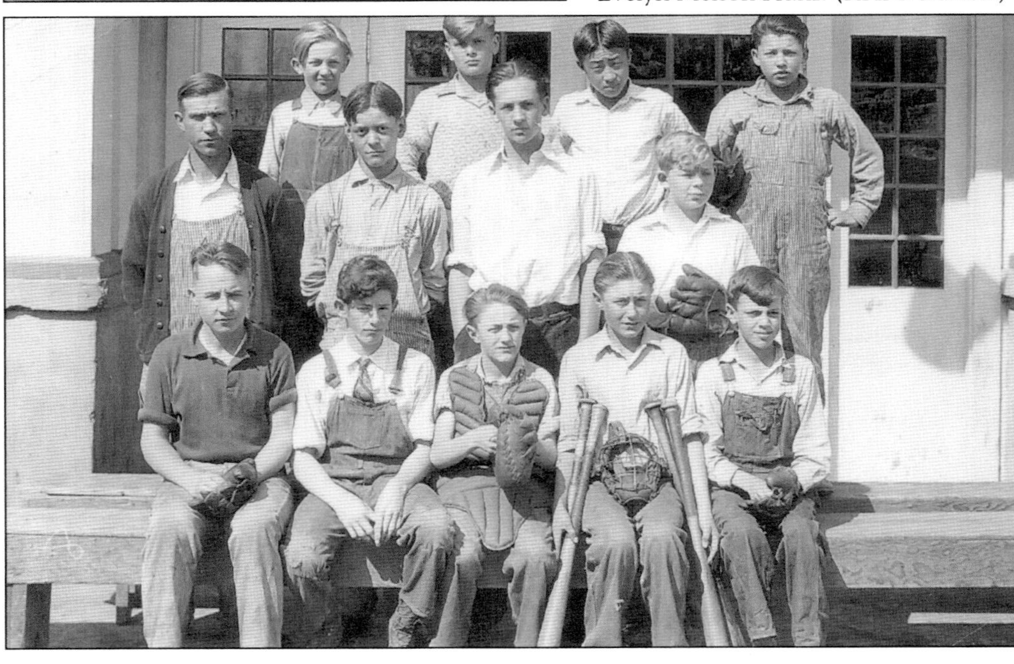

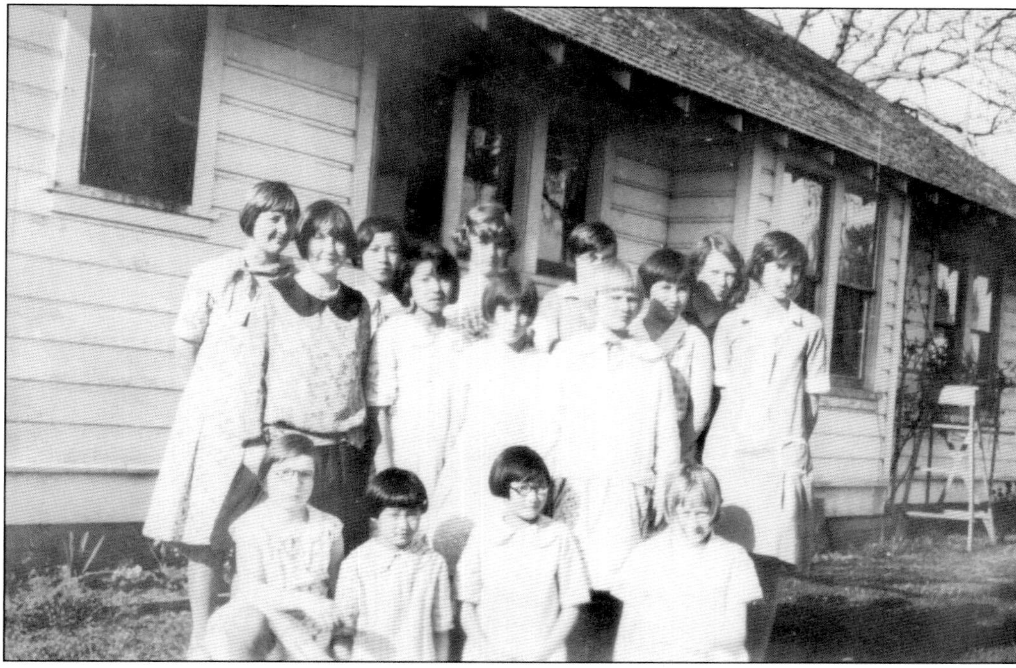

Girls of the first 4-H Club No. 6 in Keizer gather at the home of Ben and Mabel Claggett on Verda Lane in the 1930s. The schools promoted 4-H involvement, and most students were active in the club. Activities for children included team sports, 4–H, scouting, Camp Fire, and the Keizer Community Band. (KHM: Claggett.)

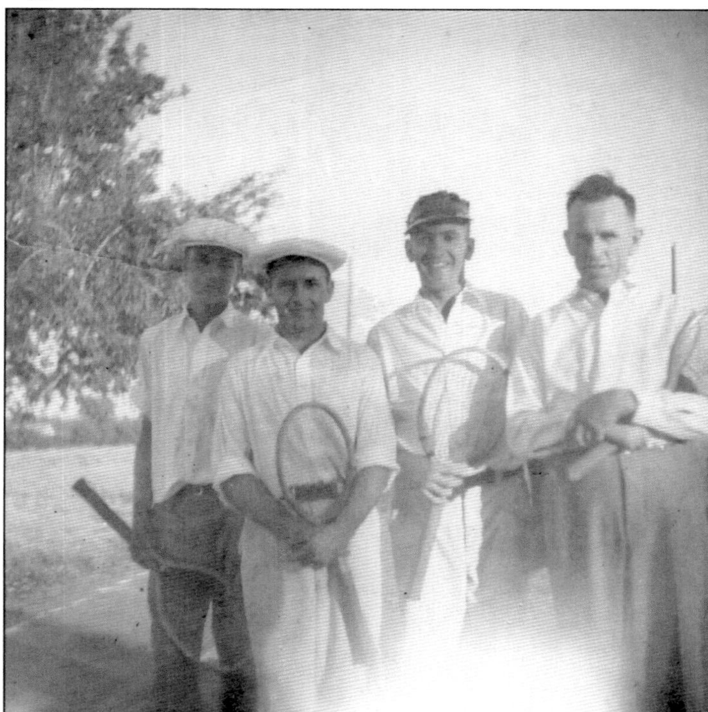

Tennis is being played at the Claggett home on Verda Lane. Usona "Sally" Claggett Baker wrote on the photograph: "From left to right: Boyd Claggett, Gilbert Savage, Glenn Savage, Daddy [Ben Claggett]. On our tennis court. Daddy & Glenn beat—notice their faces." The Frogleys and Lachmunds on Windsor Island Road also had tennis courts. The McNarys played the sport, and nearby Hayesville had a tennis club. (Claggett.)

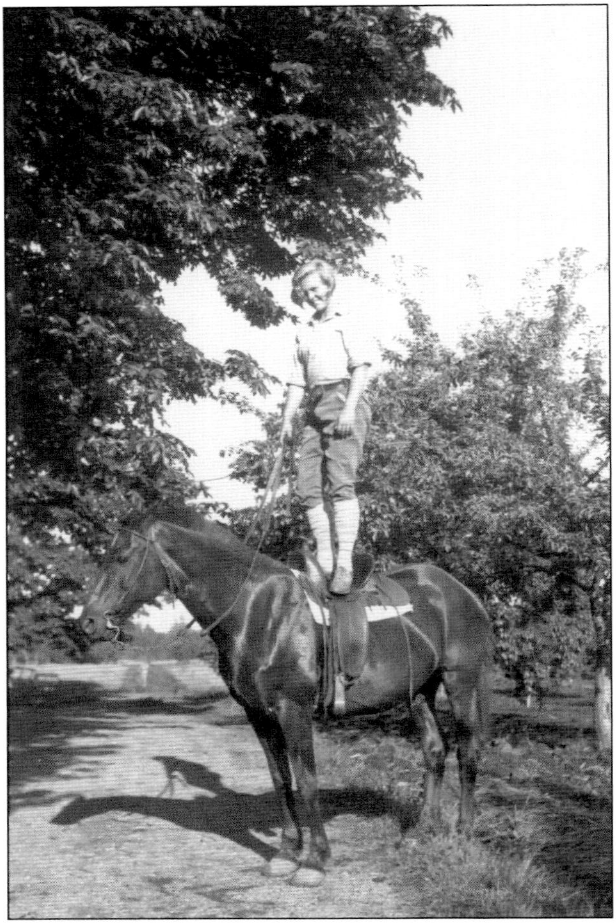

Evelyn Melson stands on her Morgan horse, Madame Queen, around 1934. Melson rode her horse all over the Keizer area and to Claggett Creek, which bordered the east side of the family's 34-acre farm in the middle of Keizer. (Melson.)

Posing in the Onion field at the Wallace Prairie is David Saucy Sr. (standing), Albert Brownlee (sitting on tractor), the unidentified "hired man" who lived on the property with his family, David Saucy Jr. (wearing cap), and the son of Albert Brownlee. David Saucy was the resident farm manager from 1922 to 1941 for property owner Asahel N. Bush. The property bordered Cherry Avenue past Claggett Creek. (Paul and Tracey Saucy Collection.)

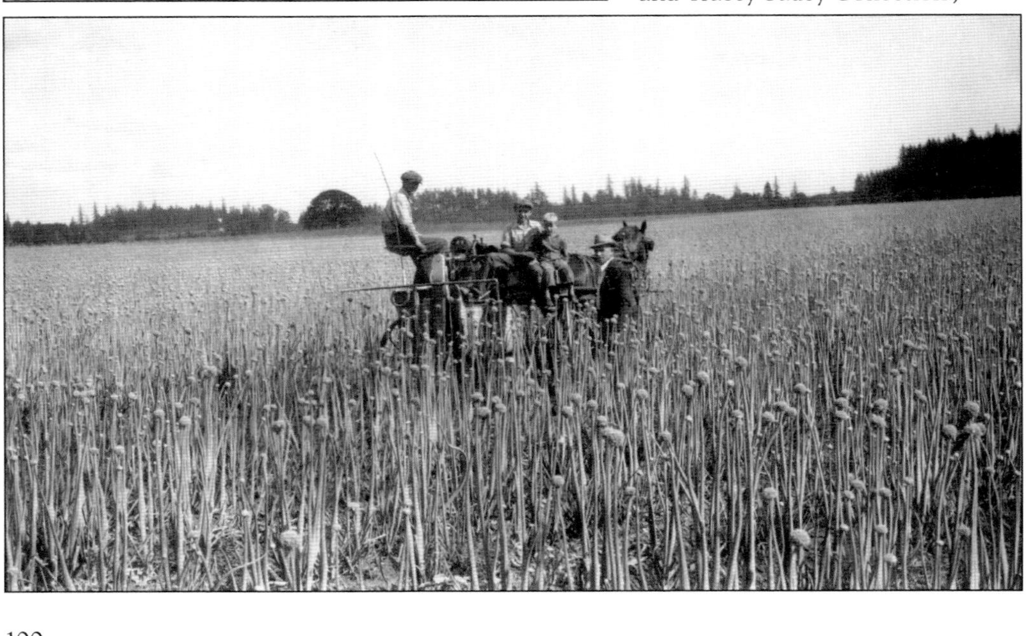

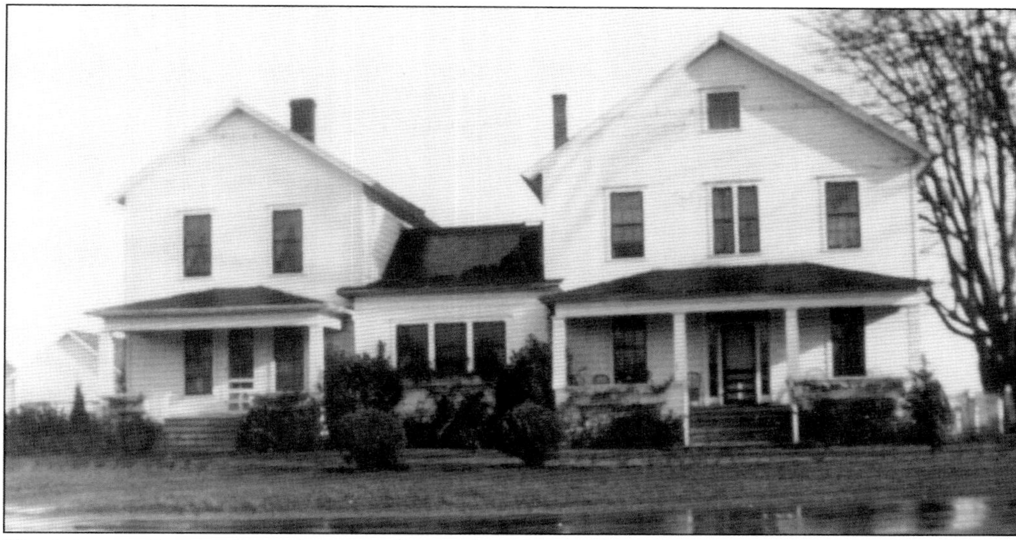

The Marion County Poor Farm was located in the south end of Keizer (now Salem city limits) in the area of old land claims of P.C. Keizer and his brother-in-law Sam Penter. In 1932, William and Margaret Oldenburg worked for the farm. The 30 acres extended to the School for the Deaf on Cherry Avenue, but the dwellings were on Front Street near Tryon Street. (KHM.)

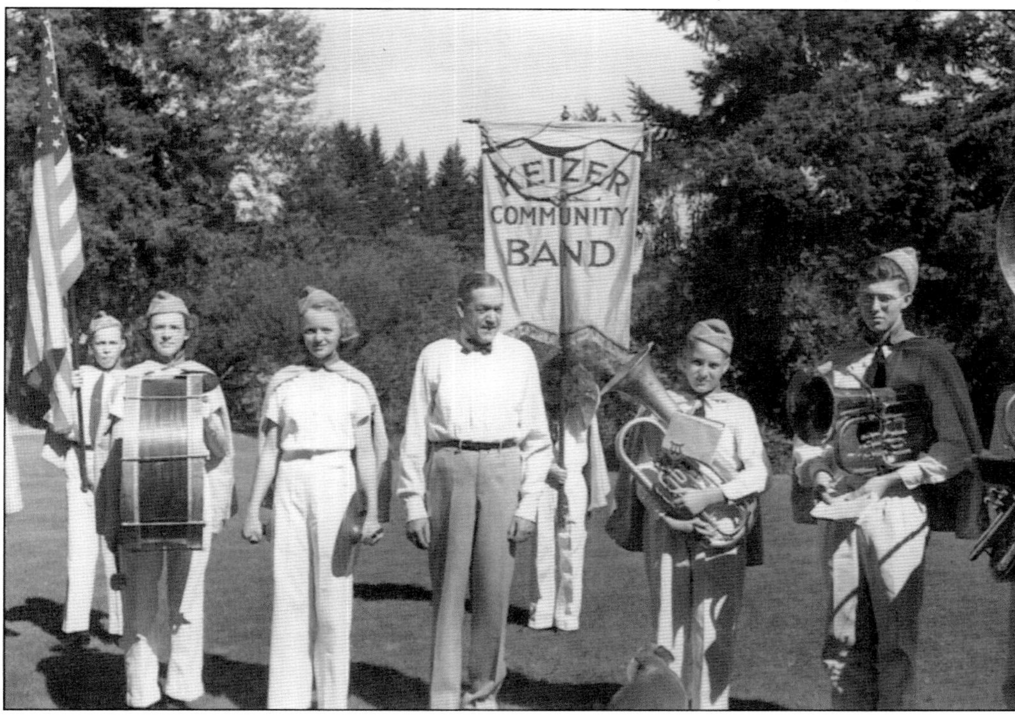

Sen. Charles McNary poses with the Keizer Community Band at his farm, Fir Cone (now the site of McNary Golf Club). McNary was campaigning as the vice-presidential candidate on Wendell Wilkie's presidential ticket in 1940. The band members are, from left to right, unidentified (flag), Verle Saucy (bass drum), Alice Rose (Jones) (cymbals), unidentified (banner), Donald Earle (tuba), Chester ?, and Milton Savage (tuba). (KHM: Jones.)

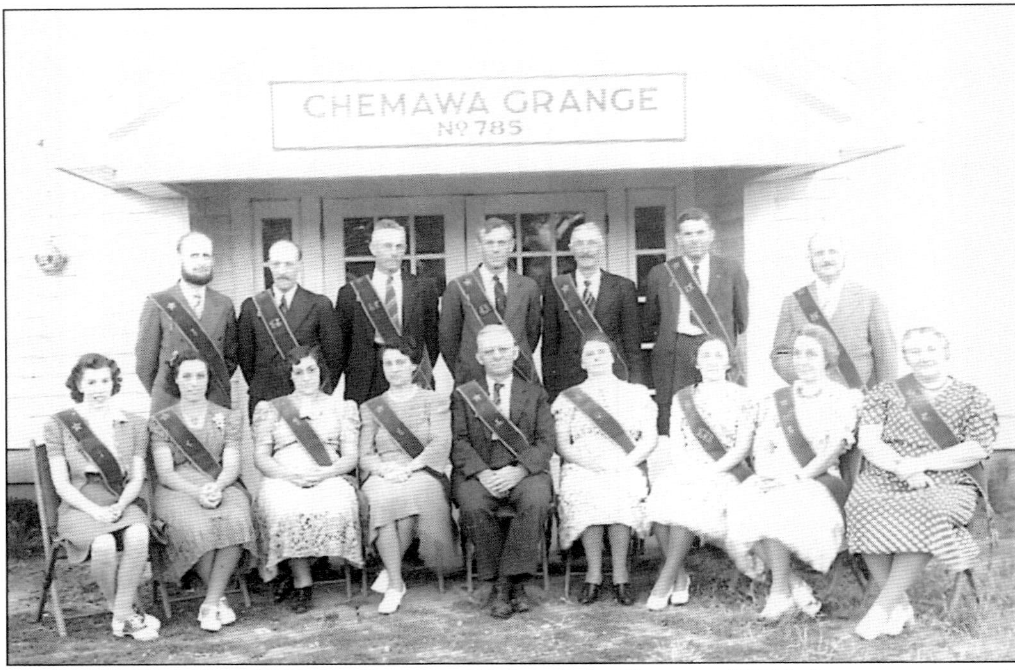

Shown are members of the Keizer Grange in the late 1940s. Ernest and Wilda Savage are on the far right. In 1931, the Chemawa Grange No. 785 was established. The national farmers' organization first met near the Indian School at the Woodmen of the World Hall. In 1938, it met at Keizer School until the new building was completed. In 1946, it became the Keizer Grange. (KHM.)

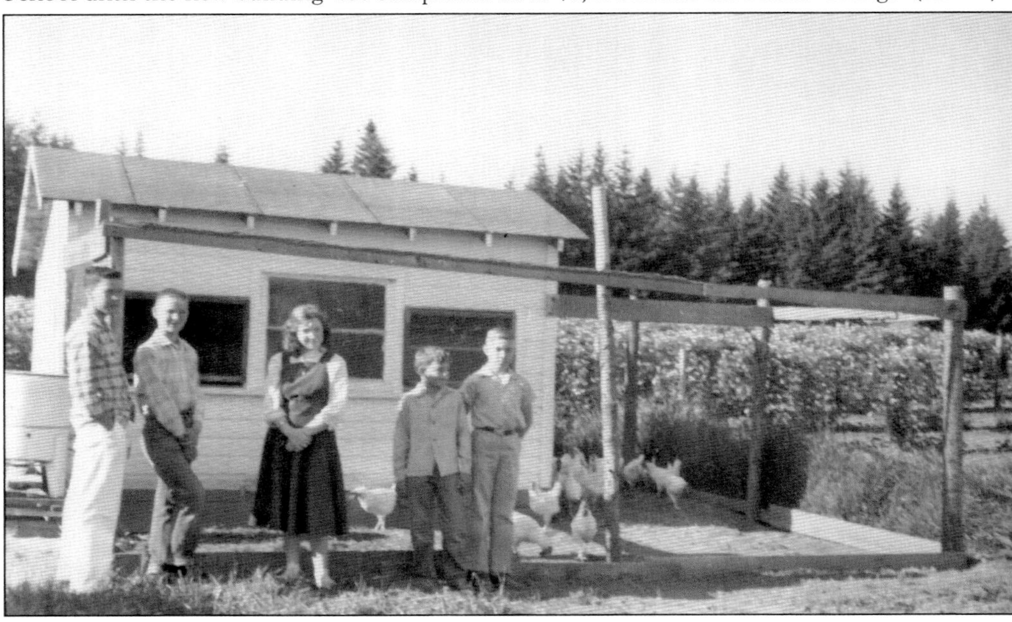

Members of the Clear Lake 4-H chicken club in 1959 are, from left to right, Dennis Schmaltz, Jack Watson, Loreen Ostrander, Victor Wilder, and James Dosdall. Berry vines are in the background at the Dosdall home at 7830 O'Neill Road. The Ostrander family also raised chickens at their home at 7005 River Road. Watson's family lived on the Strickfaden property. (Loreen Ostrander Wells.)

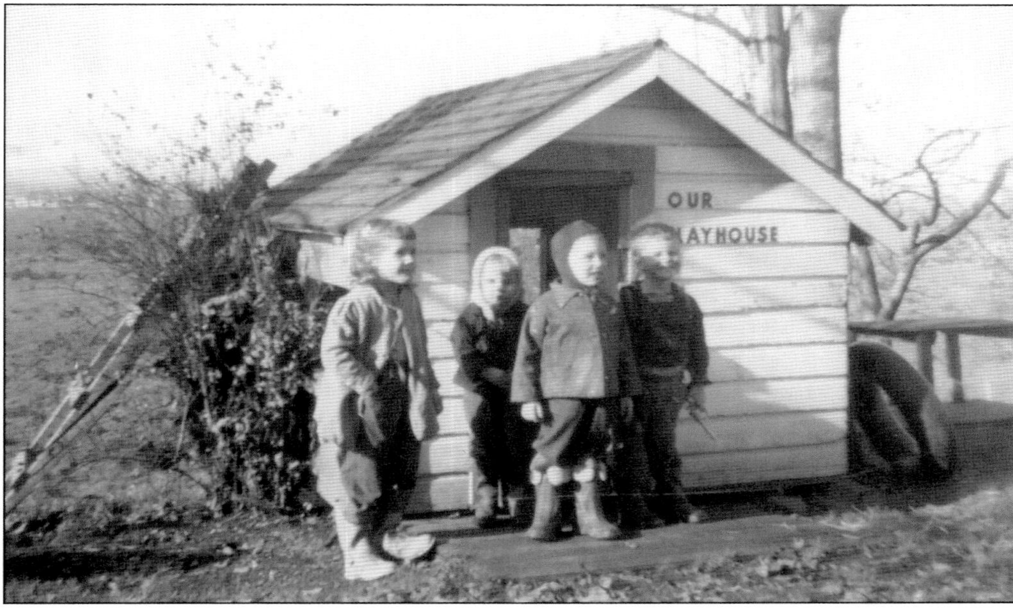

The Herber children, Tyrene and Joey, pose with their cousins, Ceci Oldenkamp and Jimmy Masten. They are enjoying the kid-sized playhouse on the Herbers' Verda Lane farm in the 1950s. The Herber family moved onto the old John Pugh farm in 1943. The Herbers were hired by the Savage family to run Keizer View Dairy. Rosalie Herber was active in the community and in the preservation of the old Keizer School. (Tyrene Herber Denlinger.)

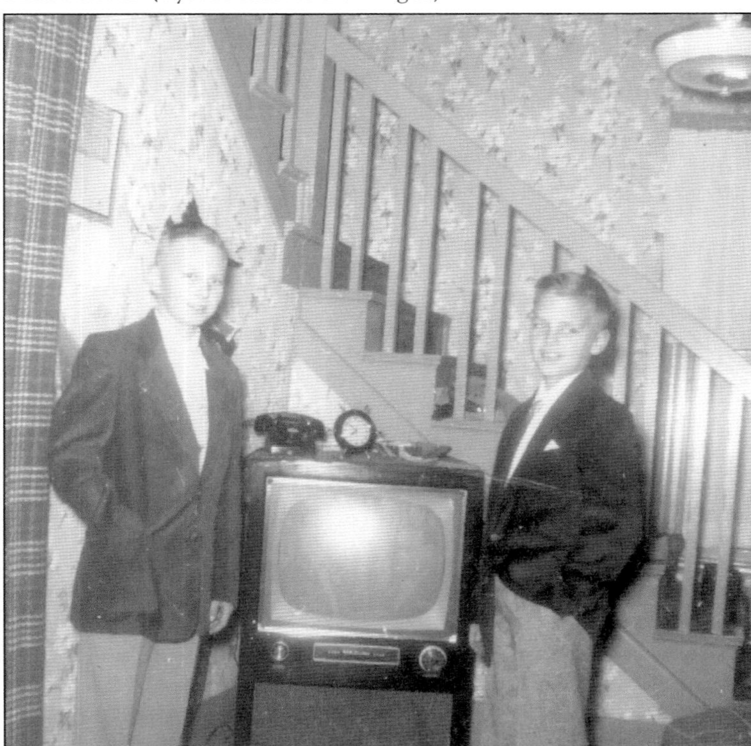

The Franz boys, Stan and Allan, are seen with their first black-and-white television set at the old family farm home (where Greenwood Apartments are now located). The advent of television changed the social dynamics for many; no longer did one need to leave the house for entertainment and news. (Melson Franz.)

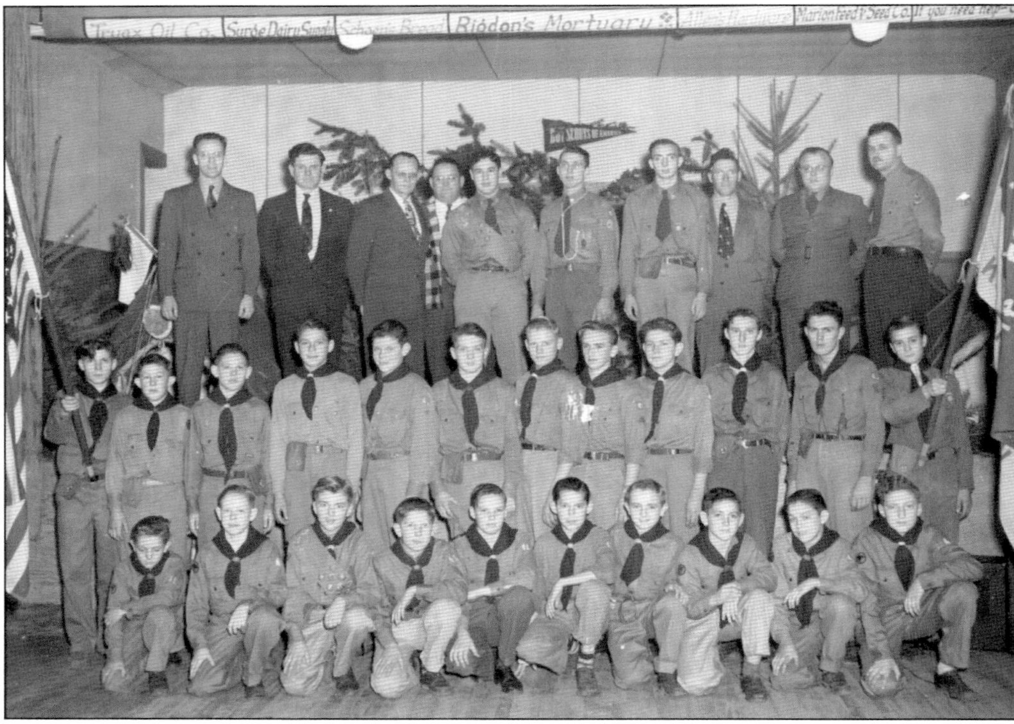

Keizer Boy Scouts Troop No. 41 is seen here around 1948 at Keizer Grange. Among those identified are Hugh Adams (third row, far left), Mickey Hickman (third row, sixth from left), Dave Adams (second row, fourth from right), and Loren Stetler (third row, far right). Hugh Adams started Troop No. 41 in Keizer in 1941 with Lyle Leighton, a Scout executive in Salem. Rusty Teets was the first scoutmaster, and Otto Yunker also served as scoutmaster. (KHM: Terry Teets.)

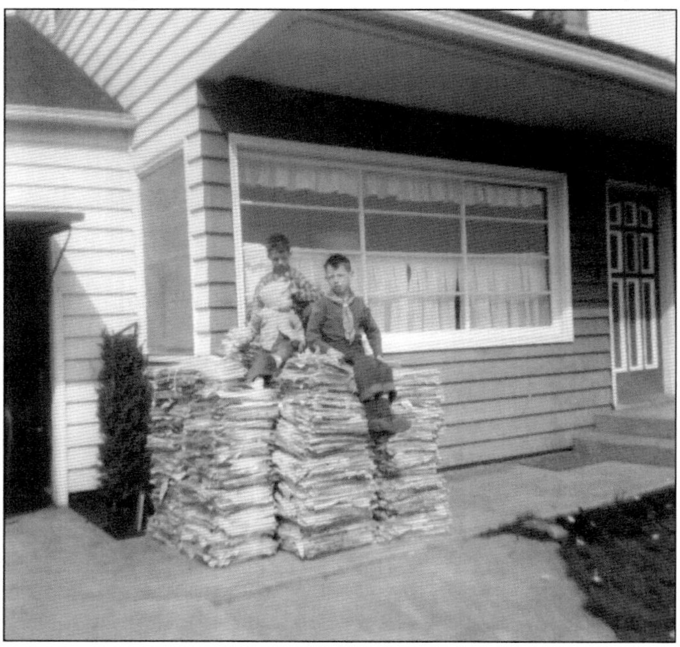

From left to right, Paul, Doug (back), and Tom McCarty perch on stacks of newspapers collected for a Boy Scout paper drive. Den leader Marie McCarty held Cub Scouts meetings in the single-car garage of their Dietz Avenue home. The McCarty family left Dietz Avenue in 1961, although Marie later returned to Keizer and is an active volunteer at the Keizer Community Library. (McCarty family collection.)

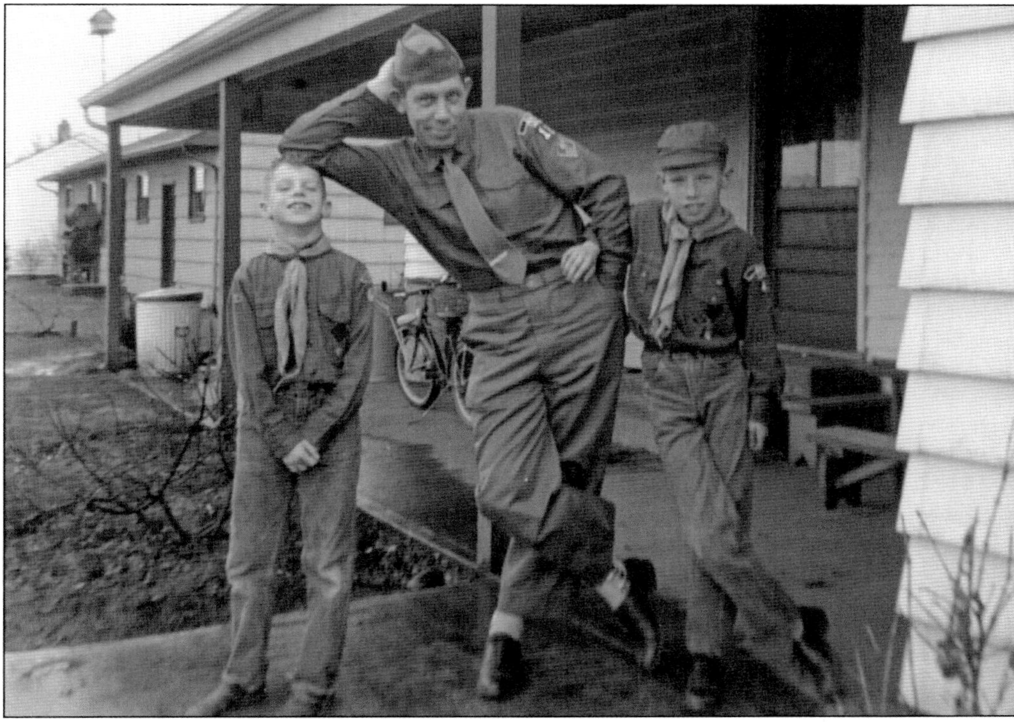

Scoutmaster Vere A. McCarty poses in the backyard with sons Doug and Tom. The McCartys lived on Dietz Avenue from 1952 to 1961. During this time, their house number changed from 1135 to 771, and the number of McCarty sons changed, from three to six. Dietz Avenue was named in 1948 by a drawing of residents' last names. (McCarty family collection.)

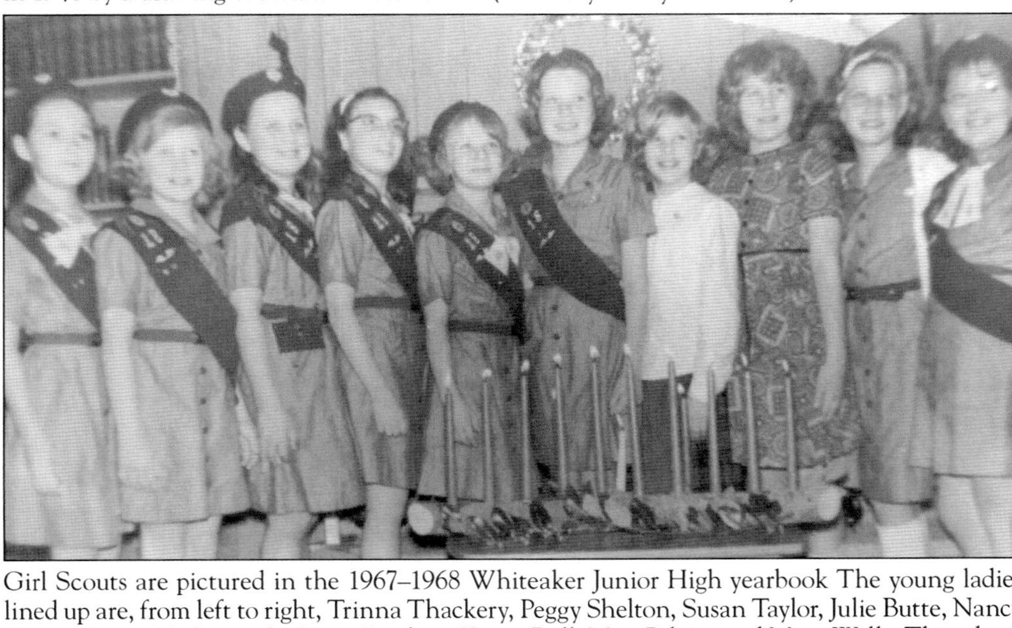

Girl Scouts are pictured in the 1967–1968 Whiteaker Junior High yearbook The young ladies lined up are, from left to right, Trinna Thackery, Peggy Shelton, Susan Taylor, Julie Butte, Nancy Drees, Nancy Nightengale, Janet Gardner, Karen Bull, Mari Prlain, and Mary Wells. The school was housed at McNary High School until the fall of 1968. (Whiteaker Junior High yearbook.)

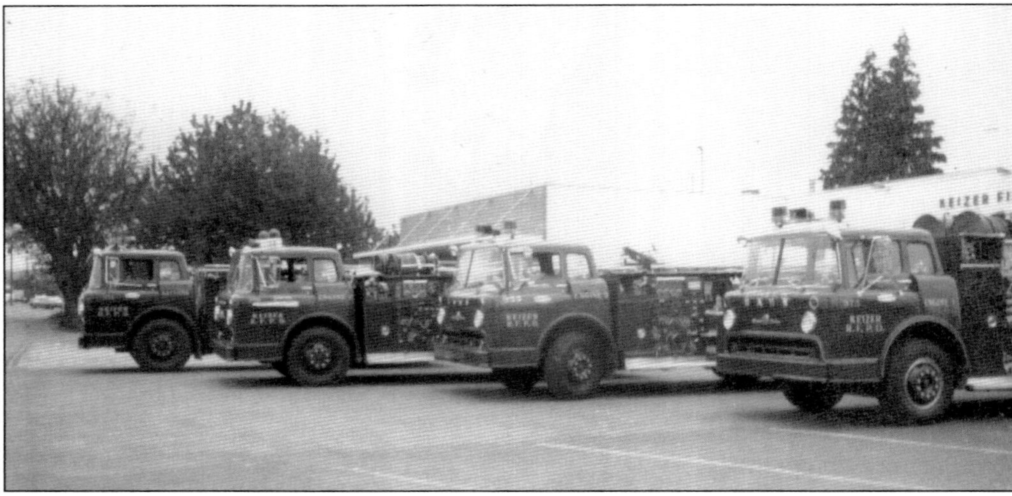

The Keizer Fire District was organized in 1948. The equipment consisted of one 1948 Ford 500-gallon pumper, which cost less than $10,000. This fire engine was housed under a lean-to shed at the Keizer Food Lockers. The first alarm involved McDermott's Variety Store. The original Keizer fire engine was fully restored by volunteers. The operational fire engine is proudly displayed at open houses and parades. (KFD.)

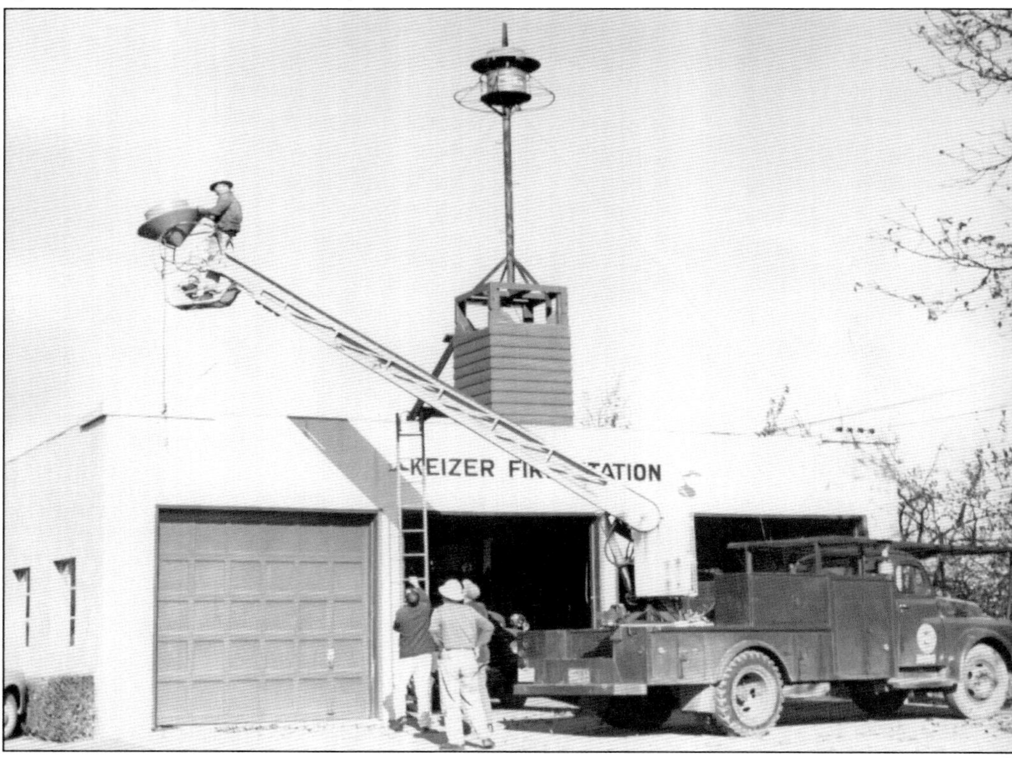

A new siren was installed at the fire station in 1959. When a fire call went out, people needed to be cautious of the volunteer firemen quickly making their way to the station. Today, the alarm still sounds each Friday at noon. The siren summoned firefighters in years past. Today, VHF radio pagers and notifications to smart phones are used. (KFD.)

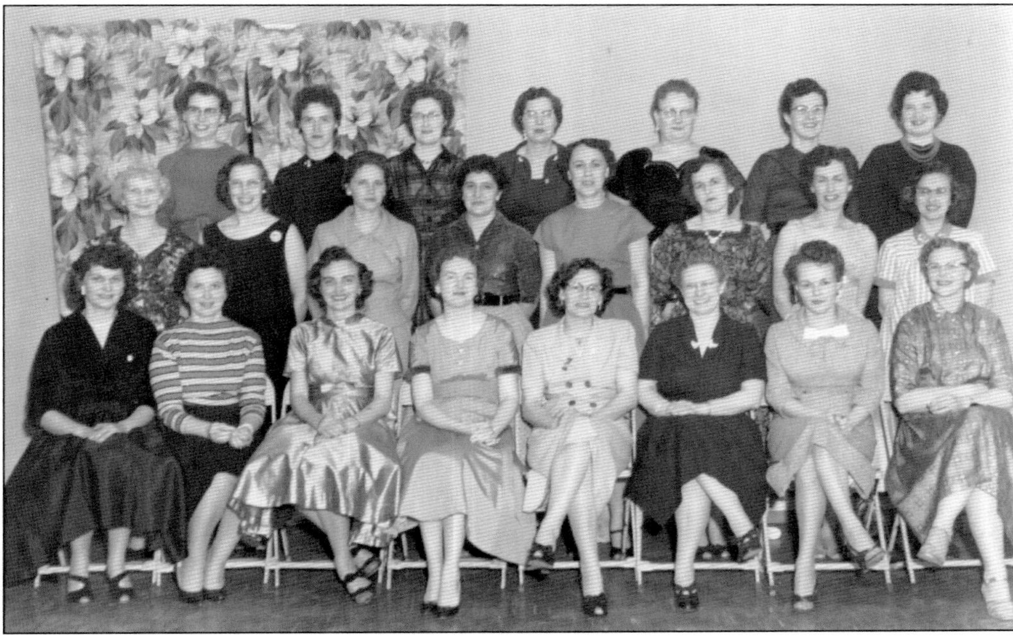

The Firemen's Auxiliary was formed in 1950 to aid and support the firemen. These women pose in January 1958. The first officers elected were Nellie Yung (president), Sally Orcutt (vice president), Olive Snook (secretary-treasurer), and Charlotte Mekker (correspondent). The auxiliary conducted first aid, food and clothing details, traffic control, and other activities. (KFD.)

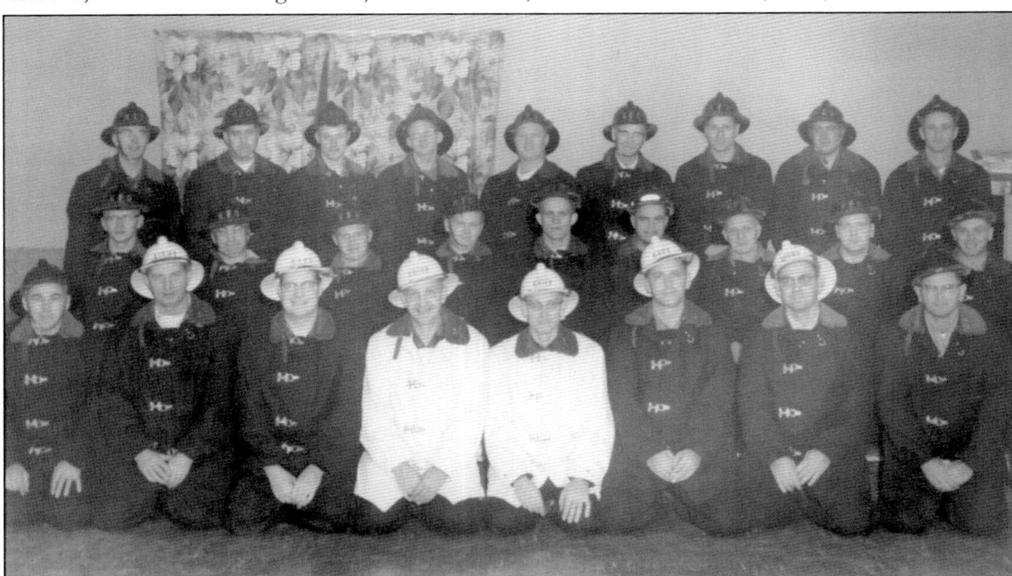

The 1959 fire volunteers shown here are, from left to right, (first row) Anderson, Lieutenant Wilson, Captain Nightengale, Chief Mekkers, Assistant Chief Snook, Captain Powell, Lieutenant Affleck, and Jensen; (second row) Hamm, Hemmer, Fish, Anderegg, Reece, Wade, Sanford, McDonnell, and Zielinski; (third row) Wood, Wilson, Kampstra, Sanford, Burright, Teets, Orcutt, Staats, and Halbeisen. Turnout equipment (pants, coats, and helmets) were purchased with proceeds from Fireman Benefit Balls held at the Lions building. (KFD.)

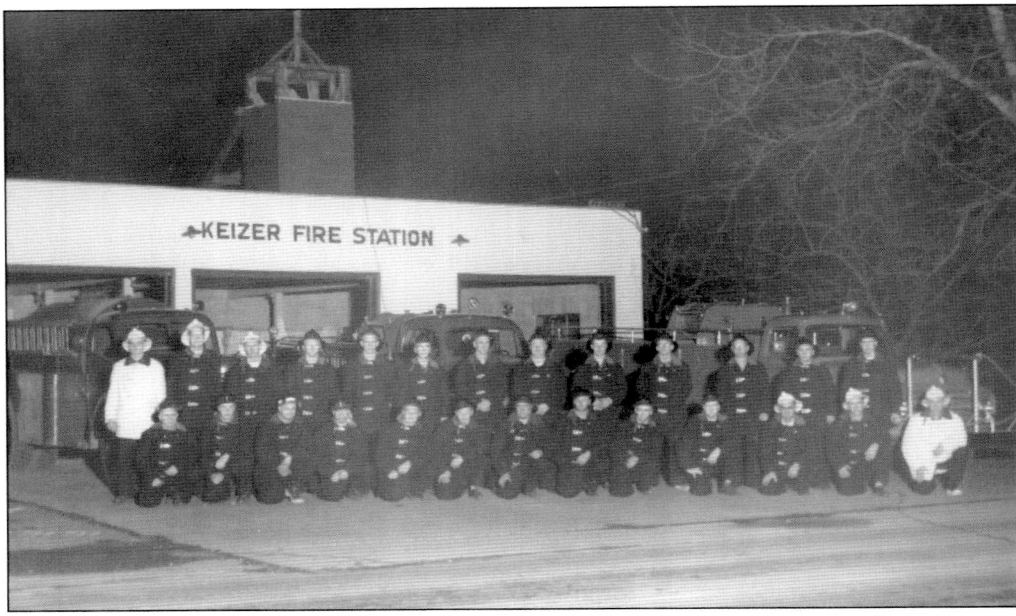

In 1949, the fire station was completed at its present location, with room for three pieces of equipment. It consisted of a multipurpose room with kitchen facilities to be used by the firefighters and community groups. The station was remodeled in 1961, when the apparatus bay was enlarged, and again in 1970, when a new multipurpose room, kitchen, and offices were added. In 1996, a new station was constructed. (KFD.)

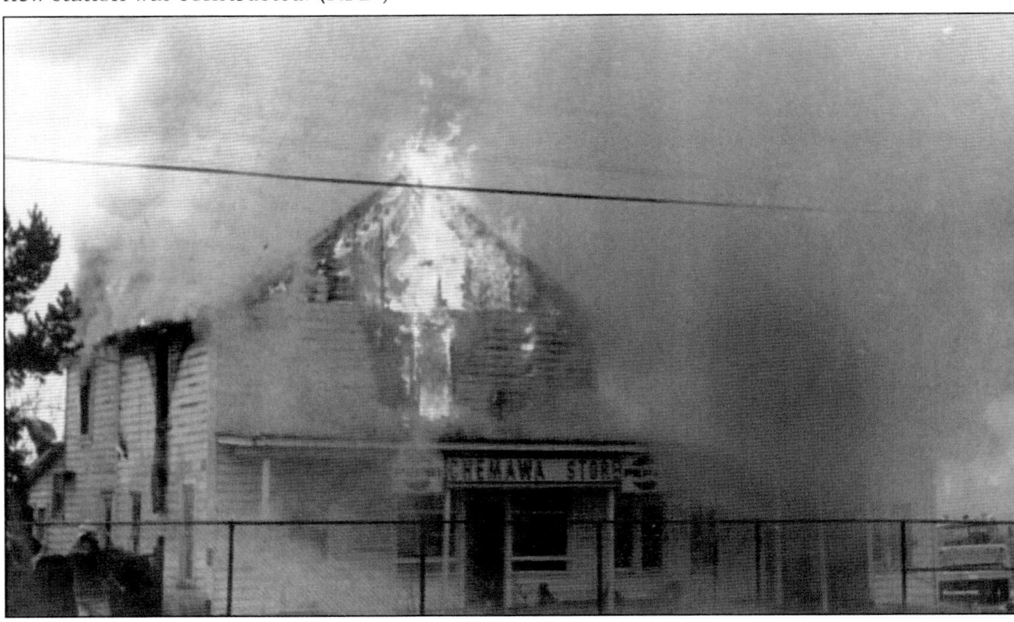

The old Chemawa structure, just west of Keizer, which consisted of the general store, gas station, and post office, is shown ablaze. The Keizer Fire District service coverage extended to the Chemawa area. The school was named after the original post office that existed in the area. Chemawa Indian School is the nation's oldest continually operating Indian boarding school, established in 1880 and relocated near Keizer in 1885. (KFD.)

Eight

Early Businesses

The earliest telephone lines in the surrounding areas were independent lines connected to neighboring farms. Salem Fairfield Telephone Association was organized in 1908. Attorney Charles McNary advised the corporation stockholders. By 1915, the Salem-Keizer Telephone Company improved service. In 1972, the last lines joined Pacific Northwest Bell.

As the farming community grew, local family-owned grocers provided basic needs to avoid frequent journeys into Salem. The first store was at Quinaby, on the east side of the Oregon Electric Railway tracks. The tiny Clear Lake community supported both Charley Pugh's Hilltop Store and Nick Vallick's Clear Lake Store.

The Savage family, who lived on the old Pugh farm on Claxtar/Claxter Road (now Verda Lane), developed Keizer View Dairy, which began after 1914. In 1927, Ward Russell's little grocery store with its hand-operated gasoline pump was the first store in Keizer. About 1940, Ray Smith built a store and gas station on Cherry Avenue. In 1947, John Coomler and Ewald Franz bought the hardware store. Keizer Supermarket opened across from Russell's, and Sam Orcutt built his IGA market.

About 1948, Clarence Rickard built a small store at the corner of Newberg Drive and Chemawa Road that still operates today. That year also saw the opening of Al's Radio Shop, Keizer Food Lockers, and Keizer Cleaners. In 1949, the Commercial Club was formed to acquaint local people with area businesses. It advertised on radio station KSLM. The club also started the *Keizer News*. Business boomed in the 1950s. Camellia Beauty Salon opened in 1952, and Boucher Jewelers began in 1953. In 1954, Berg's Market built a large store on River Road, opposite of Cummings Lane. Bauer Insurance began in 1957. Town and Country Lanes opened in 1960.

The first physician, Dr. Vernon Casterline, and the first dentist, Dr. Gerald Bowerly, arrived in 1950. They shared the new River Road professional building with Mootry's Pharmacy.

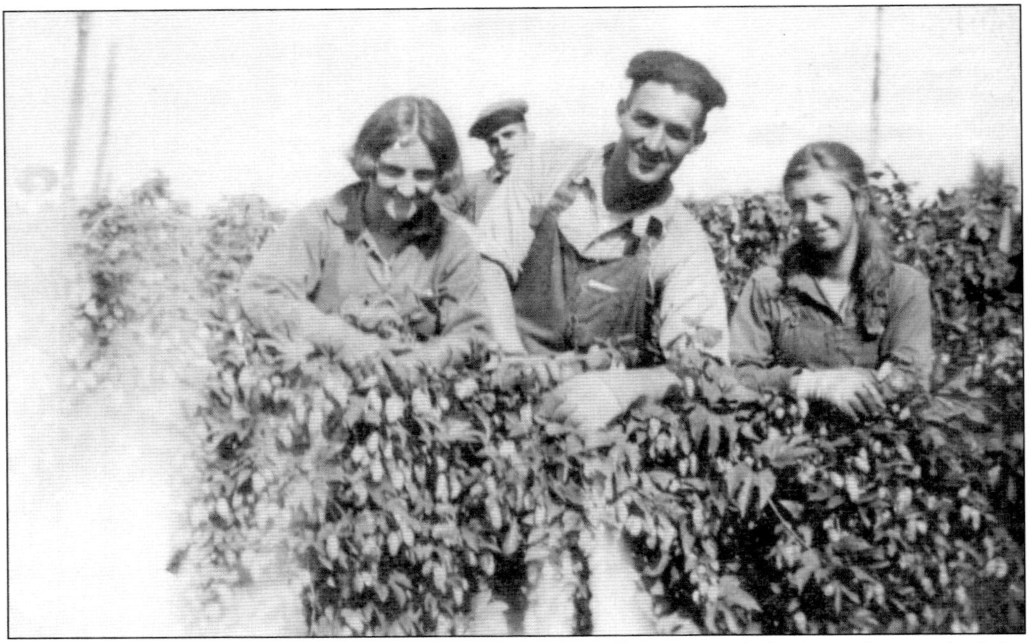

This 1926 photograph shows hop pickers happily working. Families and children often worked the fields. In the days of steamships, families from as far away as Portland would come and camp while harvesting. Hops have been grown in the Mission Bottom area for over 100 years and continue to be a major crop today. (KHM: Ann Lossner.)

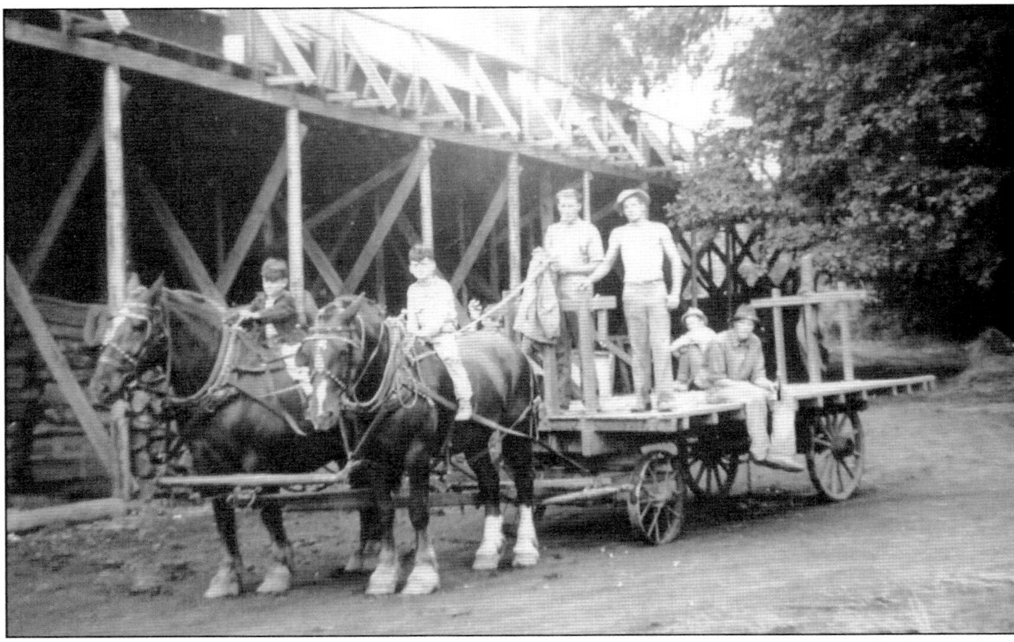

Horses Duke and Barney pull a wagon on the Fook Chong Ranch. Hank Beier (in hat) stands on the wagon behind the new hop house. The wood stacked up is for the wood-burning furnaces that heat the hop dryers. Hop Lee owned the ranch, a laundry on Ferry Street in Salem, and other businesses. He never lived on the ranch, but hired managers to run it. (KHM.)

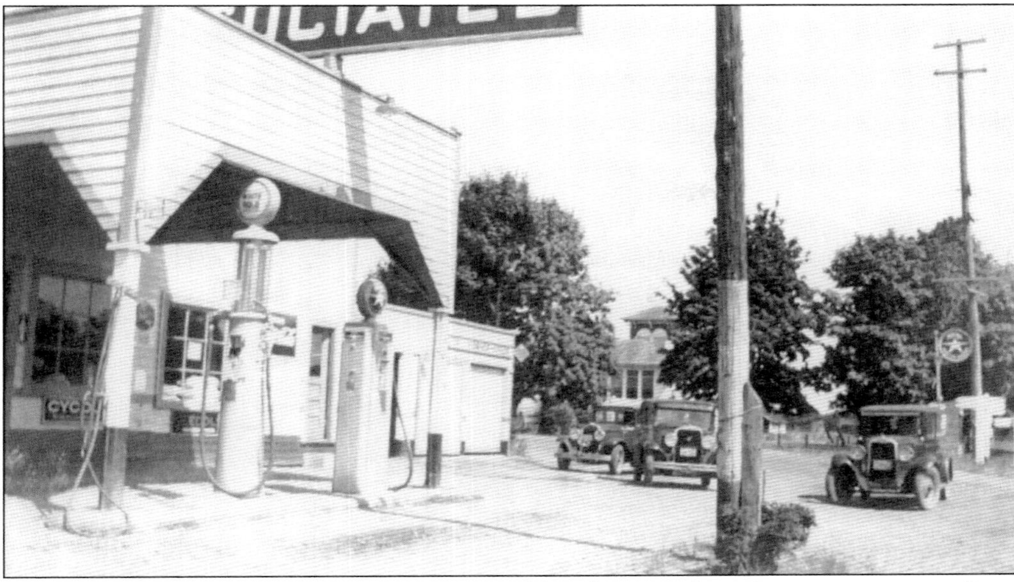

Ward and Nellie Russell's little grocery store and hand-operated gasoline pump were on River Road at the corner of Chemawa Road, southwest from Keizer School. The little store, begun in 1927, was Keizer's first storefront business. The Russells lived in a tent while they built the station and their house next door. (KHM: Russell.)

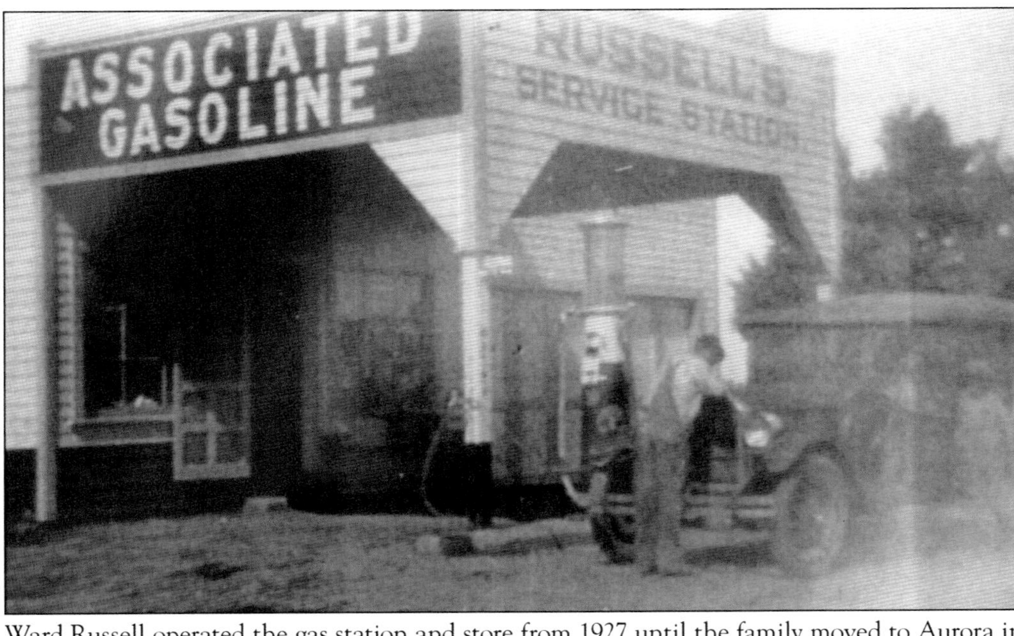

Ward Russell operated the gas station and store from 1927 until the family moved to Aurora in 1937. They had the only business at the River Road and Chemawa Road thoroughfare. Other gas stations would operate through the years at this busy intersection. As the roads were widened through the years, the business lot and access ways were decreased. The site now beautifully houses a city sign, fountain, and flagpoles. (KHM: Russell.)

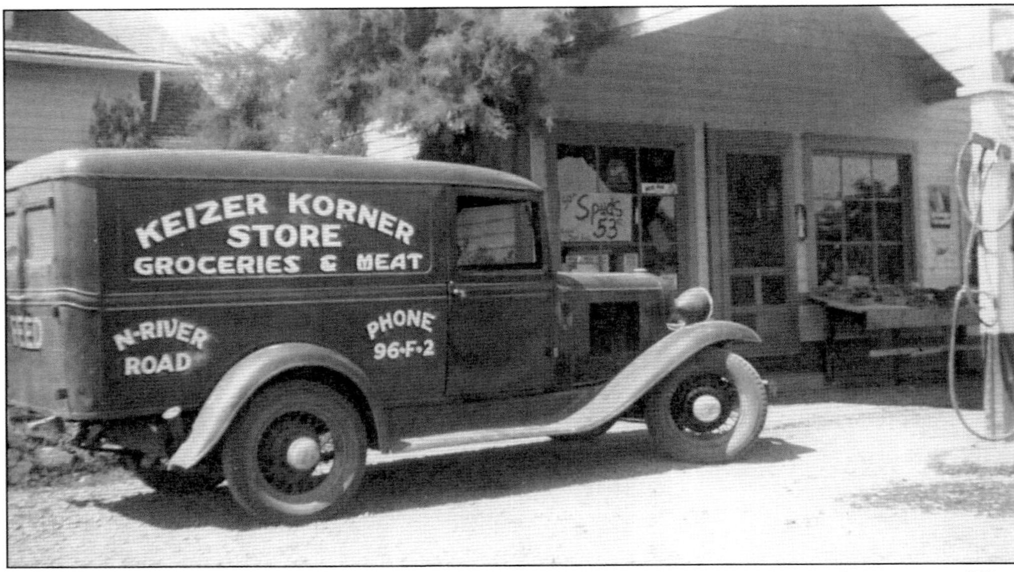

Mr. and Mrs. Hugh Shattuc owned and operated the Keizer Korner store and gas pump. They lived at the house next door on River Road that Ward and Nellie Russell ran until 1937. Walt Robinson's lumberyard was around the corner on Chemawa Road. Later, Mrs. Shattuc had their house torn down and replaced with a building that housed American Federal Bank and Dr. Casterline's office. It is currently occupied by Boucher Jewelers and a veterinary office. (KHM.)

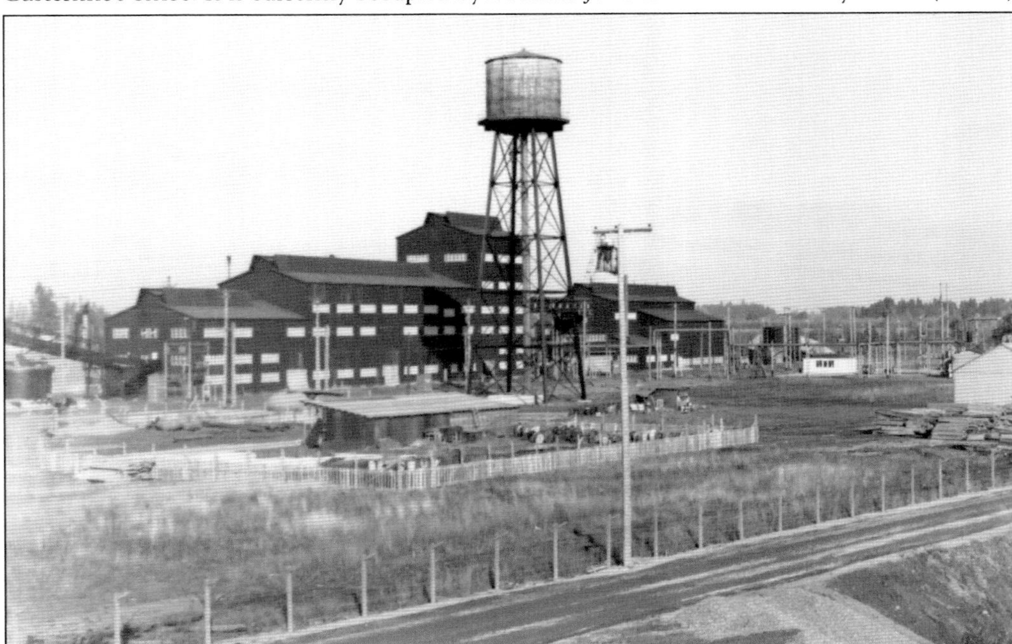

The Salem Alumina Plant was a $4 million facility used for processing alumina ore during World War II. As seen in 1945, the building consisted of varying heights; the tallest section was six stories high. The property perimeter was fenced, and a water tower stood impressively in the foreground. The plant was located on Cherry Avenue, across from where Home Depot is today. (SPL: Ben Maxwell.)

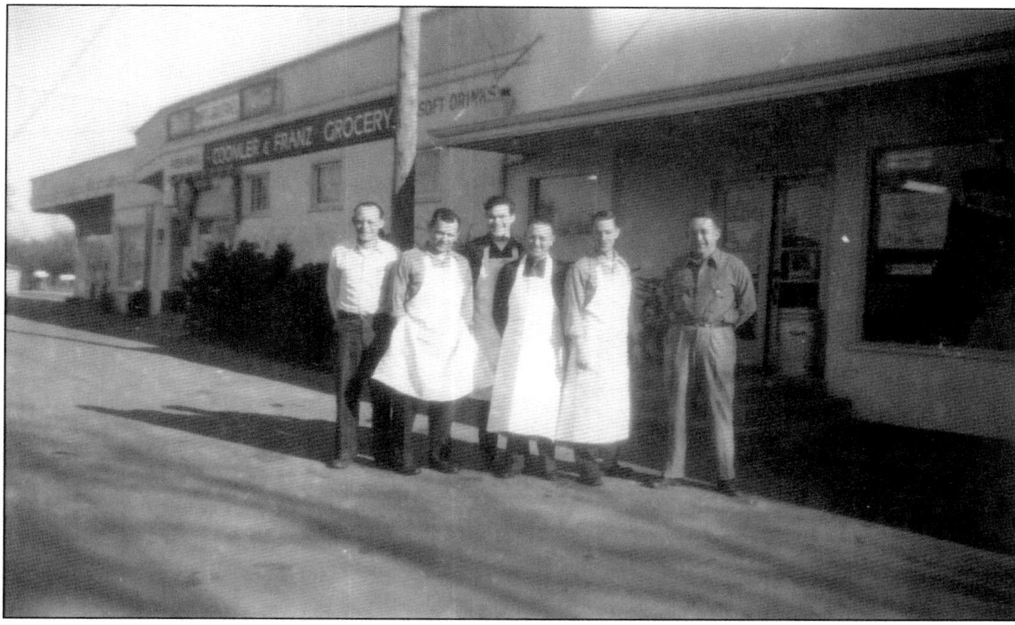

The Coomler & Franz grocery store was operated from 1946 to 1951 at the intersection of River Road and Cherry Avenue. The men standing in front of the store are, from left to right, Ewald Franz, Albert Evans, Clay Vincent, R.K. O'Connor, John Coomler, and Everett Ward. (Melson Franz.)

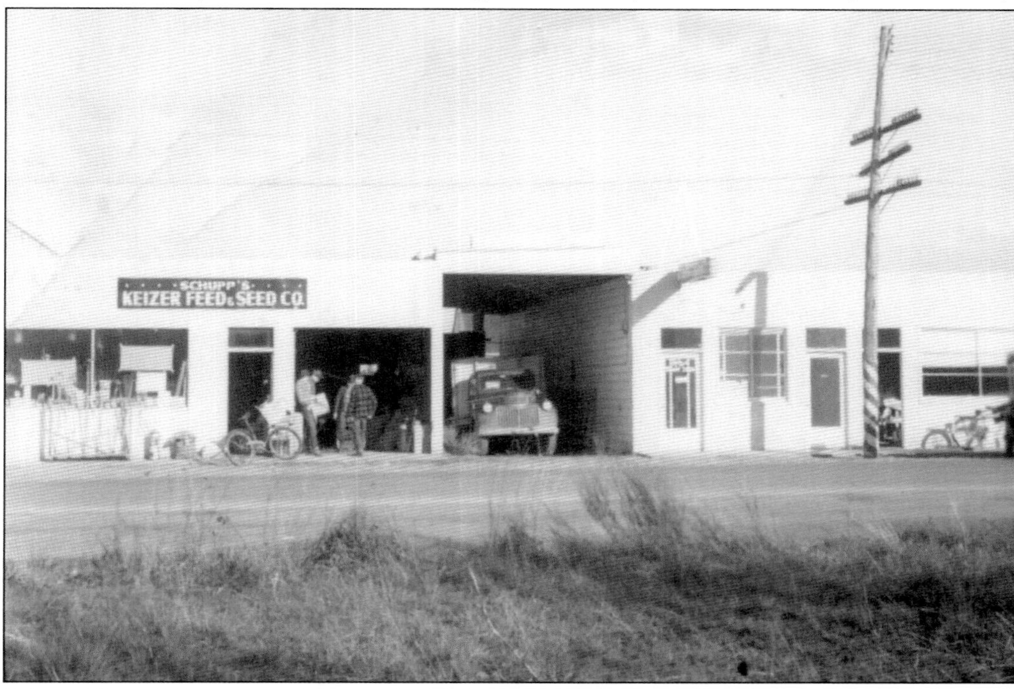

Bob and Fran Schupp owned Keizer Feed & Seed on River Road. This photograph, taken in 1946 or 1947, shows the new addition, which housed Terry Carrigan's Keizer Beauty Shop (later home to Boucher Jewelers). In 1948, Bob Schupp was one of the lead men in developing the Keizer Commercial Club. (KHM: Nannette Schupp Hickman.)

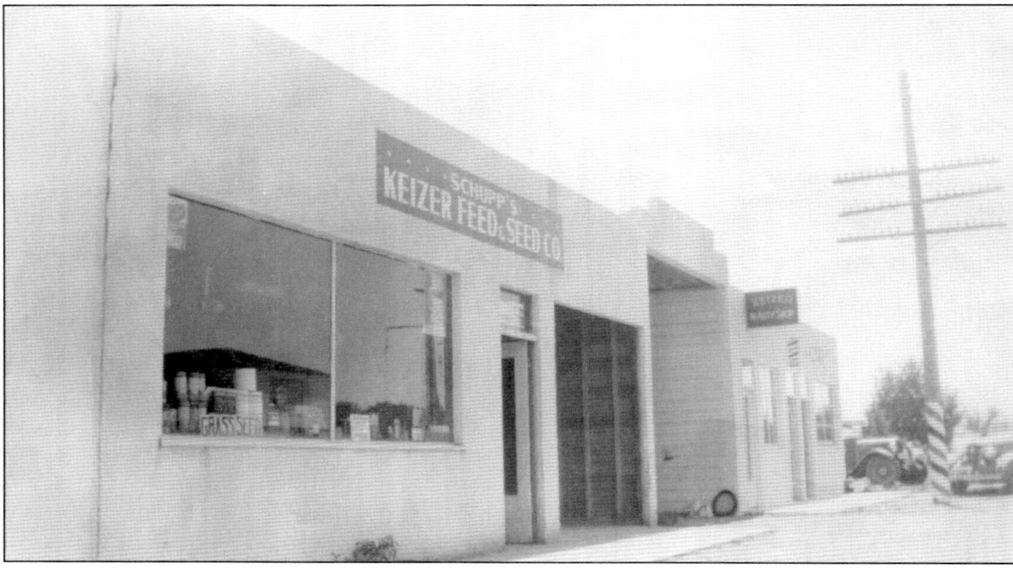

In 1946–1947, Bob and Fran Schupp built an addition to their Keizer Feed & Seed Company. Terry Carrigan opened Keizer Beauty Shop, which, in 1953 became the site of the new Boucher Jewelers. The beauty shop (with improvised barber pole) was relocated to the west side of River Road. (KHM: Nannette Schupp Hickman.)

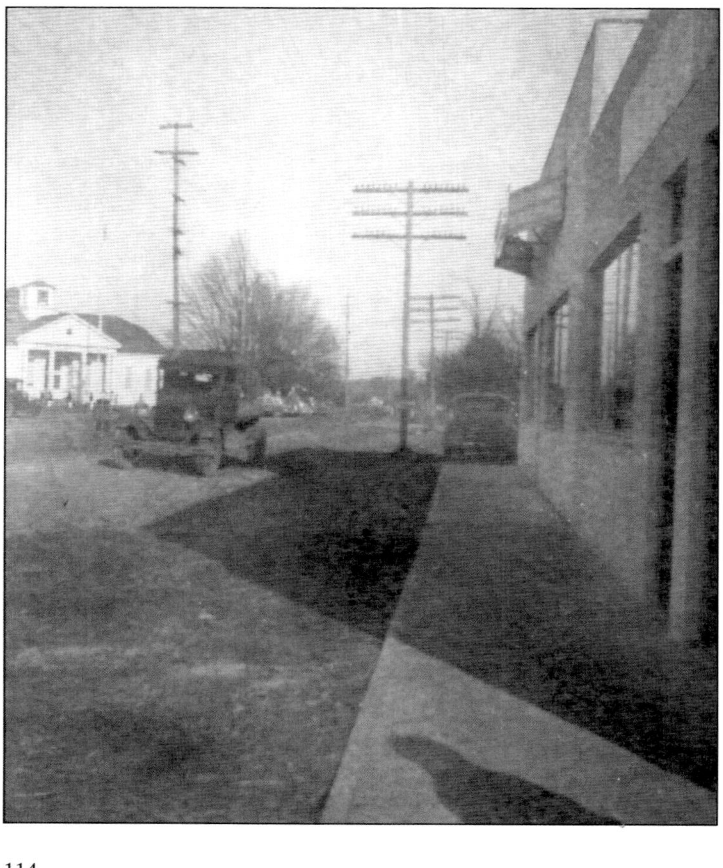

Looking north from the Schupps' Keizer Feed & Seed store, Keizer School is visible in this photograph from 1946 or 1947. In 1944, Mr. Rickard built a neighborhood market west on Chemawa Road; it was later purchased by Dean McFarland. By 1950, River Road became two lanes, and more businesses were developed. (KHM: Nannette Schupp Hickman.)

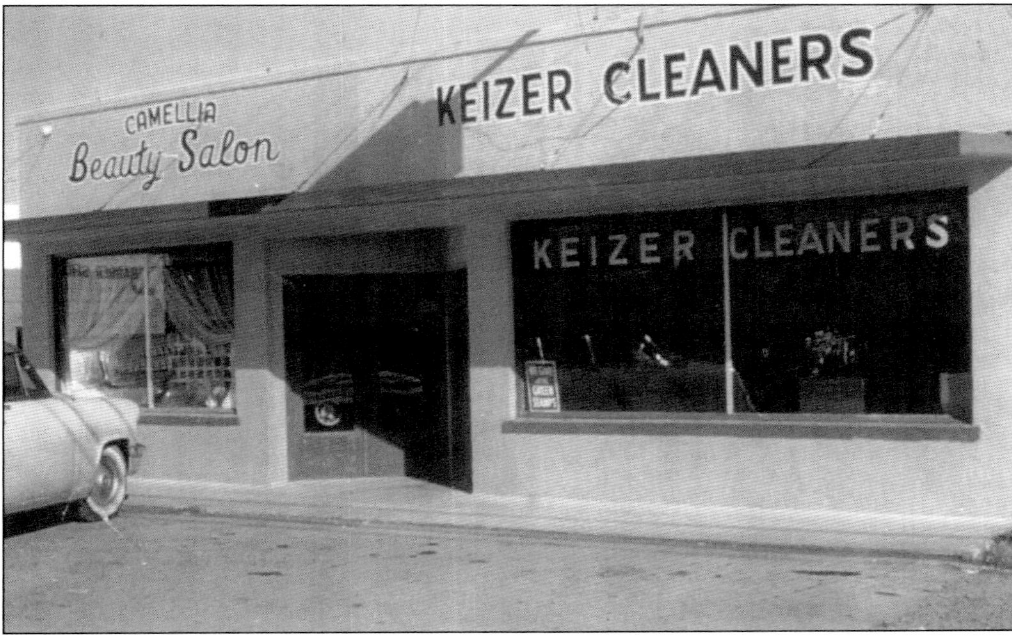

Otis and Alice Anderson built Keizer Cleaners in 1948, owning and operating it until 1960 at 4945 River Road (near Shari's today). The other side was first rented by Goldie's Dress Shop, then Modette; in 1952, Camellia Beauty Salon began. In 1961, the Andersons developed and managed Rainbow Gardens Mobile Village on the site of the former Ferrill's Nursery. (KHM: Anderson.)

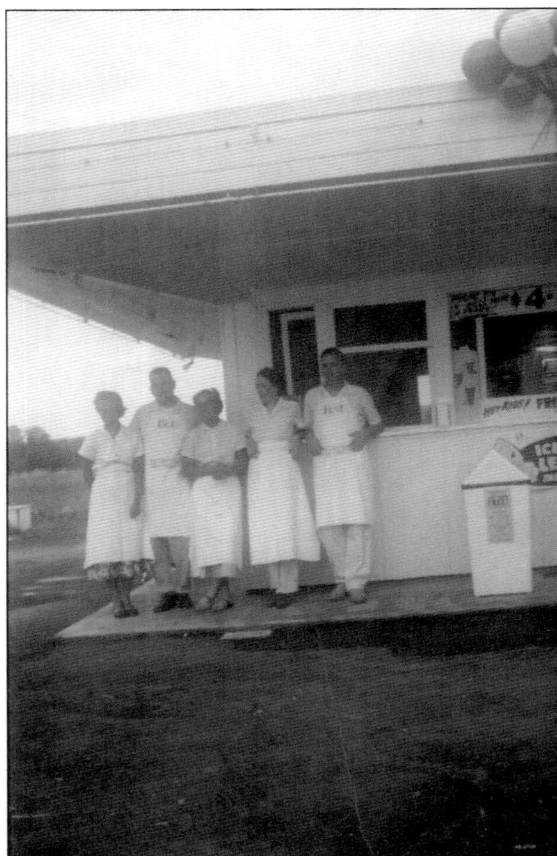

Balloons greeted customers at the 1950 grand opening of Tele-Treat Drive-In. The restaurant was co-owned by Robert and Barbara (Kurtz) Smith and "Red" and Betty Lewis. Shown are, from left to right, Evelyn Franz, Robert and Barbara Smith, and Betty and "Red" Lewis. It was later purchased by Merrill Lucas and then Don Whigham. Located at 3825 River Road, it was used as a practice burn in 1979. (Melson Franz.)

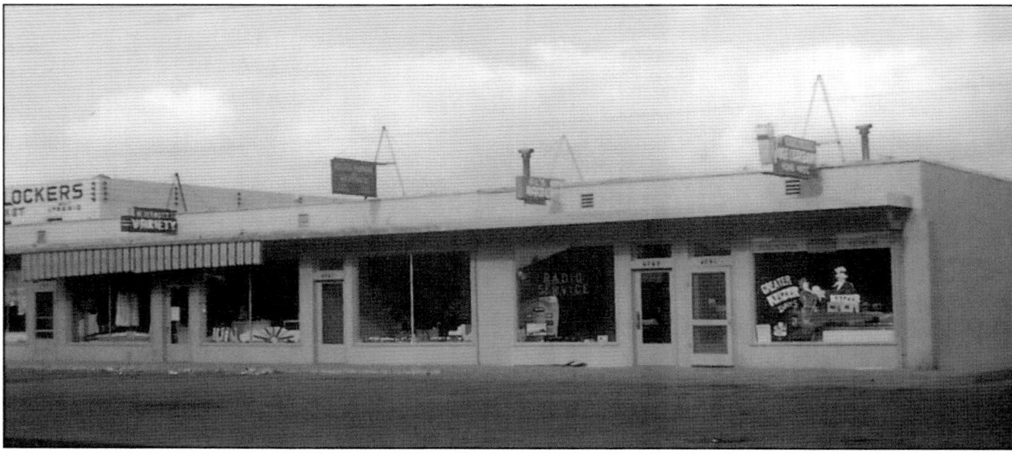

The Keizer business district is seen in 1951, with the new building owned by Don Wolf. The core businesses are, from left to right, Keizer Lockers, Teeter's Specialty Bakery, McDermott's Variety Store, Keizer Plumbing and Heating Co., Al's Radio, and Richlee's Ice Cream. (KHM.)

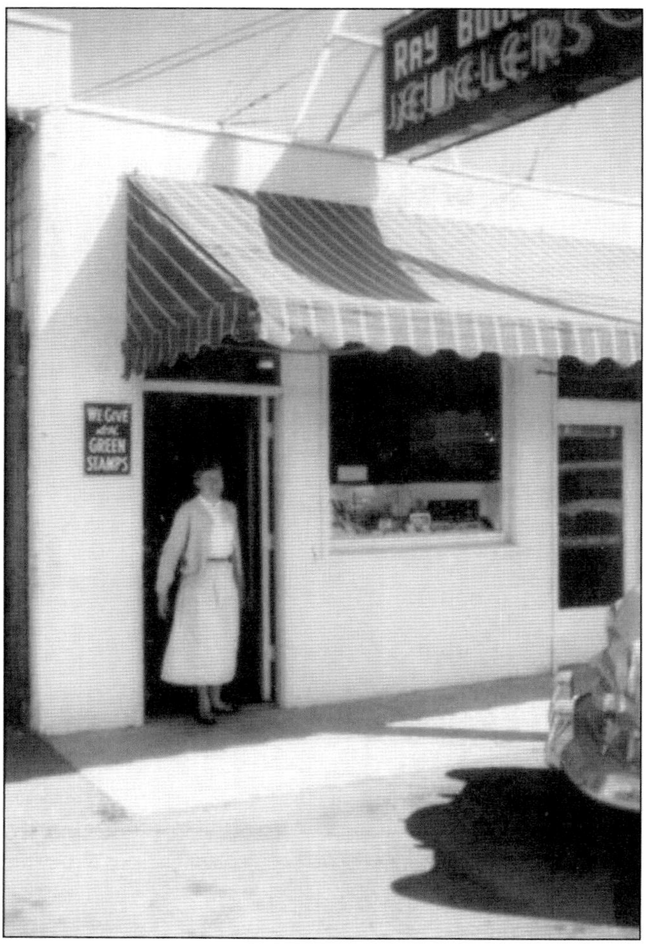

Ray and Louise Boucher opened Boucher Jewelers in 1953 next to Keizer Feed & Seed on River Road. There were few businesses at that time, mainly orchards in the area. The Bouchers made a meager income doing clock and watch repairs. Ray was a charter member of the Keizer Merchants Association. The store continues to this day, now located across the street on the west side of River Road. (Boucher.)

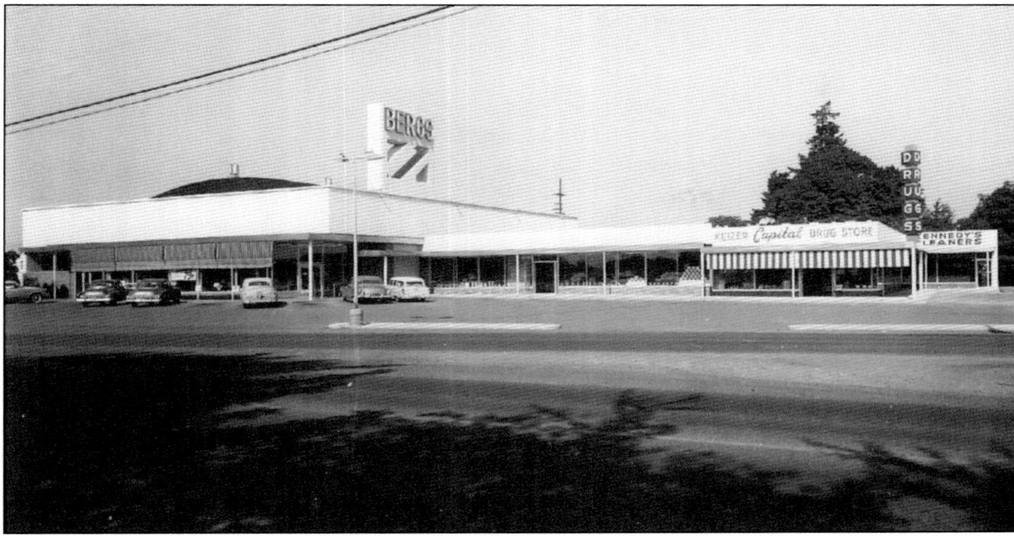

Robert "Bob" Peterson was the manager of the newly built Berg's supermarket in 1954. The large, modern store featured a wall mural of natural scenery. The self-service, ready-packaged meats and vegetables were new items for the day. Capital Drug Store and Kennedy's Cleaners were added later. (Judy Peterson.)

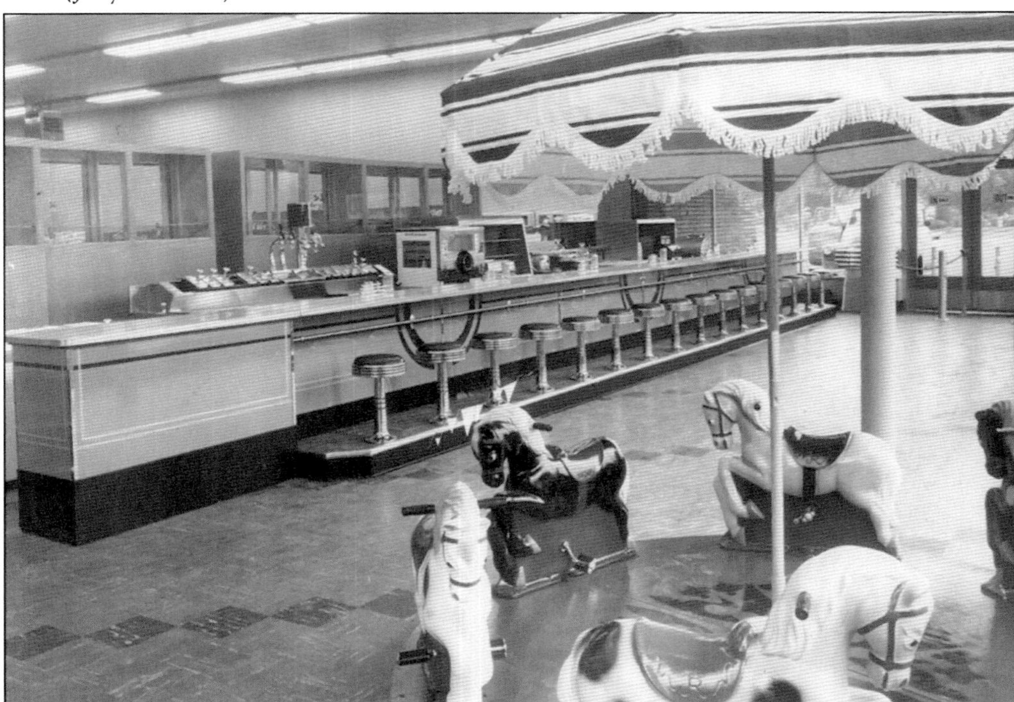

The shiny new soda fountain and carousel at Berg's supermarket are seen in 1954. The varying shades of pastel walls and the floor covered with asphalt tile of marbleized green and black squares beautified the new store. Bob Peterson, store manager, and Dick Van Osdal, assistant manager, operated the store, along with department managers Lloyd Lebold, Al Benson, Don Drees, Bill Peterson, and Dick Eckle. (Judy Peterson.)

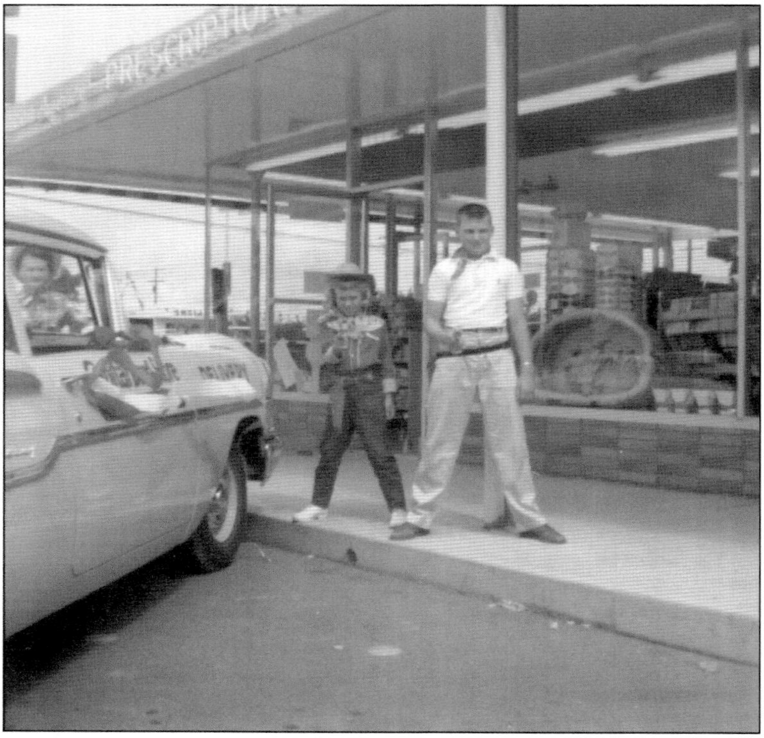

The Oregon Centennial Days Celebration in July 1959 brought out many participants in the Keizer district. Genese Franz (left) and her cousin Steven Hill show off their Western wear in front of Capital Drug Store on River Road at Cherry Avenue. (Melson Franz.)

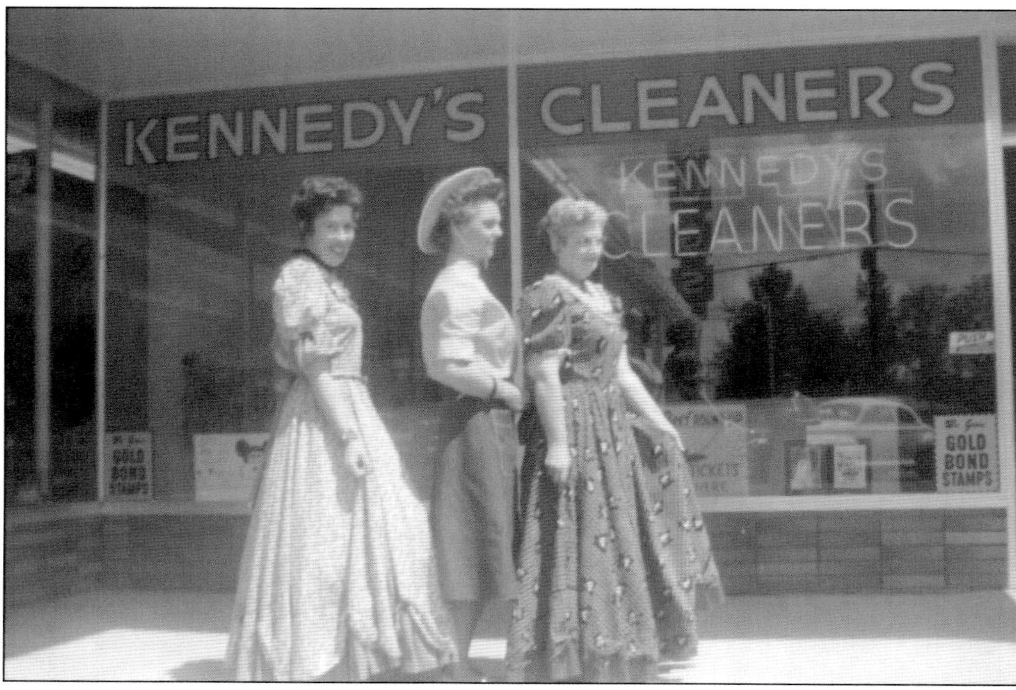

Dressed for the Oregon Centennial Days Celebration in July 1959 are, from left to right, Ila Bowden, Evelyn Franz, and Lola Davis in front of Kennedy Cleaners on River Road at the Cherry Avenue intersection. A dry-cleaning business still operates in the location today. (Melson Franz.)

Gary Young moved from California in 1964 to open Topper's Steak House (the name was soon changed) in the Keizer Plaza, on the corner of River Road and James Street. This was a new type of restaurant for the country community. Opening night saw people lined up around the plaza. The Keizer Rotary Club was established in 1965. Regular rotary luncheon meetings were first held at Gary's Steak House. (Gary Young.)

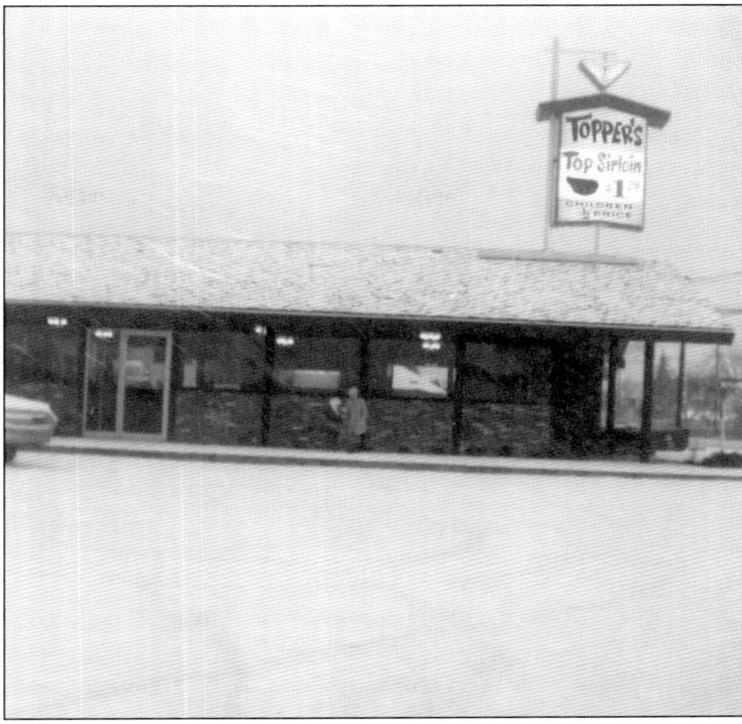

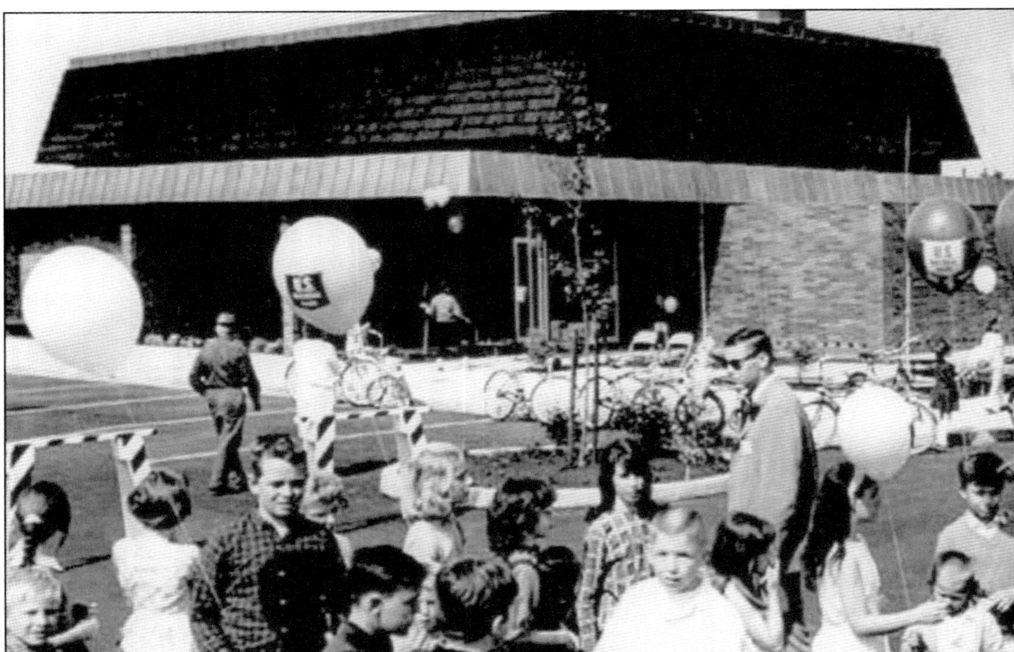

The 1965 grand opening of US National Bank on River Road is seen here. Children in the bank parking lot enjoy their balloons, given out by a bank employee. This is one of the few businesses still operating in the same location today. Its location served as an early line-up area for the Keizer parade. (SPL: SJ.)

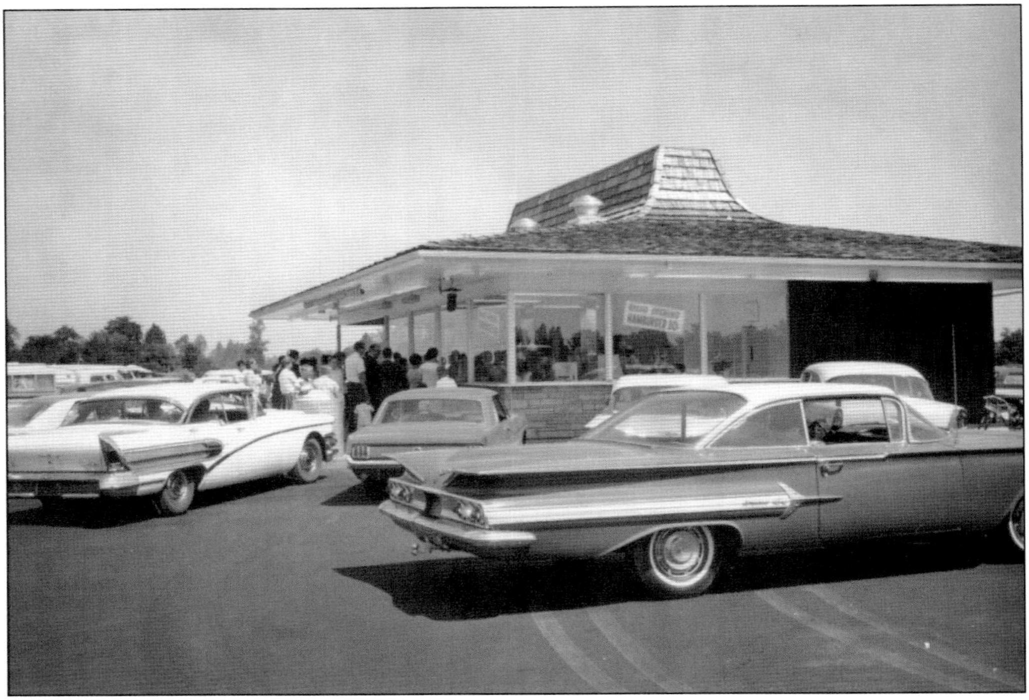

In 1965, Bob Corey opened Keizer's Bob's Hamburgers drive-in restaurant. Located on North River Road near Sandy Drive, it was a popular hangout for high school students. One of the most nostalgic fast-food restaurants in Oregon for decades, it was where kids got their first jobs, or just hung out and ate the best burgers, fries, shakes, and cones around. And don't forget about the secret sauce! (Bob's Hamburgers: Allen Wright.)

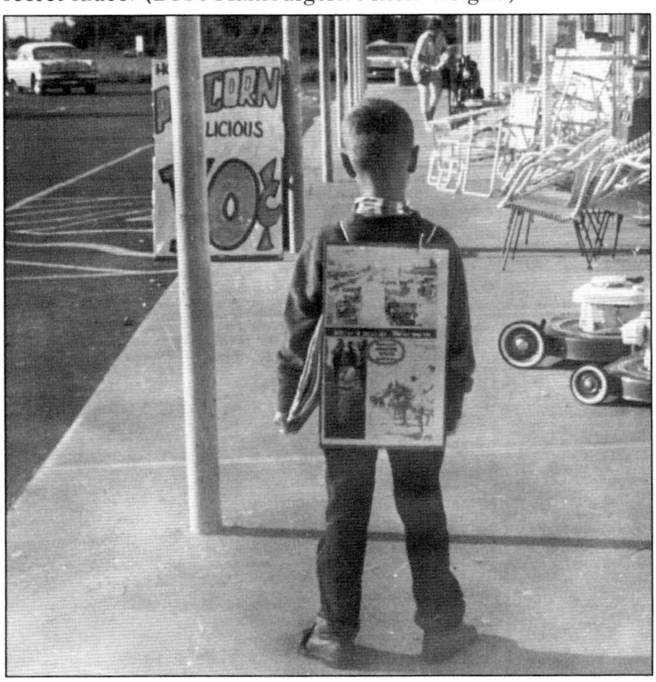

Young Leland Zaitz is a walking billboard for the *Keizer News* at a storefront in 1966. The paper was started by the Keizer Commercial Club in 1949. In 1952, Lynn Martin became editor and publisher, followed by Clarence Zaitz in 1963. His sons Les and Lyndon would later take on the role with the *Keizertimes*, which was established in 1979. (Zaitz family and *Keizer News*.)

Nine

Keizer Days Parade

Neighbors in Manbrin Gardens started having parades in the 1940s, with children dressed in costumes. The festive tradition evolved into the Iris Festival, now held each May. In 1949, the newly formed Keizer Commercial Club desired to promote local businesses, and the Keizer Days Parade commenced on Saturday, June 24, 1950.

Over the years, the parade and festivities have grown. The Keizerfest began in 1980, sponsored by St. Edward Catholic Church. Added to the lineup of events were a carnival, a run, and musical entertainment. In 1974, the Keizer Junior Miss scholarship program was included, among other activities.

According to the Keizer Chamber of Commerce (previously Keizer Merchants Association), today's parade brings over 25,000 spectators to River Road. With the nearby Schreiner's Iris Gardens (operating since 1925 and the nation's largest retail grower of iris), the festival promotes and celebrates Keizer as the Iris Capital of the World.

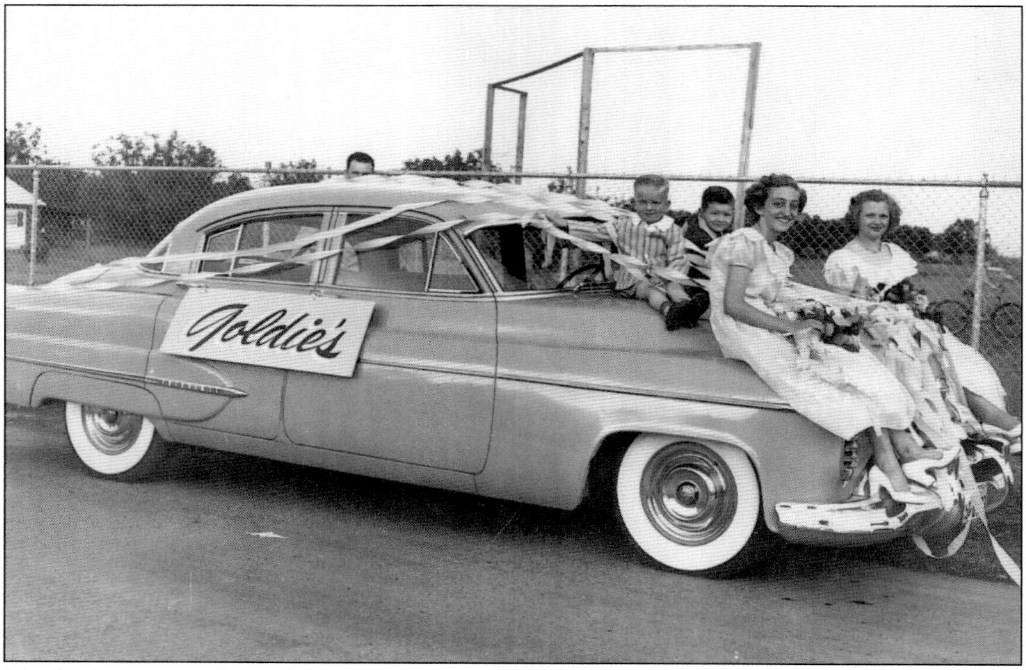

The first Keizer parade was held in 1950, sponsored by the Keizer Commercial Club to promote area businesses. The kids on this car are part of the Goldie's dress shop entry. The business was located next to Keizer Cleaners. The car is parked at the old Keizer School baseball field. (KHM.)

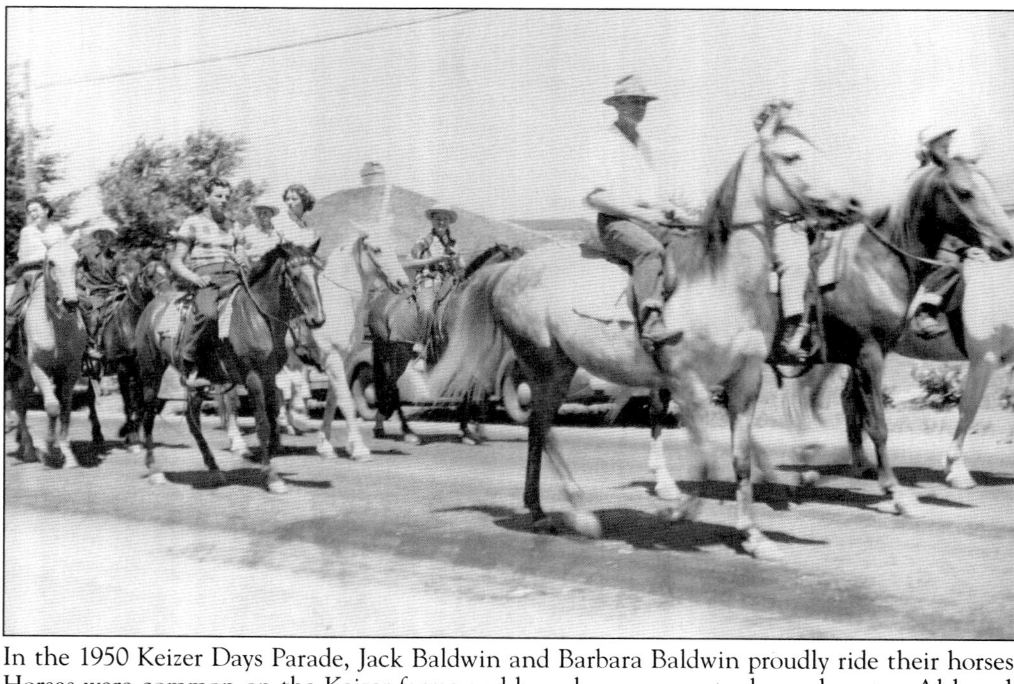

In the 1950 Keizer Days Parade, Jack Baldwin and Barbara Baldwin proudly ride their horses. Horses were common on the Keizer farms and have been a perpetual parade entry. Although the staging areas, direction, and length of the parade has varied over the years, the route has continued down Keizer's main street, River Road. (Barbara Baldwin Knighton.)

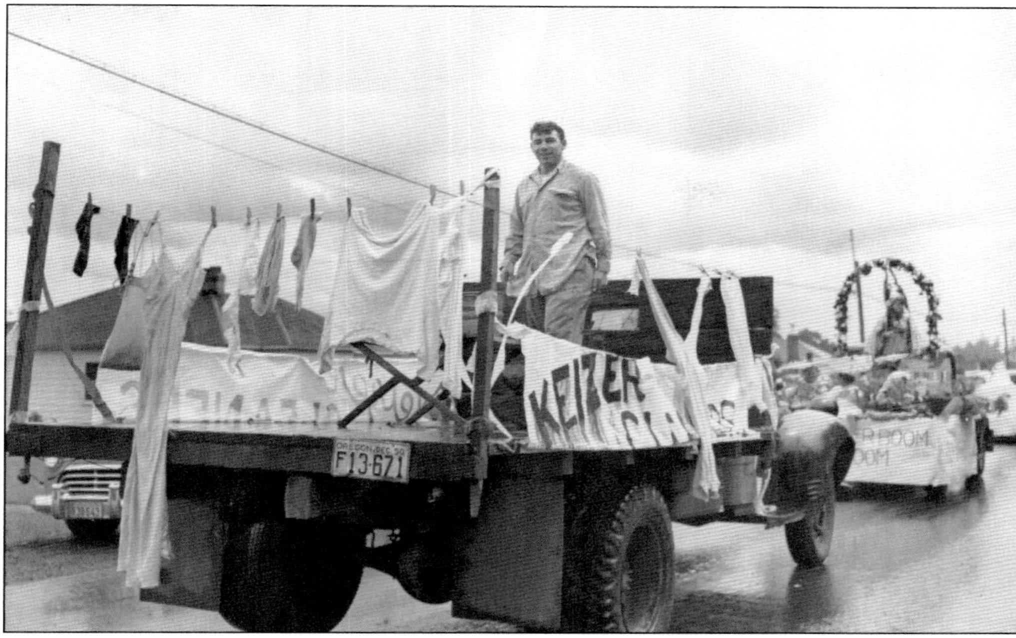

Otis Anderson of Keizer Cleaners is shown with his parade entry in 1950. The business owners united to help promote their industries and encourage new customers. State police were on hand to help the fire department control traffic along the parade route. There were more than a dozen large floats, which became bedraggled in the downpour. (KHM.)

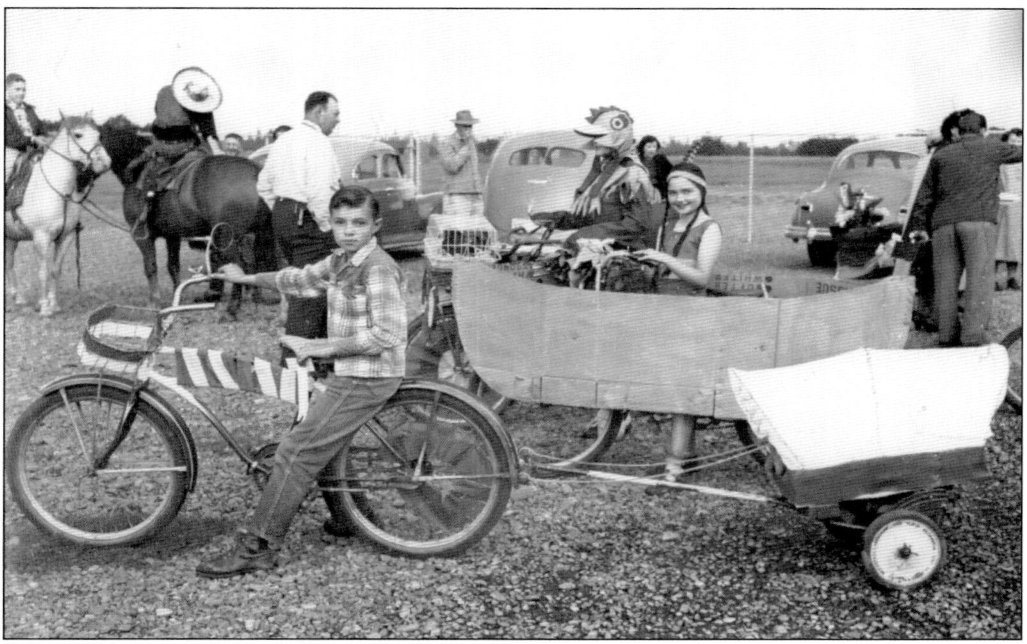

The kids had many creative costumes to go with their bikes. More than 100 excited marchers and bicyclists gathered at the Keizer School long before the appointed time of 1:15 p.m. At 1:30, decorated bicycles were judged. Heavy rain marked this first parade as it traveled the six blocks to Orcutt's Market at 4200 River Road, where J.C. Pizzeria is located. (KHM.)

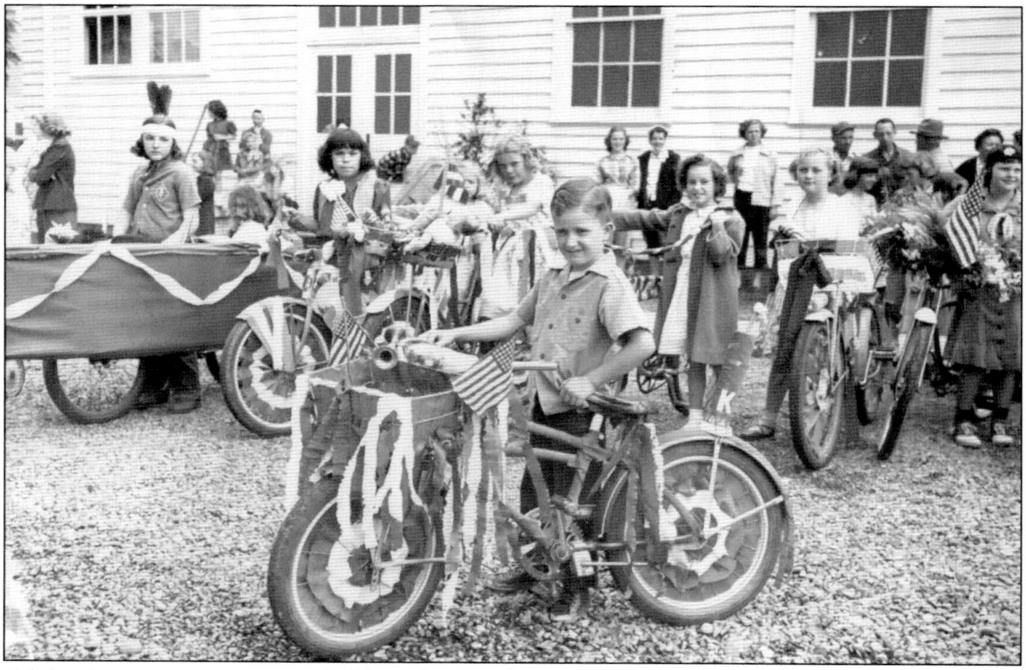

A bike-decorating contest was held on the day of the parade. The happy children and their festive bikes were displayed and judged at the Keizer School. Over 100 anxious marchers and bicyclists gathered at the school. (KHM.)

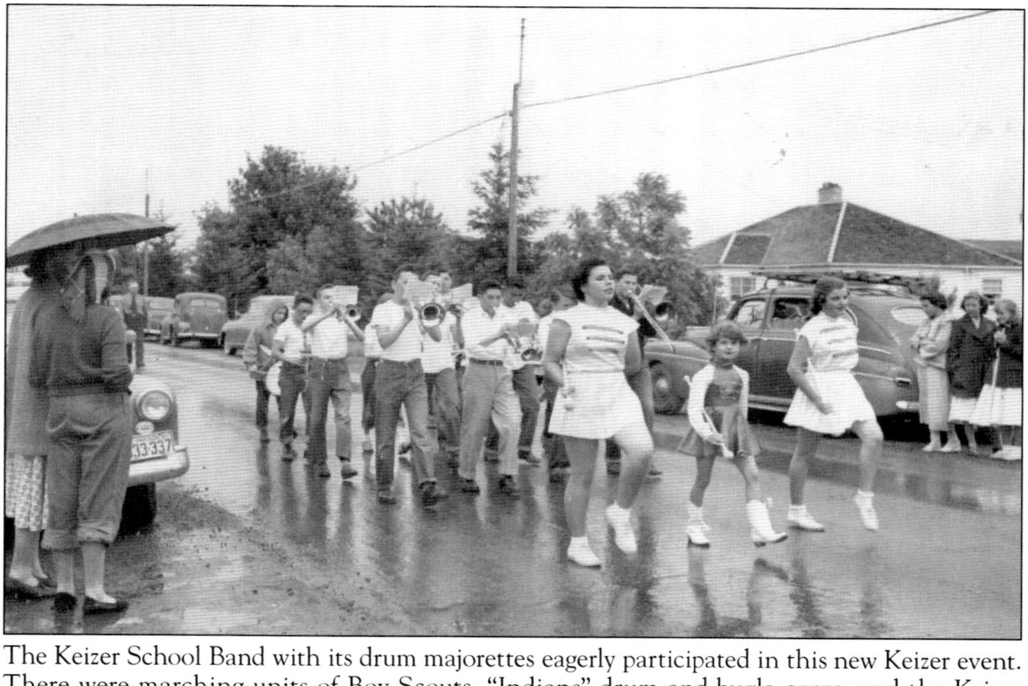

The Keizer School Band with its drum majorettes eagerly participated in this new Keizer event. There were marching units of Boy Scouts, "Indians" drum-and-bugle corps, and the Keizer School Band with its majorettes. There was a Keizer Community Band in addition to the school Band. (KHM.)

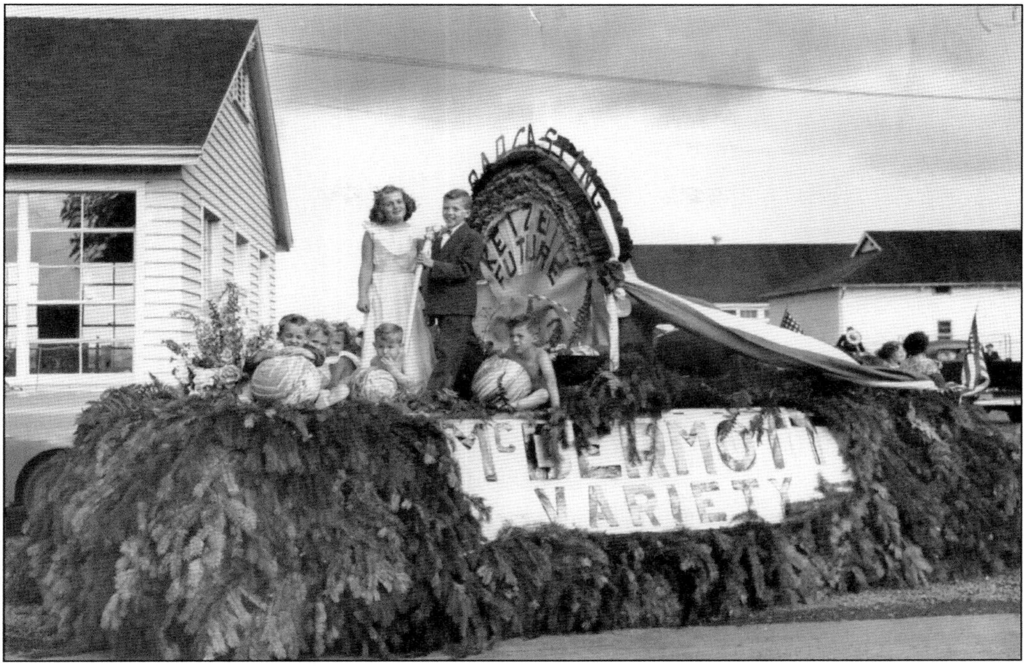

This float by McDermott's Variety Store showcases "Broadcasting Keizer Future." It was a prophetic slogan, as viewed now in these students' future. The Keizer School was the gathering place for many community events. Most of the stores closed their businesses during the parade, and every business had a Keizer Day special. (KHM.)

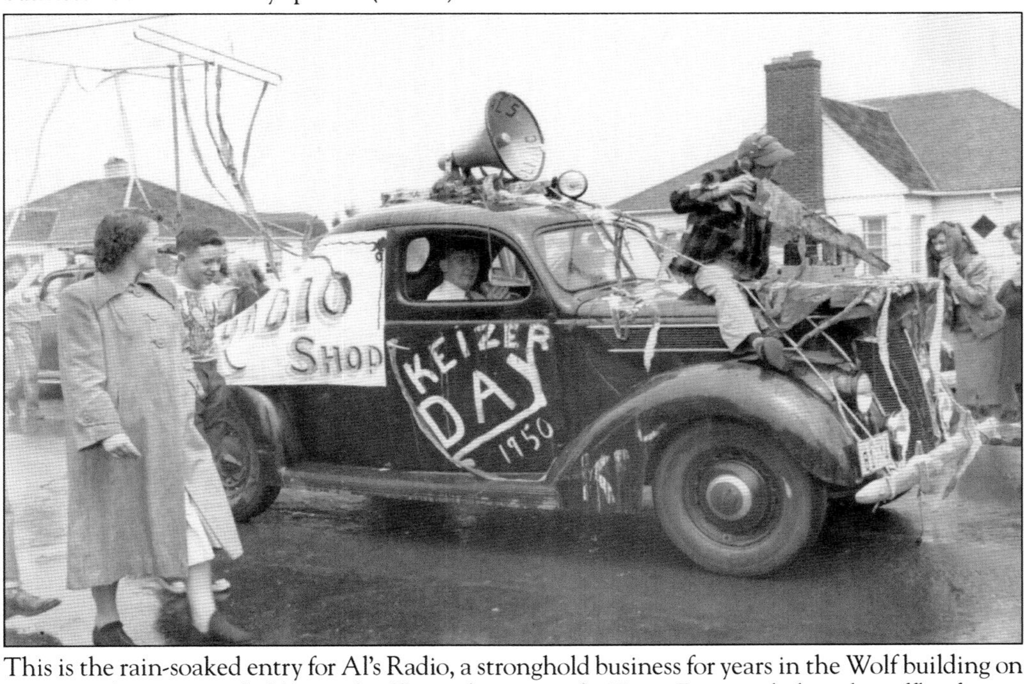

This is the rain-soaked entry for Al's Radio, a stronghold business for years in the Wolf building on River Road. Businesses held special raffles and activities for Keizer Days, including the raffle of a cow that would be penned along River Road. There were more than a dozen large floats. (KHM.)

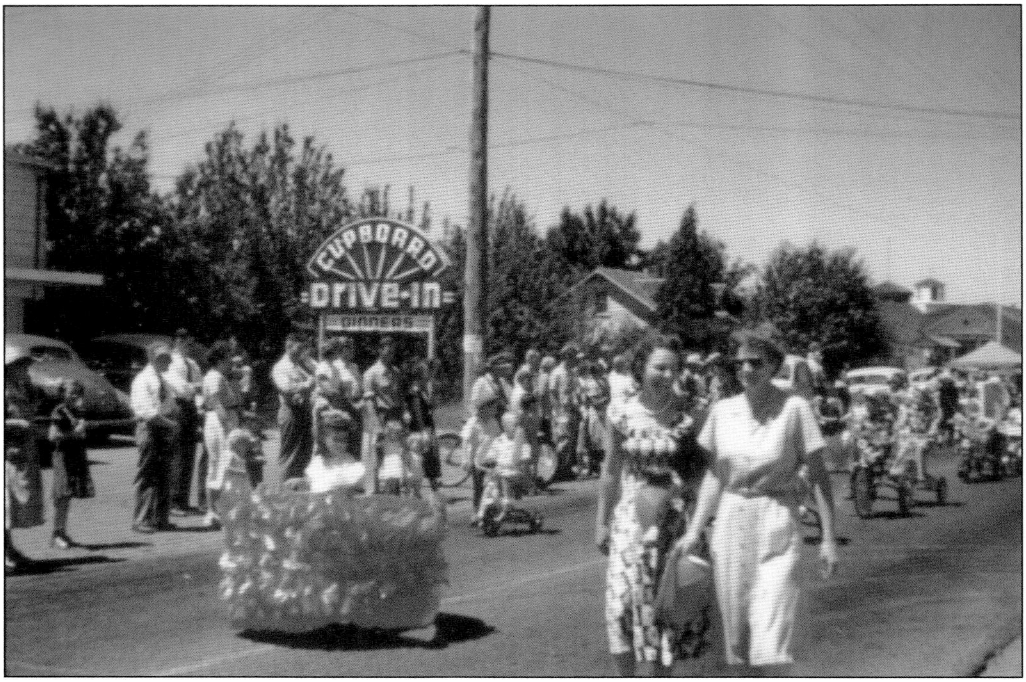

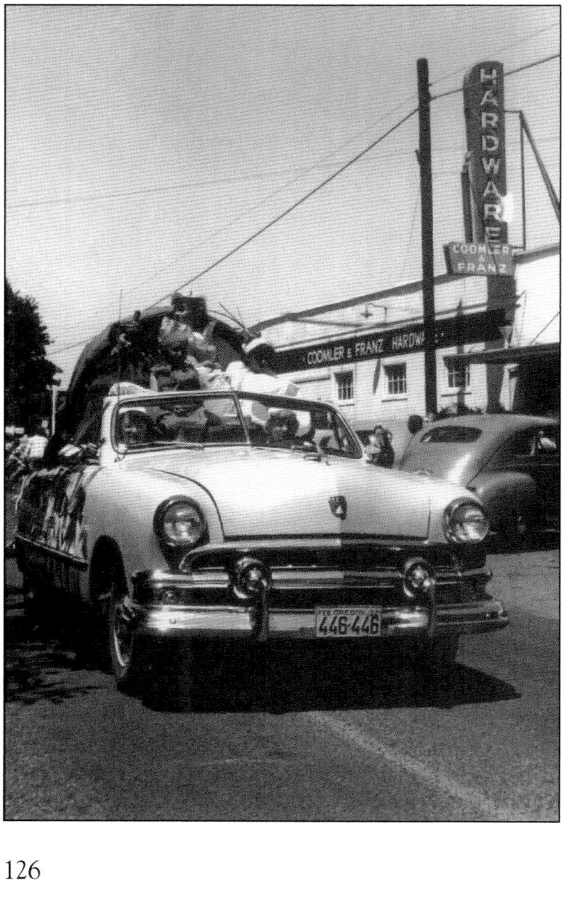

Walking from Keizer School, these women are leading the pack of bicyclists that ride past Shattuc's store and gas station, then past the favorite Cupboard Drive-In. The Greater Keizer Days began with grand openings and anniversary special sales, as well as an open house at the Keizer fire hall. There was also a baby contest. (KHM.)

Coomler & Franz Hardware, located at the intersection of River Road and Cherry Avenue, had this automobile entry. The event was a highlight for business members and their families. Parade day is an exciting event for young and old alike. Concluding the day's events were dances at the fire hall and the grange hall. (KHM.)

About the Keizer Heritage Museum

The Keizer Heritage Museum, housed in the 1916 Keizer School, opened in 1999. It displays historical artifacts from the community and the old school, collected by the Keizer Heritage Foundation. The displays cover a wide range of history, from the days of the Oregon Trail wagon train, through the City of Keizer's beginning in 1982, to the present. A variety of items relate to "The Old School" and its many teachers and students. Many local families have contributed their histories to display boards, scrapbooks, and display cases.

The landmark school stands prominently at 980 Chemawa Road, a few blocks from the original location on River Road. The completed move and restoration of the old Keizer School gives residents a place to connect with the past and learn about their agricultural heritage. Along with the museum, the Keizer Art Association Gallery and Keizer Community Library are located in the facility. The historic building and grounds are available to rent for events and weddings.

The museum has local history books for sale. Discover more at keizerheritage.org. (Marcus Berg, Unique Angles Photography)

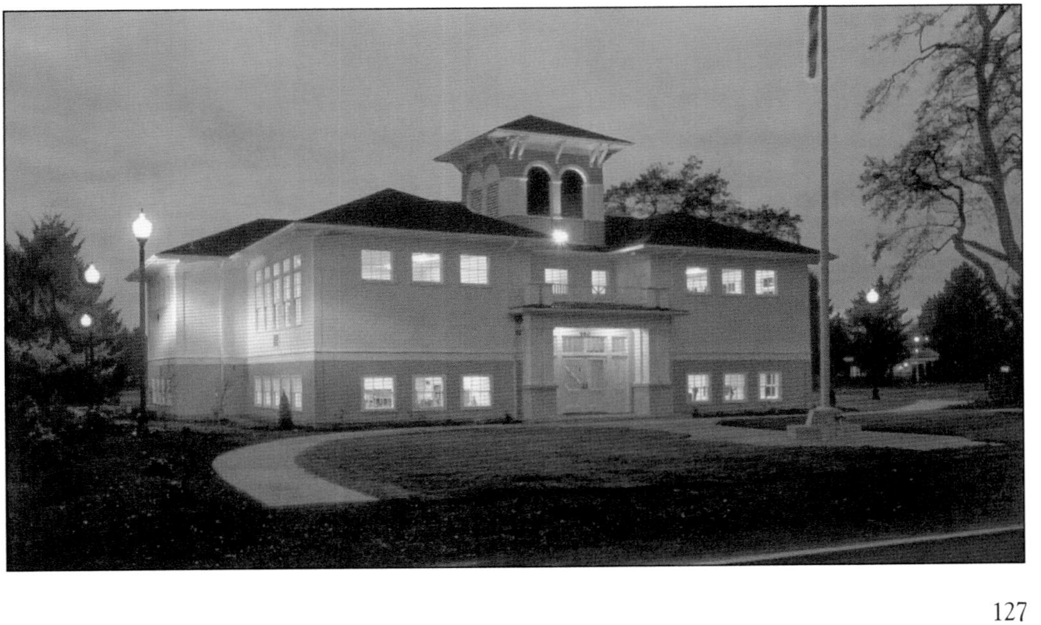